New Jewish Voices

SUNY Series in Modern Jewish Literature and Culture
SARAH BLACHER COHEN, Editor

New Jewish Voices

Plays produced by the Jewish Repertory Theatre

Edited
by EDWARD M. COHEN

Benya the King	RICHARD SCHOTTER
36	NORMAN LESSING
Elephants	DAVID RUSH
Friends Too Numerous to Mention	NEIL COHEN and JOEL COHEN
Taking Steam	KENNETH KLONSKY and BRIAN SHEIN

State University of New York Press
ALBANY

Published by
State University of New York Press, Albany

Printed in the United States of America

For information, address State University of New York
Press, State University Plaza, Albany, NY 12246

Library of Congress Cataloging in Publication Data
Main entry under title:

New Jewish Voices.

(SUNY series in modern Jewish literature and culture)
Contents: Benya the king / by Richard Schotter—
36 / by Norman Lessing—Elephants / by David Rush—
Friends too numerous to mention / by Neil Cohen and
Joel Cohen—[etc.]
1. American drama—Jewish authors. 2. American drama—
20th century. 3. Jews—Drama. I. Cohen, Edward M.,
1936- . II. Series.
PS628.J47N48 1985 812'.54'0808927 84-8799
ISBN 0-87395-996-5
ISBN 0-87395-997-3 (pbk.)

10 9 8 7 6 5 4 3 2 1

Contents

The editor wishes to express his gratitude to the following organizations for their support of his work and the work of the JRT Writers' Lab:

Associated YM-YWHA's of Greater New York, Emanu-El Midtown YM-YWHA, Jewish Art Subsidy Fund of Federation of Jewish Philanthropies of New York, National Endowment for the Arts, National Foundation for Jewish Culture, New York State Council on the Arts.

Introduction

EDWARD M. COHEN

Theatre is an art form which cannot be separated from the society in which it exists and the audience which it serves. Poems and paintings can be artistic entities without listeners or viewers; plays require production to be complete. While it is certainly true that getting produced is no guarantee that a playwright will turn out a major work, it is equally true that important playwrights develop only as they are produced and plays are produced based on the dictates of an age.

The American theatre today is in a state of change, different from any in its history. Theatre is no longer a mass-market medium. That role, for better or worse, has been assumed by film and television. Theatre has become an art form created in small spaces: off-off Broadway, in lofts and cellars, on the experimental stages of the regional theatres, in universities—and theatre is meant to appeal on an intimate, personal level.

Plays written for these spaces are more likely to be produced, and writers speaking to limited, defined audiences can now be heard. Any playwright thinking of writing an historical epic or a sociological study of urban life or a science fiction ensemble piece requiring a cast of thirty would be better served by film or television. These media have become the mirrors of our external realities and they do so with such sophistication that audiences will no longer accept the theatre's shortcomings in these areas. Theatre has become the place where we investigate internal struggles: interpersonal, psychological and spiritual.

Added to these elements is the fact that American audiences are hungry for individual definition and identification. No longer are assimilation and conformity the ideals of this society. The "me" generation has produced a hunger for individuality and a pride in ethnic roots.

In the 1940s, only Broadway playwrights with wide audience appeal were heard. In the sixties, daring experimental writers responded to the times. The seventies was the era of politically aware writers, of Joseph Papp's Public Theatre.

The reality factors affecting the theatre of the eighties—space, competition from other media, economics, the needs of the audience—combine to create a breeding ground for ethnic theatre. Those playwrights involved in the Jewish theatre movement are very likely to flourish in this environment.

1. The Jewish Theatre Movement

The existence of a Jewish theatre movement in this country can be verified by activity. More and more plays on Jewish themes are being done, on Broadway and off, than ever before. Broadway has always seen its share of Jewish plays because of the large New York Jewish audience, but as the number of Broadway productions shrinks, that share grows larger and, more impressively, of higher quality and greater ethnic authenticity. In recent seasons, Broadway has seen productions of C.P. Taylor's *Good,* Lanford Wilson's *Talley's Folly,* Jules Feiffer's *Grown Ups,* Isaac B. Singer's and Eve Friedman's *Teibele and Her Demon,* Neil Simon's *Brighton Beach Memoirs,* Martin Sherman's *Bent,* and the award-winning *Torch Song Trilogy* by Harvey Fierstein. Off-Broadway has contributed James Lapine's *Table Settings,* Wendy Wasserstein's *Isn't It Romantic?,* Jean-Claude Van Italie's *Early Warnings,* Ronald Ribman's *Buck,* Jean-Claude Grumberg's *The Workroom,* Dick Goldberg's *Family Business,* and *March of the Falsettos* by William Finn.

All of these, after their New York runs, find productions in regional theatres and attract large audiences. In addition, there are constant regional productions of the Jewish writers of the past and a current interest in the work of Clifford Odets who has been represented regionally and on Broadway with major revivals of *Awake and Sing!,* *Rocket to the Moon,* and *The Big Knife.*

New York's non-profit theatre includes two professional companies exclusively devoted to plays in English related to the Jewish Experience. The American Jewish Theatre at the 92nd Street YM-YWHA has produced such revivals as *The Caine Mutiny Court Martial, In the Case of J. Robert Oppenheimer, The Tenth Man,* and has had a notable success with *The Rise of David Levinsky,* a new musical based on the Abraham Cahan classic. The Jewish Repertory Theatre is sponsored by the Emanu-El Midtown YM-YWHA and its repertoire is discussed throughout these pages.

Jewish community centers have expanded the movement by building new theatre facilities to house amateur and semi-professional companies and many of these seek out exciting new fare and encourage the production of new plays. Such work is being done at JCC theatres in Cleveland, Baltimore, Rochester, Buffalo, Berkeley, and Toronto.

The California-based Traveling Jewish Theatre tours with a rotating repertoire of company-created pieces, as do many notable actors doing one-person shows. Courses on aspects of Jewish theatre are being offered at major universities and several important books and articles have been published in the field.

The National Foundation for Jewish Culture has become a coordinating body of this activity. It organized the Jewish Theatre Conference and Festival (New York, 1980), sponsored American participation in the first International Conference and Festival of Jewish Theatre (Tel Aviv, 1982), publishes the resource catalog *Plays of Jewish Interest,* sponsors the annual Berman Playwrighting Award Competition for the best new play illuminating an aspect of Jewish life, and awards Playwrights Travel Grants which enable theatres to bring in playwrights for the rehearsal period of premiere productions.

In October 1983, the Foundation co-sponsored, with the University of Pittsburgh and the United Jewish Federation of Greater Pittsburgh, the Jewish Playwrights Conference which included two productions of plays of Jewish interest by the University of Pittsburgh Department of Theatre Arts, readings of participants' plays by drama students, a series of informal round-table discussions, and public addresses by prominent members of the theatre, academic and Jewish communities.

This abundance of activity is certainly evidence of a movement. Each time leaders in Jewish theatre meet, there is agreement on one point: you cannot have a theatre movement without plays. The question of whether good, modern, Jewish plays will develop out of this environment is of major concern and it brings with it the enormous problem of defining a modern play, defining a good play and, heaven help us, defining a Jewish play. To seek the answers to some of these questions, we must first look to the past to, at least, see what prevented us from finding the answers previously.

2. *Jewish-American Playwriting*

In the 1930s, Clifford Odets became the first Jewish-American playwright to use his heritage as a powerful force, perhaps the single most powerful force, in his plays. Such plays as *Awake and Sing!, Rocket to the Moon,* and *Paradise Lost* are political, ideological, sociological and, certainly in the case of *Awake and Sing!,* universal. But, first and foremost, they are familial and ethnic. They are about a very specific set of values which are often in conflict with the societal values surrounding the family unit; the drama in the plays evolves out of this primary conflict. The fact that these families are Jewish is as crucial to the dynamics of the plays as is the fact that they take place in 1930s America.

Odets came to prominence in a generation of Jewish-American writers—S. N. Behrman, Lillian Hellman, Sam and Bella Spewak, George S. Kaufman, and Moss Hart—but none of these writers dealt seriously, courageously, or successfully with ethnic themes. Behrman turned to his roots in his 1958 autobiographical play, *The Cold Wind and the Warm.* It was a failure in its original Broadway production both because of script problems and because the production was so decidedly un-ethnic; the very talented Maureen Stapleton was dreadfully miscast as Behrman's Aunt Ida. Ironically enough, this play was a success in its first New York revival twenty years later at the Jewish Repertory Theatre. Lillian Hellman also had a failure late in her career when she dealt with a Jewish family in *My Mother, My Father and Me.* But, other than that, the issue was a minor strand in her work.

This group of playwrights was followed by the 1940s generation of Jewish American playwrights including Arthur Miller, Arthur Laurents, and Irwin Shaw. These writers also struggled with the issues that Odets had brought to the theatrical scene, but never too hard and never for very long.

Laurents's first success, *Home of the Brave,* dealt powerfully and honestly with anti-Semitism, but thereafter he chose to inhabit less personal, more intellectual realms with such works as *A Clearing in the Woods* and *Invitation to a March,* both failures. Many years later he made another significant contribution to the American theatre with the creation of the Jewish "Mama Rose" in *Gypsy,* but there had been many arid years between successes.

Miller presents the same problem. One of the major critical complaints about *Death of a Salesman* has been the lack of ethnicity in the characters. Mary McCarthy expresses this view in *Sights and Spectacles:*

> A disturbing aspect of *Death of a Salesman* was that Willy Loman seemed to be Jewish, to judge by his speech-cadences, but there was no mention of this on the stage. He could not be Jewish because he had to be "American." All the living-rooms, backyards, stoops and fire escapes of the American School claim to be "America," while containing no particular, individualized persons of the kind that are found in the plays of other nations and in novels. The absence of any specific information seems to guarantee profundity . . .
>
> "Attention must be paid," intones the shrill, sing-song voice of the mother, ordering her sons to take notice of their father's plight. "Attention, attention, must finally be paid to such a person." She is really admonishing the audience that Willy is, as she says, "a human being." But that is just it; he is a capitalized Human Being without being anyone, a suffering animal who commands helpless pity. The mother's voice raised in age-old Jewish rhythms ("Attention must be paid" is not a normal English locution, nor is "finally" as it is used, nor is "such a person") seems to have drifted in from some other play that was about particular people.*

Later in his career, Miller came out of the ethnic closet and created a full-blooded Jew, the junk dealer in *The Price,* and he revealed a humor, a humanity, a specificity in his writing that had never been seen there before. More recently, he has established an informal working relationship with the Jewish Repertory Theatre. In 1981, the company mounted a successful revival of *Incident at Vichy.* Miller

* "Sights and Spectacles," Farrar, Straus and Cudahy, New York, 1956.

then authorized JRT to produce the first New York revival of *After the Fall.* In 1983, Miller gave the company the rights to produce the New York premiere of *Up From Paradise,* the musical he and composer Stanley Silverman had adapted from his *The Creation of the World and Other Business.* Irwin Shaw's *The Gentle People,* an ethnic play which had faded from the theatrical scene, was revived by JRT in 1979. Of course, Shaw had long since wandered off, not only from such personal material, but from the theatre itself.

In addition to the growing policy of avoidance fostered by these writers, their very prominence and appeal created another side effect. Over the years, they had attracted an audience of middle-class Jews and when, in the late fifties and sixties, many of these writers fell into silence or turned to Hollywood, a huge gap was left. As usual in the arts, the gap was filled by promoters.

There followed a stream of commercial vehicles for such stars as Sam Levene, Menasha Skulnick, Gertrude Berg, Molly Picon. Plays like *The Impossible Years, Seidman and Son, Uncle Willie, A Majority of One, Fair Game, Milk and Honey* could open with sizeable advances, run for a season or two despite lukewarm reviews, and disappear forever from memory.

But they reduced Jewish characters to stereotypes. They overused and demeaned ethnic traits without investigating their roots. They skimmed the issues and probed no deeper. Often they were well done. Often they were successful and, as the technique and the response grew, their appeal expanded to a wider audience, resulting finally in the phenomenon of Neil Simon's stream of comedies about New York Jews sanitized of all ethnic traits.

One can only guess how the bitter aftertaste from these years affected Jewish-American playwrights, but the upsurge of ethnic writing in the late seventies produced no Jewish work comparable to Albert Innaurato's *Gemini,* Leslie Lee's *First Breeze of Summer,* John Guare's *House of Blue Leaves,* Pinero's *Short Eyes,* and *Zoot Suit* by Luis Valdez. The crop of Jewish-American writers who emerged in the sixties and seventies, including Arthur Kopit, Ronald Ribman, Israel Horovitz, Mark Medoff, shied away from these issues. Where were the playwright equivalents of Philip Roth, Bernard Malamud, Saul Bellow, Bruce Jay Friedman, Leonard Michaels, Cynthia Ozick?

In a *New York Times* interview of November 1978, Nobel Laureate Issac Bashevis Singer said:

Literature is completely connected with one's origin, one's roots. The great masters were all rooted in their people. Tolstoy, Dostoyevsky and Gogol were as Russian, as Ukranian, as they could be. Dostoyevsky himself even became a Pan Slavic. The only real writer who had no roots was Kafka. He was a Jew, but he was kind of an assimilated Jew. At least, I would say about Kafka that he was looking for his roots. He tried to get them. But when you take a man like Koestler, who tries so hard to show that the Jews are not even Jews, he fails also as a writer. A Jewish writer who denies his Jewishness is neither a Jew nor does he belong to any other group.

You cannot write a love story of two human beings without dealing with their background. To whom did this person belong, and what language did his father speak at home, and so on. Of course, we know that you are writing about a man. But the question is: What man? Where does he come from? You have to give his address. Of course, an address in literature is different from an address on an envelope, but the idea is the same.

3. The Jewish Repertory Theatre

Ran Avni, the founder and artistic director of the Jewish Repertory Theatre, wished to form a theatre in which the central issue of the material produced was the "address" of the characters; not a theatre restricted to plays by Jewish playwrights, nor plays with Jewish characters, but one concerned with plays about Jewishness, about roots, about their value, their loss, the search for roots, the distaste for roots, the joy of roots. This is a truly ethnic theatre. Certainly, in New York City, he assumed that such a concept would be valuable to artists and audience, and if the productions were done on a professional level, they would appeal to more than Jews. The theatre would research and revive older plays, would discover new playwrights dealing with such topics, would offer encouragement to more established playwrights seeking an opportunity to explore these avenues.

Avni started the Jewish Repertory Theatre as an off-off Broadway company in 1974. This was a period of great activity in non-profit theatre. Broadway was in a steady decline, certainly in terms of the production of new American drama, and government and private funding was being increased to try and stem the tide. Institutional theatres throughout the country were being created and enlarged. In New York, off-off Broadway theatres were gaining the respect of critics and attention from audiences by presenting the works of talented new playwrights and by keeping the repertoire of important American drama alive.

Many of the New York theatres created in that flurry have not survived the budget cuts of the eighties. Among those that have survived are the Manhattan Theatre Club, Playwrights Horizons, Ensemble Studio Theatre, Negro Ensemble Company, Puerto Rican Traveling Theatre, and the Circle Repertory Company.

In the 1974–75 season, without a permanent home, the Jewish Repertory Theatre produced Sholom Asch's *God of Vengeance* in the first revival since its 1910 Broadway production, and Leah Goldberg's *Lady of the Castle,* an American premiere of a play about survivors of the Holocaust.

During this initial season, Avni approached Donald Geller, Executive Director of the Emanu-El Midtown YM–YWHA, about starting a theatre in the "Y," a relationship which was not without precedent. The 92nd Street YM–YWHA had long been famous for its series of poetry readings, dance and music concerts, and children's theatre programs. The 50th Street YMCA was the original home of the highly successful Playwrights Horizions.

The Emanu-El Midtown YM–YWHA is a neighborhood center which includes a music and dance school, art classes, a nursery, a Hebrew school, a senior citizens program, a photography gallery, and a health club. It serves a community of about four thousand people in mid-Manhattan, including Stuyvesant Town and Peter Cooper Village, middle-income housing developments directly across the street from the center. All available space on all four floors of the Midtown Y is booked all day, the hallways are teeming with youngsters, the telephones are always ringing, and the mimeo machine is always spewing out notices.

But Geller and the Y Board were attracted to the concept of a Jewish Repertory Theatre. They felt this kind of theatre was needed in New York and, most certainly, in the community served by the Y. They offered initial funding and a large dance rehearsal room which was free in the evenings.

Avni set to work, removing ceiling tiles so lights could be installed, converting an adjacent kitchen into a light and sound booth and, with only basic physical necessities, he produced four plays at the Y during the 1975–76 season. They were *A Night in May* by A.B. Yehoshua, an award-winning play about an Israeli family in the besieged Jerusalem of 1967; *The Closing of Mendel's Cafe* and *Relatives* by Eve Able, two original one-act plays; *Andorra* by Max Frisch, a drama exploring anti-Semitic attitudes in an imaginary country; and *East Side Justice* by Isaac Metzker, a semi-documentary adapted especially for the theatre.

In the 1976–77 season, still working around dance classes and rehearsing often to the strains of the senior citizens' discos from downstairs, Avni expanded his series from four to six plays and had his first popular hit. The play was *Cafe Crown* by Hy Craft, a touching and nostalgic comedy originally presented on Broadway in 1942. The play takes place in a cafe where actors of the Yiddish theatre congregate and it is based on an actual coffeehouse which existed in the very neighborhood of the Emanu-El Midtown Y. Word got around about the local connection and, by the middle of the run, Avni was selling out. He had found a neighborhood audience which he was never to lose and which was to serve as the backbone for his theatre's growth.

The other plays presented that season were *Middle of the Night* by Paddy Chayefsky, a revival of a Broadway play presented twenty years before; *Jonah* by Guenter Rutenborn, a parable of the Biblical story; *The Condemned of Altona* by Jean Paul Sartre, a drama about an ex-Nazi officer in post-World War II Germany; and *Ivanov* by Chekhov, an early play about an individual who cannot cope with Russian society.

Besides attracting an audience, the theatre was beginning to attract writers, directors, and actors, some of considerable repute like Stefan Schnable who appeared in *The Condemned of Altona* and Allan Swift who was in *Cafe Crown*. These artists were obviously drawn to the kind of material the theatre was doing and the concept of the theatre itself.

The 1977–78 season opened with *The Cold Wind and the Warm*. By this time, consistently large audiences were made up of old friends who clearly felt connected to the theatre and often vociferously expressed their opinions, sometimes during the performances. One newcomer to the theatre said that the feel of the evening was similar to that of a Black revival meeting because the intensity of the connection between performer and audience was so great, as was the connection of both to the material.

This intimacy between audience and stage is one heritage of the Yiddish theatre that remains intact. The material has changed, the point of view has become more worldly, acting and writing styles have been modernized, audiences are now assimilated, but the JRT subscribers still feel about their theatre as passionately as the immigrant audience did about theirs.

The Cold Wind and The Warm was followed by *Dancing in New York City* by Julius Landau, a new play about middle-aged bachelors and the women they meet at singles dances; *The Merchant of Venice; Anna Kleiber* by Alfonso Sastre, a contemporary political drama; *I Am a Camera* by John Van Druten, based on Christopher Isherwood's *Berlin Stories;* and *I Am a Zoo* by Bonnie Zindel, a new comedy about an American family.

A major breakthrough occurred for the theatre when Thomas Lask of the *New York Times* reviewed *I Am a Camera.* The theatrical world of New York is still a provincial one-paper town and in order for an off-off Broadway group to rise out of the anonymous mass of theatres functioning in the city, a *Times* review is essential. The *Times* reviewers are very wary of what they cover and their acknowledgment is enough to attract theatre people, other reviewers, and funding sources.

Major changes were made to keep up with the growth of the theatre. A subscription program was started and the initial mail order drive produced two hundred subscribers for the 1978–79 season. A Board of Directors was formed with Alfred L. Plant as Chairman. The facilities were renovated and expanded.

Avni opened the 1978–79 season with *Triptych* by Ernest A. Joselovitz, whose play, *Hagar's Children,* had been produced at Joseph Papp's Public Theatre, and followed it with *The Halloween Bandit* by Mark Medoff, author of the highly acclaimed *When You Comin' Back Red Ryder?* and *Children of a Lesser God.* Both plays were New York premieres, both plays centered on Jewish themes, and the fact that something of ethnic and theatrical significance was happening was acknowledged by Mel Gussow in his *New York Times* review:

> The appearance of a new play by an acclaimed writer at the off-off Broadway Jewish Repertory Theatre is no accident. Though,

as it begins, "The Halloween Bandit" seems far removed from that experience, it eventually deals with such concerns as assimilation and conformity to a protestant ethic.

It was during this season that a literary advisor joined the staff and started the JRT Writers' Lab to seek out and develop new playwrights and new scripts.

4. The JRT Writers' Lab

By then it had become clear that the success of the theatre depended on the production of new plays instead of continued reliance on revivals. From a practical point of view, the repertoire of revivals is not unlimited and new plays attract younger audiences, greater funding, and critical attention. This is particularly true in Jewish-American theatre which has been so entrenched in the past, has so often appealed only to older audiences, has yet to gain critical respect from mainstream publications. While JRT and other theatres still do many revivals of Jewish plays exploring the past, the JRT Writers' Lab is alone in exploring the present and laying the groundwork for the future of American Jewish theatre.

The one undeniable fact of theatrical production, however, is that good new plays do not come in over the transom. Playwriting is an art different from any other form of writing because, in the end, the script is only one element in the creation of the final work—the play as produced on a stage before an audience.

There may be many levels of appreciating plays, but the immediate response of an audience is essential to a play's success. "It doesn't work! " is the constant cry of a theatre professional—meaning it does not matter what the intent was, it does not matter how philosophically significant the speech is, it does not matter what will be revealed after hours of reflection—if it "doesn't work" in the immediate moment, it is not good theatre. Often the writer is dependent on his collaborators—actors, designers, director—to make the moment work so that his more significant intent can linger and expand in the mind of the audience, but the playwright must learn to use his colleagues' talents as well as to respect their input.

The essentials of a play development program are nourishment and feedback. The purpose is to take the talented playwright out of isolation, to introduce him to a community, to encourage him to allow other artists to have some impact on his work. He may as well learn this early in order to reduce the trauma once rehearsals begin.

The JRT Writers' Lab offers many different services to talented playwrights, depending on the needs of the script and the level of development of the writer. The literary advisor reads all scripts submitted, now averaging one hundred and fifty yearly, and responds personally to any glimmer of talent with a letter, a phone call, a meeting. This alone has become a rare service due to the "closed to unsolicited manuscripts" policy of the larger non-profit theatres. Very young talents need only this much encouragement to go on and write another play. If a script has potential but is not yet ready for audience exposure, a "closed reading" is scheduled. This experience, often a first for young talents, allows the playwright to hear his play read by professional actors under the guidance of a director and then to talk with all involved about the problems and values of the script.

The next level offered is an open reading. These are produced on an admission free basis, and a loyal audience of theatre people and neighborhood devotees has been developed which, along with the writer's guests, creates a friendly and supportive atmosphere. The day after the reading, there is a discussion attended by the playwright, the director, the literary advisor and the artistic director. At this level, the aim is to keep the experience intimate, unpressured, focused on the script and the developmental process.

The theatre also has a group of writers-in-residence. This constantly expanding group, now including six playwrights and two composers, meets with the literary advisor on an intermittent basis throughout the season. The basic aim is to connect the writers with the theatre in a continuing and committed way. These writers have input in the direction of the theatre's growth and a voice in artistic policy. They are invited to all major productions, to make their thoughts known to management about repertoire, to interact with directors and other artists. By allowing writers a sense of community and importance, by inviting them in on planning, the possibilities of their continued work and commitment are increased.

In addition, the writers are exposed to one another and their works. Each writer has a project proceeding through the developmental stages, culminating in a "mini-production": a fully rehearsed, fully staged reading with necessary props, set pieces, lighting, presented for an invited audience for two performances.

Such a play development program is not unique. Other organizations, such as the O'Neill Theatre Center and Playwrights Horizons developed these techniques and have effectively demonstrated that new works and new writers can shape the course of modern theatre. What is interesting about this program is that the aim is to produce good plays related to the Jewish experience.

Many of these writers previously, for various reasons, did not wish to be labeled as "Jewish writers" and shied away from Jewish material. They wrote science fiction, political tracts, cowboy spoofs, non-verbal performance pieces, but they were reluctant to deal with what they knew best. Even when they did, they resisted ethnic identification.

A case in point is that of a talented playwright who submitted a charming comedy about intellectuals on a Midwestern campus in the 1960s. The playwright had labeled his oddball characters as "New Yorkers" but not Jews. It was only after a reading and discussion that he acknowledged that their Jewishness was central to his play; it was the reason his characters were out-of-step in their environment, it was the reason they clung together, it produced the essential conflict in the play, and he had twisted himself into knots to avoid it. "You have defined my vision for me," he said.

Playwrights are very practical people. They wish to be produced. They need response. Once they discover a producer seeking something they have, they will use it, and true to Isaac Singer's statement, when Jewish writers write Jewish plays, these ethnic connections are so deeply entrenched with early memories and emotional nerve endings, that such plays are more likely to be personal, more deeply felt, and richer in every way.

One playwright responded to an invitation to submit a play to the Jewish Repertory Theatre by saying "I don't write religious plays." Such thinking must be attacked in writers, as well as in audiences and producers. A program such as this expands the horizons of Jewish playwrighting by allowing the writers to define a "Jewish" topic, by opening this movement to writers of talent without prejudging their religiosity, and by giving them the opportunity to get in touch with their ethnic past in their own way. It is the philosophy of the Lab that if a writer wishes to deal with self-hatred, so be it. Only when a sense of loss and hatred and rage and deprivation has been channeled into creative work can pride and love in one's heritage emerge. It is the role of the artist to expand our personal horizons by voicing the questions no one else dares ask. The Jewish theatre movement is only going to be pertinent and alive if we allow our writers to take us on voyages through uncharted waters.

Many of the scripts developed in the JRT Writers' Lab have gone on to further production at the JRT itself, as well as at Ensemble Studio Theatre, Playwrights Horizons, American Jewish Theatre, Manhattan Punchline, Counterpoint Theatre, Siesta Key Actors Theatre of Sarasota, University of Tel Aviv, Whole Theatre Company of New Jersey, and Jewish Community Centers of Cleveland, Baltimore, Toronto, and Buffalo.

The five plays included in this volume went on to full production at JRT. In addition to these new works, JRT produced the musical *Vagabond Stars* by Nahma Sandrow, Raphael Crystal, and Alan Poul and *Luna Park,* a one-act adaptation by Donald Margulies of Delmore Schwartz's *In Dreams Become Responsibilities,* which was done on a double bill with Schwartz's play *Shenandoah.* The theatre has continued to do revivals of forgotten American plays such as Gertrude Berg's *Me and Molly,* John Howard Lawson's *Success Story,* as well as of classics such as Pinter's *The Birthday Party,* Michel de Ghelderode's *Pantagleize* and Odets's *Awake and Sing!*

But it has been the increasing number of new plays produced each season that has brought JRT its greatest attention, and it is the shared vision of these contemporary writers, the process by which their work has been developed, and an understanding of the new paths they are treading which are the major concerns of this volume.

5. *The Plays*

The first shared attribute of these plays is that they all went through the developmental process described and there is no question that the maxim about plays being rewritten, not written, has been proven.

Norman Lessing's *36* arrived as a three-act fantasy with metaphysical overtones in which the central character ended in heaven and an ominous black angel hovered throughout the action. In the course of the readings and rewrites, an entire act was dropped, fantasy figures fell by the wayside, and the play settled comfortably into a broad comic style more appropriate to the material.

Benya the King also experienced a remarkable change in tone as it became, in the developmental process, more the playwright's play than the original story writer's, which is as it should be in theatrical adaptations. Little by little, Isaac Babel's hard cynical tone merged with the funnier and sweeter voice of Richard Schotter.

Friends Too Numerous to Mention lost well over an hour's playing time, several characters, confusing subplots, growing slowly into a tight, tense farce. David Rush's *Elephants* went through a year and a half of new second acts until the proper one emerged.

Most dramatic of all, perhaps, was the evolution of *Taking Steam* which arrived in the mail from Canada as a one-act series of vignettes set in Toronto's decaying steam bath. The play had no plot, no central character, no unifying theme, but it did have a wonderful sense of place, beautifully drawn characters, and exquisitely funny dialogue. Over a period of two years and several readings, a central event was created and all else fell into place around it. What had started as disconnected blackout skits had become a play.

It is interesting to note that the playwrights had circulated the first draft throughout Toronto, where one would have expected it to attract a great deal of interest because of the neighborhood connection, but no local theatre was able to offer the writers the encouragement, support, feedback, and services they needed to build what they had into a play. Last season, *Taking Steam* returned in triumph with its Canadian premiere at Toronto's Leah Posluns Theatre.

The other immediately apparent similarity between the plays is their comedic point of view. The plays deal with serious enough issues; *Steam* is about death, *Elephants* about isolation in old age, *36* about loss of faith, *Friends* and *Benya* about corruption; yet the tone is light-hearted, the rhythms are quirky and sharp, the jokes always come before the tears. This is not only a quality of current Jewish writing, but of all American playwrights of the day. It seems that these perilous times do not allow for the somberness of O'Neill, the poetry of Williams, or the rage of Odets. Seriousness of tone is left these days to soap operas; our important playwrights are flirting with an awful despair and, when they get too close, they are forced to be funny.

The humor and rhythm are also inescapable because these plays are rooted in urban landscapes where everything has to be fast and furious in order to be heard; there is never time for long speeches, and poetry gets lost in the traffic noises. The plays are set in Cincinatti and New Jersey and Toronto and Chicago. *Benya the King* is set in Odessa, but Richard Schotter tells a revealing story about its evolution.

The play was inspired by two very short stories in Isaac Babel's *Tales of Odessa,* but Schotter wrote the first draft out of memories of the corner toughs in the 1950s Bronx, where he was raised. Once the draft was done he decided to do some historical research to verify his imaginings. To his amazement, he was told he had captured the feel and tone of Odessa before the revolution perfectly.

The point is that these are not immigrant plays, nor depression plays, nor Holocast plays, nor *shtetl* plays. They are not set on the lower East side nor in the woods and farmyards of Europe. These playwrights are not Talmudic scholars, nor pained immigrants, nor alienated children of immigrants, nor self-hating, second-generation Americans bobbing their noses and changing their names. Wandering Jews no more, these tough, modern, street-wise playwrights are downtown, right in the middle of the action. The past however, has a very stong hold on their moral and philosophical concerns, and it is the conflict between this tug of the past and their vivid involvement in the present that creates the electricity in their writing.

Although these writers are quick-witted and sharp-tongued, there is a deep moral strain in each and an awareness and respect for their ethical and religous heritage. It is significant that two of the plays, *Elephants* and *36,* take place in synagogues. In *Taking Steam,* one health club member calls another to discuss his life's miseries. "Should I go to *shul* or should I come to the club?" he asks. The answer? "Of course you'll come to the club!"

In each play there is a Solomon-like Rabbi figure, either on stage or off, available for either respect or ribbing but always omnipresent. He is a central character in *36,* this Reform Rabbi climbing the ladder of suburban success who, in the process, has lost his faith. Surely the character of Dr. Berk, who arrives at the climax of *Friends Too Numerous to Mention* to solve all the problems, is being kidded for his rabbinical posturing and rhetoric, as is the off-stage Rabbi in *Taking Steam* who inflicted such shame on Max, the loud-mouthed character, by hollering in *shul,* "Max Glass—silence!" The entire tale of *Benya the King* is seen through the eyes of Reb Arye Leib, and the irony in the plot is that Benya, the charming criminal, eventually takes over as the town's Rabbi/Judge/Wise Man figure.

These writers, for all their modernity, continue to struggle with the authority figures of the past, though they are writing about the wheeler-dealers of the present with equal admiration and awe. Their heroes are out to make it big in this new world, even if it takes a denial of faith to do it.

Certainly that is the Rabbi's problem in *36*. It is true of the gang of thieves in *Friends Too Numerous to Mention* and the *Shamus* in *Elephants.* Lenny Zavitz, the character in *Taking Steam* who has died and sparks the play's action, starts off as the most admired club member and is revealed to be unscrupulous, untrustworthy, and morally despicable. "Lenny Zavitz didn't give a damn! He didn't give a damn about anybody! " is the wrenching first-act curtain line.

The writers reveal, at crucial moments in every play, a hunger for ritual to connect them to the past. Witness the locker-opening scene in *Taking Steam,* the candle lighting/cocaine snorting in *Elephants,* the funeral and weddings in *Benya,* and the family meetings in *Friends.*

The trouble is that these connections are not working. These plays are about a world where the traditional structure has collapsed, the past no longer offers protection for the present, the old are left to die alone, the thieves succeed and are admired, the voices of authority have no relevance; even in *36,* the most optimistic of these plays, we come fairly close to the end of the moral world as we know it.

The dilemma is most effectively dramatized in the last line of *Elephants* with its total rejection of community, faith, nature, morality, responsibility, and even God. It is not the *Shamus* of the synagogue who has the last word, but the bag lady of the streets. The playwright has recorded it as violently, as accurately and as vividly as possible; still the line pains more than it shocks bcause it reverberates with an awful sense of despair and an acute awareness of the loss.

These then are undeniably Jewish plays. They are, each and every one of them, about the relationship of the individual to his tribe, his community, his extended family. It is interesting to note that there is not one adolescent-family-memory play herein; the traditional forte of young writers. These playwrights are dealing with concerns that are more than strictly familial and personal, concerns that have been passed down by Jews from generation to generation: the loss of the homeland, thievery and corruption, adapting to changing moral codes, hanging on to a sense of self through ritual and tradition, turning to the wise man to learn how to survive, "making it" despite all odds.

It is not only that these plays are stocked with Jewish characters, written with an ear for Jewish rhythms and humor, connected to Jewish tradition. Dr. Margaret Brenman-Gibson, in a recent lecture on Clifford Odets, defined the state of being Jewish as "coming to terms with living apart from the comfortable majority." More than anything else, it is this state that informs these plays and defines them as Jewish.

These writers are not always happy about their alienation. They mock it, sneer at it, deny it, want desperately to drop this burden of bondage to the past. That tension can be felt in the plays. It may not make leaders of the Jewish community happy to claim these plays, but that is not to say that their "Jewishness" can be denied.

These plays are written with a voice that has not been heard before on the stage: the modern, successful, assimilated, urban Jew—still racked with problems. That, together with the fact that they are witty, compassionate, theatrical, dramatic, and enormously entertaining, makes them valuable and significant.

Benya the King

a play by

RICHARD SCHOTTER

Inspired by *Tales of Odessa* by Isaac Babel

For Roni, who was always there

Richard Schotter, *Benya the King.* (Photo: Adam Newman.)

RICHARD SCHOTTER is Associate Professor of English at Queens College, CUNY. He holds a Ph.D. in Dramatic Literature from Columbia University and has been a theatre critic, an editor of *The Drama Review,* and a Fulbright Scholar. From 1971 to 1973, he was Literary Manager of The American Place Theater, New York, and he edited the anthology, *The American Place Theatre: Plays* (Delta, 1973).

Mr. Schotter's first play, *Medicine Show: An American Entertainment,* was produced at Theater at St. Clement's in New York, toured the United States, Canada and Europe and, in 1973, was nominated for an "Obie" award.

For *Benya The King,* he received a New York State CAPS grant in Playwriting and the National Foundation for Jewish Culture's 1983 Berman Award for the best play on a Jewish theme. After its production at the Jewish Repertory Theatre, the play was done at the Cleveland Jewish Community Center Theatre in 1982.

Critics and audiences have consistently responded to its combination of charm and bite. Clive Barnes, in the *New York Post,* wrote, "The story of Benya's rise, fall and rise again comes over like an updated folk tale where a smidgen of cynicism has replaced a large pinch of sentimentality." In *Park East Magazine,* Vineta Colby had this to say: "It is a deceptively light play, concealing a powerful anger and protest. Babel, a loyal supporter of the Russian Revolution, was himself the victim of the Stalinist purges of the late 1930s. If his memory were to survive only in Schotter's *Benya The King,* it would serve to remind us of the persistence and resilience of human idealism—no small claim to immortality."

Benya The King was first produced by the Jewish Repertory Theatre in December 1979 with the following cast:

REB ARYE LEIB	Michael Marcus
BENYA KRIK	Brian Kale
LEVKA KRIK	Jeff Lorber
DEVORAH KRIK	Gay Baynes
CRAZY MAN	Willy Switkes
LYUBKA SCHNEIVEIS	Hope Arthur
EPHRAIM ROOK	Jerry Rockwood
RUVEN TARTAKOVSKY	Harold Herbstman
JOSEPH MUGINSTEIN	Willy Switkes

SAVKA BUTKIS	John Martello
CHAIM BLIT	Willy Switkes
THE BEAUTIFUL WOMAN	Gay Baynes
TSILYA EICHBAUM	Ellen Newman
THE COSSACK	John Martello
	Willy Switkes
MUSICIANS	Mary Beidler
	Libby Richman
	Andy Stein

Directed by Roger Hendricks Simon
Music by Ken Collins
Sets and costumes by John Scheffler
Lighting by Jeffrey Beecroft

The play takes place in Odessa circa 1912.

Act I

SCENE 1

The lights come up slowly on a short, impish-looking old man. He looks at the audience, examines them a moment or two, and speaks.

LEIB: I am Reb Arye Leib, a proud Jew dwelling by the dead. For seventy years I've sat on the cemetery wall and watched the Jews of Odessa, the people of the Moldavanka, kill each other with craft and guile or be killed by Cossacks riding red death horses though the night. For a Jew in Odessa, my friends, life can be as cold as the Russian Winter. But for one Jew, one special Jew, life was warm as a dancing flame and not even Cossacks put fear in his heart. His name, need I tell you, was Benya Krik. What can I say of Benya Krik that you don't already know? Close your eyes tight and imagine this if you can. You are a lion. You are a tiger. You are a cat. You are twenty-five years old. You can spend the night with a Russian woman . . . and satisfy her. If rings were fastened to heaven and earth, you'd pull them hard and draw heaven and earth together with your fists. If you can imagine all this you already know Benya Krik without meeting him. Imagine that for a father you have a drunken ox of a scrapman whom the town in terror calls Mendel Pogrom.

(At back of stage, a slovenly, crude-looking man with a strap in his hand drinks from a bottle of vodka. He continues as LEIB *speaks.)*

What does such a father think about? Drinking a glass of vodka, smashing in someone's face, horses, and nothing more. If you want to live, he makes you die ten times a day. If you stand up to walk, he trips you and laughs when you fall. But then, one November night, without a sound, terrible Mendel Pogrom drops down fast on the barnyard floor *(The figure standing and drinking, clutches his chest and falls to the floor. As he does, three figures are seen standing over him—two men and a young woman.)* leaving you, your brother Levka, and your unfortunate sister, Devorah alone in the world except for the company of unpaid bills, a half-dead horse, and a broken cart that hardly pulls. What would you have done in such a situation? You would have done nothing. But Benya Krik did something. That's why he was the king and you . . . tomorrow, you'll sit taking orders at your desk. And imagine. Tonight, my friends, I'll show you what might have been. Tonight I'll show you how a king is made . . . not born. Watch as Benya Krik makes a first decision and never again looks back.

(Lights down on LEIB, *up on another part of the stage where* LEVKA KRIK, *sits at a desk sorting, exasperated, through a pile of papers. He is* BENYA'S *brother, a man in his late twenties, well-built but flaccid and already showing signs of a bent back. He is dressed in dark colors. He sits there a few moments when his brother* BENYA, *age twenty-five, bursts onto the stage. He wears an orange coat, red boots, a scarlet scarf. When he speaks, he has the lilt of youth and confidence about him.* LEVKA *doesn't lift his head from the papers as* BENYA *enters and speaks.)*

BENYA: And a lovely evening to you, brother Levka. Your smile lights up the night.

LEVKA: What do I have to smile about? Papa dies and you disappear into the air. A week later you show up grinning like a fool.

BENYA: Why so mean, brother? Why so rough? The world's a wonderful place. You should see more of it. Come on, Levka. Live your life and let the dead lie still.

LEVKA: That's how you talk about your father?

BENYA: My father was a drunk who now is dead. What more is there to say?

LEVKA: Plenty when a father dies. Plenty and more.

BENYA: Some father he was, Levka. Beating his children black and blue behind closed doors at night but in the day, when the Cossacks rode by . . . I saw what he did then, Levka. I saw.

LEVKA: What did you see, Benya? What did you see?

BENYA: One day when the sun was shining hot and he was piling junk on his cart, two Cossacks on thunder horses stopped fast by his side. One of them, an ugly man with a beard of lice, started kicking at father's cart. He kicked and kicked with hate on his face, until the cart was empty in the sun and the yard lay strewn like a garbage heap. The other laughed out loud and dared our father with his eyes to defend what was his. And what did he do? Our father who terrorized the town and feared no man on earth? Meek as a child he walked up to the ugly one, leaned his head into his horse's flank and kissed, long and hard, the Cossack's boots. So don't talk to me about respect for the dead, brother. The dead had no respect for himself. Now that he's gone, a new life can begin for me. Today, in the square, two bluebirds sang me a song as I walked past their tree. This you would not have believed.

LEVKA: Tell your stories to Devorah. She'll listen to anything.

BENYA: These birds were singing me life songs, brother. Telling me not to be a scrapman's son all my days. I want to share their meaning with you. There are more things in life than we ever thought there could be. Just lift up your eyes and look around. Everywhere there are things you can have.

LEVKA: Like those clothes you're wearing?

BENYA: I see you noticed.

LEVKA: Who gave them to you? Lyubka the Whore?

BENYA: Leave her out of this, if you please. Handsome, aren't they, Levka? The best the street has to offer.

LEVKA: You look like a clown in the circus.

BENYA: Twenty South Americans worked a month to sew the boots. The cloak is finest Russian wool. And the scarf. Feel it, Levka. Like a woman's hair it slides through your fingers.

LEVKA: *(Refusing to touch):* Very pretty. Very nice.

BENYA: You can have it too. This and much more. All you have to do is put your pencil down, lift your legs on the desk and dream a little.

LEVKA: I've heard it all before, Benya. A hundred times. Just take off that suit and get to work in the back where you belong. I don't have time for your stories anymore.

BENYA: Make the time, Levka. Listen to the dreams I bring and you may never write an order again.

*(*DEVORAH *enters. She is older than* BENYA *and* LEVKA*; not ugly but not attractive either. She is nearing the age when she may never find a husband. She is open and responds freely and emotionally to the things around her.)*

DEVORAH: Is that my Benya standing there? You look so handsome, so . . . different.

BENYA: And look what I have outside. *(He takes her aside. They look out.)*

DEVORAH: An automobile, Benya. Like a ruby it glows in the moonlight.

BENYA: The horn plays a pretty tune when you push. Music to tell people you're coming.

DEVORAH: Will you take me for a ride?

LEVKA: Some other time, Devorah. Tonight we have bills to do. *(To* BENYA*)* You'll tell me now where you got the car?

BENYA: That's a long story that I'm sure you don't want to hear.

LEVKA: Try me, I'll listen.

DEVORAH: Go ahead, Benya. I love to hear you talk.

BENYA: Okay. Okay. I'll tell you everything. Two days ago, I was walking down Sofieska Street on my way to the square, when a crazy man runs up to me.

(A disheveled-looking man enters with a red cardboard cut-out car around his waist.)

His eyes were rolling around his head like eggs in a skillet. *(The man shows us what* BENYA *means.)* Down his chin ran spit like a horse with the bridle too tight. I was afraid of this man. Believe me, I was afraid of him. But before I could put one foot in front of the other, he grabs my arm and whispers quick in my ear with breath as hot as fire . . .

CRAZY MAN: Good gentleman. Here's a hundred rubles for your kindness. A favor I musk ask you in return. The car I am driving, this very pretty car, is, unfortunately, not mine. A week ago Tuesday I stole it from a man in Pinsk. A week ago Wednesday, this man declared he wished me dead. If he sees me in the car, I'm dead on the spot. Therefore, I must give the car to you. That way we'll both be safe.

BENYA: This was, you can imagine, a surprise. No, no, I said to him. I can't take such a gift from a stranger. But before I could repeat my words again, he sat me behind the wheel . . . *(The*

CRAZY MAN *puts cut-out car around* BENYA.*)* and ran off down the street. *(*CRAZY MAN *exits.)* So, I figured, God gave me a present to spare my feet, and I drove it away. That's how I got the car. By luck.

DEVORAH: That's what I call an exciting story.

BENYA: And that's the way it's going to be, sister. Luck and style and boldness in the sun will take me farther than I ever thought. I know how it can been done.

LEVKA: I have a feeling you no longer want to work in my shop.

BENYA: So now it's your shop, is it Levka? Under such conditions, I've got better things to do than work in your shop.

LEVKA: What could be better than working in my shop? Tell me that, Mr. Bigshot.

BENYA: I've got plans, Levka, to make us rich in land and fortune. Schemes to take you out from the counter for good. Dream of houses in the country with flowers in front. Of servants in and out, up and down, cooking and cleaning and washing your clothes. Of horses that run like fire through the woods with their tails making initials in the wind. Of money enough to go to Moscow each Spring and come home with jewels trailing from your pockets like stars. Of women, Levka. Beautiful women, kissing your neck with their wet-warm lips and whispering all the time, now, Levka. Now. This and more I offer you. Join with me and we'll be partners in crime. The greatest the town has ever known.

DEVORAH: A gangster, Benya? Like the Cossacks?

LEVKA: That's a life for thugs and killers. Not for respectable Jews.

BENYA: Who said anything about killing? I'll do it all with brains and style and lots of dash. An unbeatable combination. I've chosen my gang already. An organization in need of new ideas.

LEVKA: Play the gangster today brother, and you won't be welcome under my roof tomorrow. I'm warning you.

BENYA: I won't be needing your roof, Levka. I'm building one of my own. A roof with tiles of gold.

LEVKA: In that case, good luck to you Benya. Don't ask me to pay for your funeral.

BENYA: Good luck to you, Levka. May you prosper from hard work.

DEVORAH: Oh, Benya. Please take me with you.

BENYA: Stay with Levka and take care of business, Devorah. You weren't made to be a lady gangster. But make sure he treats you well, you hear? If he doesn't, he'll answer to me.

DEVORAH: I'll stay if I have to, Benya, but inside, I'll be with you. Make me a promise, though?

BENYA: Anything you want.

DEVORAH: You'll be careful with yourself, yes? When you die, you should be in one piece.

BENYA: Don't you worry about me, Devorah. I plan to be alive a long, long time. Soon enough, you'll be hearing the name of Benya Krik around the square.

(Lights down.)

SCENE 2

REB LEIB *is sitting on the arm of a sofa on which are sitting* BENYA *and a woman in her thirties wearing a sexy dress. Her name if* LYUBKA SCHNEIVEIS. *She is a handsome-looking woman who is beginning to show signs of age around the eyes and the middle. The two are slightly drunk and hold champagne glasses. After* LEIB *speaks, he disappears behind the sofa.*

LEIB: Where does a young man go the first night he's free? Benya Krik goes where others only dream. And he goes there all the time.

BENYA: A toast, Lyubka. I propose a toast. To Lyubka the Whore. May her breasts always point toward heaven.

LYUBKA: Thanks for the compliment, Benya. But they point the other way these days.

BENYA: Don't be silly, Lyubka. You're as new and fresh as a sweet young girl. And ten times more exciting.

LYUBKA: And you've got more and use it better than any man in the Moldavanka.

BENYA: That night in your purple bed, when you made me a man. I still get dizzy remembering.

LYUBKA: It was nothing.

BENYA: Nothing, she says. Satin smooth and soft as fur. That's how it was. Your arms were full and warm around me. And your hips moved three ways at once. Like the cavalry at a charge. I'll never forget that night, Lyubka. Never.

LYUBKA: Wait till a pretty girl comes your way with hair that smells like grass. You'll forget my name in a minute.

BENYA: Not after what you've given me. I'm going far and I'm going fast but a man does not forget deep favors, gracefully done. I could never forget a woman like you.

LYUBKA: Where are you heading so fast, Benya? You just left the shop and already you're gone. Like a lightning streak you move.

BENYA: I'm making connections, Lyubka. Establishing positions. Let my brother scrape and bend his back if he likes, but the sun is going to shine on Benya Krik. Bright and warm on Benya Krik.

LYUBKA: I believe you, Benya. You don't have to shout in my ear.

BENYA: If a man doesn't shout, no one hears what he says. And I intend to be heard.

LYUBKA: Tell me, Benya. Where you're going, there's room for extra passengers?

BENYA: Come now, Lyubka. When a man starts out in life, he has to travel alone. You told me so yourself.

LYUBKA: Always alone, Benya. Always thinking. Sometimes I wonder if, inside of you, there's room for anything but fancy dreams and schemes.

BENYA: Of course there is, Lyubka. I'm a man, aren't I? But not now, understand. Now Benya Krik has other things to do.

LYUBKA: What kind of things?

BENYA: First thing tomorrow I offer my services to one-eyed Ephraim Rook.

LYUBKA: Ephraim Rook? The wool merchant?

BENYA: Wool merchant by day, but by night, a fearless stalker of the moonlight docks. Rook is looking for a man like me. He just doesn't know it yet.

LYUBKA: Watch out for Ephraim Rook, Benya. He's a rough customer with a heart of lead.

BENYA: You know something about Rook? Let me hear.

LYUBKA: I'll tell you a story about Ephraim Rook. You make up your mind.

(We see ROOK, *standing next to* LYUBKA. *He is a powerful man with an eye patch over his right eye. He is gruff and unkempt. He looks like a pirate captain without his ship.)*

It was Sunday night when Rook came in. He had a mean look in his one good eye when he told me his desire.

ROOK: I want a girl and I want her quick. She should have long black hair and make lots of noise. I have no time to waste.

LYUBKA: I have just the girl for you, I said to him. The famous Marina Yevtushenko who once spent a night with the Tsar.

ROOK: She better be good and she better be fast. The last one I had lay like a whitefish under the sheets half an hour without a stir. I'm a simple man with simple tastes. I want no second-rate girls.

LYUBKA: I'll make a guarantee, I said to him then. Sweet Marina tickles your fancy or your money back, with interest.

ROOK: Money means nothing if she's second-rate. I want satisfaction guaranteed.

(ROOK leaves.)

LYUBKA: And he took Marina, a sweet young thing, down the hall to room number two. Five minutes later, her face red with blood, she runs to me in fear for her life. Ephraim Rook was beating her black and blue. And why? Because he objected to the color of her underpants.

BENYA: Young girls he can beat, but not a man like me. When I'm through with my pitch, he'll beg me to join his gang.

LYUBKA: And if he breaks your legs like chicken bones?

BENYA: You underestimate my talents, Lyubka. For talking fast and thinking quick, no one is better than Benya Krik. I'll be a member of the gang by tomorrow night. And after that . . . who can tell? Another drink, Lyubka. To send me on my way.

LYUBKA: No more drinks, Benya. I have customers coming in, one every hour. In my business, everything is turnover.

BENYA: A kiss then, for good luck.

LYUBKA: One kiss but then you go.

(They kiss.)

BENYA: Now I can go in peace, Lyubka. Out your door and into the moonlight future.

LYUBKA: But will you come back, Benya? That's what I want to know.

BENYA: I'll move fast as desire can go, Lyubka, but I'll always come back to you. Tomorrow night we'll be drinking another toast. To Benya Krik, first-night gangster, and lovely Lyubka the Whore. That's what I call . . . a couple.

(BENYA and LYUBKA freeze as LEIB comes out from behind sofa and addresses the audience as Scene 3 begins.)

SCENE 3

As LEIB *speaks, the lights fade on* BENYA *and* LYUBKA *and rise on* ROOK *sitting behind a desk at another part of the stage.*

LEIB: The next morning, as the sun rose orange above the sea, Benya Krik, in his bright red car, paid a visit to Ephraim Rook.

(The cardboard car of BENYA, *with* BENYA *inside, moves from the wings, across the stage, and over to* ROOK'S *office.* BENYA *is dressed in another gaudy outfit. The car moves as* LEIB *speaks.)*

What thoughts were in his mind as he rode through the square, only God above can know. We on earth know only what we hear—that he took a breath, shook fear from his heart, and left the past behind.

*(*LEIB *exits.* BENYA, *who has gotten out of his car, barges in on his would-be employer.)*

BENYA: Good morning, comrade Rook. Now down to business.

ROOK: Find your way to the door, Mr. Whoever-you-are. I don't speak to children.

BENYA: I want a minute of your time.

ROOK: A minute's too much.

BENYA: A minute can change a man's life.

ROOK: Who are you? Where do you come from? And what do you want with me?

BENYA: My name is Benya Krik and I've crawled out from beneath a pile of scrap. I desire that you take me on. I want to climb aboard your ship, lift high the sails, and let the winds of life carry me far out to sea. Give me a chance and I'll transform your organization into an empire of crime.

ROOK: Go take up space somewhere else, Mr. Baby. I'm finished with cocker spaniels with big ideas in their heads. Once I had a talker like you. Long-legs Hershel, that was his name. A safecracker with a body like a cat. He could scale any building. Climb any wall. That was his claim to fame. The first night on the job, he fell off a boat and drowned. After I paid him fifty rubles. In advance. Pick some pockets for a year and a half and come back with skills.

(Snaps his fingers. Two thugs come out. To BENYA.*)*

My associates. Mr. Bender and Mr. Bullock.

BENYA: Pleased to meet you, gentlemen.

THUGS: Likewise, I'm sure.

ROOK: They will now accompany you to the alley where they will relieve you of your teeth. Good day, Mr. Benya the Baby.

(He signals and they ominously approach BENYA.*)*

BENYA: You're making a mistake, my friends, when you treat me so rudely. Stay with your old ways too long and the world will pass you by. You'll end up a fossil, Monsieur Rook. A relic behind your warehouse walls. I'm warning you.

*(*ROOK *signals his men again. They approach.)*

ROOK: You're warning me, Mr. Benya Krik?

BENYA: To be warned is to know better. No excuses later on.

*(*ROOK *signals his men to move back.)*

ROOK: Explain to me then how I am making a mistake. And convince me. For your own continued health.

BENYA: It's simple, Rook. Extremely simple. You are a wealthy man in this town and yet you live, pardon the expression, like a rodent in the garbage. *(The thugs approach.)* No offense intended. *(The thugs back off.)* I ask you, Monsieur Rook, why load wool all day just to hide what your warehouse holds? Why not be a crook in the open, like the Cossacks and the police? Why not walk through the square with a hat on your head and a cane in your hand? Or be an elder of the synagogue? A member of the board of trade? Maybe the mayor himself? You can do it,

Rook. All you have to do is listen to the lesson I'm teaching, and the world will open up before you like magic.

ROOK: Speak to me one word at a time, Mr. Head-in-the-Clouds. And make yourself clear.

BENYA: A new age is coming in Odessa. An age when men with brains and style and luck, men like you and me, can be the kings of the world. Anything we want, we can get and we don't have to beat people on the head to get it. All we have to do is walk out bold in the sun, take what we want, and after we're through, do it again. No more shadow hiding or running scared in the night. This is the way of the future, Monsieur Rook. Shake hands now and I'll show you how it's done. I report to work in the morning.

ROOK: You're an impressive man, Mr. Benya Krik. But not impressive enough for me. Before I take you in, you must perform a test. Do you agree?

BENYA: What you say I'll gladly do.

ROOK: I have an enemy in the town.

BENYA: This I am sad to hear.

ROOK: Bigger and stronger than any Jew alive.

BENYA: He is suffering already. Tell me his name.

ROOK: Ruven Tartakovsky is his name. Better known as Jew-and-a-half.

BENYA: Jew-and-a-half?

(When the name of JEW-AND-A-HALF *is mentioned, we see a large, hungry man staring stony-eyed at us. He devours a huge turkey leg while staring straight ahead. He continues eating and staring as* ROOK *speaks.)*

ROOK: Meaner than a Cossack. Fiercer than a hurricane. Not a man, but a force of nature. This is Tartakovsky. A hundred men count his money every night. And a hundred more check the figures later. Nine times I've tried to rob his shop and nine times I've left with empty hands. So, I leave the job to you. One week you have to unline the pocket of Jew-and-a-half. Fail and I make you a first-class funeral. Succeed and you're part of the gang. What do you say to that?

BENYA: I commend you for your keen eye and intelligence, comrade Rook. To the assignment I say . . . O.K. First I will write a note.

*(*BENYA *takes out a piece of paper and a pen and starts writing.)*

BENYA: "Highly respected Ruven Tartakovsky, better known as Jew-and-a-half, be kind enough to place under the rain barrel, on Saturday, all the money you have in your possession. Vault included. If you refuse, know that a great disappointment awaits you in your private life. Respects from Benya Krik, whom you will know soon." Well, my friend. The robbing of Tartakovsky has begun.

ROOK: You think he'll answer such a note? He'll kill you once and then he'll kill you twice.

BENYA: A man must take chances in this world, Ephraim Rook. If your enemy makes no reply, I will be forced to take strong action. For now, I await his answer like a gentleman. In a week, you'll have yours and I'll have mine. It's as simple as A . . . B . . . C . . .

(When he says "C," LEIB *appears, standing next to* JEW-AND-A-HALF. *As* BENYA *lifts the note in the air,* LEIB *hands a note to* JEW-AND-A-HALF *who immediately springs into frenetic action. Running around. Reading and re-reading the note.)*

SCENE 4

JEW-AND-A-HALF'S *shop.*

JEW-AND-A-HALF: Such a letter is an insult to respectability. I must protect myself from this maniac who thinks he can rob a man with a note. They're trying again, God. To take from me what you in your bounty have given. Such is the ingenuity of evil that always are there new plans and schemes. But they will not succeed. The record of Tartakovsky will last forever. Nine tries and never a ruble touched. Locks must be locked. Bolts must be bolted. Joseph! Joseph Muginstein! Come up here this moment! *(He rushes off. Comes back a moment later with a huge leg of lamb. Looks around. Shouts again.)*
Joseph! Joseph! Where are you when I need you?

(A meek, thin, undernourished young man comes in, carrying two enormous sacks of grain on his frail shoulder. He drops them down and speaks.)

JOSEPH: I came as quick as I could. There was a rat in the cellar. I tried to kill it, but it got away.

JEW-AND-A-HALF: Keep away from rats, Joseph. Rats are good for cellars. Like little policemen they prowl the floor eating the bugs that eat my grain. Bugs, tiny animals you hardly see, can ruin a man's business in a week. The rats should not be killed Joseph. Rats are my partners. My friends.

JOSEPH: But the rat I saw was eating the grain himself.

JEW-AND-A-HALF: Don't be a stupid boy, Joseph. The rat hides himself in the grain till a little bug comes along. Then, like a hungry lion, he stalks him down—slow, steady—until he bites the bug in half and smiles, happy he's saved the grain of Tartakovsky and thankful for a good meal. The rat, he is like you, Joseph.

A protector of the grain. An important person. What was that sound?

JOSEPH: I didn't hear anything.

JEW-AND-A-HALF: Check the backstairs. Lock the lock. All protection I want against this letter-writing lunatic. The guards. Are they on danger alert?

JOSEPH: Twenty-five men with guns in the street.

JEW-AND-A-HALF: Then we are safe, Joseph. Safe. *(He lifts a large bell on the counter.)* All I have to do is tinkle my bell and foolish intruders are cut down like weeds. I tell you, Joseph, if this demented scribbler appears now, it will be by magic.

*(*JEW-AND-A-HALF *grabs his stomach in pain and drops to the floor.* JOSEPH *is upset.)*

JOSEPH: I'll run get the doctor.

JEW-AND-A-HALF: Do not leave me now, Joseph. It's only the pains that tell me it's time for lunch. By noon, I'm too weak to think. Listen to me, Joseph, and listen well. I am giving you now an urgent assignment. You must not fail. Understand?

JOSEPH: I think so. I hope so.

JEW-AND-A-HALF: Good. Very good. Run to the Balkan restaurant and order lunch for Tartakovsky. Rare leg of lamb with wild mint jelly. Two pounds kasha with gravy floating. One dozen dumplings, not too greasy. And bring a finger bowl with nice warm water. Once I've eaten, I'll fight ten men myself. Are you ready for the assignment, Joseph? *(*JOSEPH *nods timidly)* Then hold on to your courage, and charge.

(As JOSEPH *turns to leave,* BENYA *jumps out of a grain sack with a gun in his hand.)*

BENYA: Raise your arms high, gentlemen, and shake hands with God. Benya Krik has come special delivery to your till.

JEW-AND-A-HALF: Thief. Hoodlum.

BENYA: Vermin. Hog.

JEW-AND-A-HALF: Gangster. Rogue.

BENYA: Reptile. Dog.

JEW-AND-A-HALF: Upstart warthog. Infidel of the day. You won't get away with this. *(He picks up his bell and rings it.)*

BENYA: Your men are lying down on the job, Jew-and-a-half. My men are standing over them. Your record has been broken for good.

JEW-AND-A-HALF: Animal. Lunatic. Maniac. Scum.

*(*JEW-AND-A-HALF *makes a titanic sound of pain, clutches his stomach, and falls to the ground in pain.)*

BENYA: *(Bending over him):* Pardon my intrusion, Monsieur Jew-and-a-half, but you will have to postpone your midday meal a few moments. We have some important business to transact. I will now put some cotton in your mouth which you may chew on if you like. *(He turns to* JOSEPH.*)* Mr. Clerk?

JOSEPH: Yes? Yes?

BENYA: Fill my sack with the assets of your employer. And make it snappy, if you don't mind.

JOSEPH: Anything you say, Mr. Gangster, anything you say.

*(*JOSEPH *runs about putting money and belongings in the sack and* BENYA *turns his attention to* JEW-AND-A-HALF *writhing on the floor.)*

BENYA: Now, Mr. Jew-and-a-half. While your clerk is insuring the security of my future, I will speak to you of what's on my mind. Explain to me why, upon receipt of a friendly note, you could not reply in kind? We could have eaten a meal, had a business drink, smoked big cigars and discussed my proposition, gentleman to gentleman. "Now my balance sheets are low," you might have said. "Give me a month to pay in full." Arrangements could have been made. Low interest and all. But no. You cast out civility and treat a fellow human like he is lower than a toad. You were greedy and proud, Jew-and-a-half, and now you will suffer for your sins. Have you anything to say.?

(He pulls off the gag for a second. JEW-AND-A-HALF *shouts.)*

JEW-AND-A-HALF: You'll regret this day forever. Mr. Benya the Terrible. Every ruble you take will be drop of your blood.

BENYA: *(Puts back the gag)* I see the day's events have taught you no lessons. I am sorry for that. Extremely sorry.

*(*JOSEPH *has come back with the sack full.)*

JOSEPH: Here you are Mr. Sneak Thief. Everything that was his is yours.

BENYA: Good work, my clerk. Excellent work. Now, if it is not too much trouble for you, take the jewels from the pocket of your employer and transfer them to my hand.

JOSEPH: Here, Mr. Robber. Here they are.

BENYA: Thank you, my good man. I appreciate your efforts. Very pretty, Jew-and-a-half. You have a keen eye for shimmering things.

JOSEPH: You have everything, Mr. Gangster. Please leave us in peace.

BENYA: I was just on my way out. Thank you for your decency and good manners. At least there's one gentleman at this address. May God shine down on you many long years.

(He turns to go when a man with a gun, obviously drunk, enters. He is SAVKA BUTKIS, *one of* BENYA'S *men.* BENYA *turns his gun on him as he enters.* BUTKIS *calls out.)*

BUTKIS: Don't shoot, Benya. It's only Savka Butkis late for work. Give me a sack and I'll carry too.

BENYA: Idiot, you're drunk.

SAVKA:No, Benya. No. I'll show you how sober I am. *(Pulls out his gun.)* That bird shivering over there. *(Points to* JOSEPH.*)* I'll part his hair in the center of his head without giving him a wiggle. You'll see. *(He points the gun.)*

BENYA: Out, Savka. This is no time for games.

SAVKA: Come on Benya. It's nothing to me. Watch.

(He fires. JOSEPH *clutches his chest and drops to the floor.)*

BENYA: What have you done, Butkis? Guns are for shooting in the air, not at people. My sincerest apologies, Jew-and-a-half. But accidents do happen. You'll forgive me. I'm sure.

(He goes to JEW-AND-A-HALF *and takes off his gag.)*

JEW-AND-A-HALF: An eye for an eye, Benya Krik. A clerk for a clerk. I saw it all. All.

*(*BENYA *quickly puts back the gag.)*

BENYA: Then you also saw who pulled the trigger, and you know it was not me. I'll make it up to you Tartakovsky. You have my word on that. Benya Krik is a respecter of innocent life. I swear on my father's grave, Butkis, you'll lie next to him. I believe it is time to make an exit.

(He grabs BUTKIS *and drags him out hurriedly. From the counter,* LEIB *walks forward. He unties* JEW-AND-A-HALF *who picks up the dead* JOSEPH *in his arms and carries him off.* LEIB *follows this for a moment. Then he turns to the audience and speaks.)*

LEIB: Are words necessary, my friends? A man was, and is no more. Such a twist of fate, such quick misfortune. What did it do to Benya Krik? Did it stop him fast or cut short his amazing climb? No, my friends. It inspired him instead to bolder deeds. Watch as he demonstrates to Ephraim Rook the workings of the new age of man and raises the morning sun in the middle of the night.

SCENE 5

Lights up on BENYA *and* ROOK.

ROOK: Do you know what you have done today, Mr. Benya Krik? You have ruined my good name in the town with your murderous baby games.

BENYA: He was a nice fellow that clerk. I meant him no harm. I saw his eyes when he fell. First there was fear and then there was nothing. Nothing. I didn't mean for that to happen.

ROOK: It's not what you meant that counts. It's what you did. You have made a mistake and now you'll pay the price. *(He opens a large knife.)* Our discussion is at an end.

(He snaps his fingers and the same two thugs from before reappear.)

BENYA: Don't be acting fast and thinking slow, Mr. Rook. You do not see the situation as I do. From moldy cream, tasty cheese is made. From bad luck, good fortune can rise. In the new age of man, every misfortune has inside the sprouting seeds of benefit. You only have to plant it right.

ROOK: Don't talk your fancy talk to me, Mr. Benya Krik. Murder is murder. You can't bring the dead back to life.

BENYA: Yes you can, my friend, if you act fast and lightening bold. Here we have a case of old thought versus new. I will teach you a lesson.

ROOK: Do it fast, Benya Krik. I have no time for riddles.

BENYA: A murder is either a tragedy or an opportunity. How you see it makes it what it is. And how you make others see it, makes you either a killer or a hero. Simple is simple, yes? I intend to make poor Joseph a saint, the killer a devil and you and I heroes in the town, Monsieur Rook. And I'll do it all before the moon turns pale tomorrow. You just need to trust me, gentleman to gentleman. What do you say to this?

ROOK: I trusted you once, Benya Krik. And look what you did.

BENYA: Trust me again and I'll deliver, Rook. If I don't, you have my permission to throw my head in the sea without my body. I won't even make a noise.

ROOK: What do you intend to do to make this right?

BENYA: Tonight, I myself will pay a visit to the unfortunate Tartakovsky, without guns or knives in my hands, and when I leave, a miracle will have taken place for all Odessa to remember. You and I will benefit, my friend. And your reputation will be saved.

ROOK: Stay away from Tartakovsky, Benya Krik. He's a man of terrible passion.

BENYA: To have passion, a man must have money in the bank, Mr. Rook. Take away his money, and his passion disappears as fast as his friends. That's when I move in, not with guns but with a razor tongue. By tomorrow you'll see what I'm saying is right.

ROOK: By tomorrow you'll be seaweed in the tide if you fail. Remember that well, Benya Krik with big ideas.

BENYA: I won't fail, Ephraim Rook. On that you can rely. Just send a messenger to Tartakovsky and leave the rest to me.

ROOK: A messenger to Tartakovsky? Who'd be crazy enough to go?

(REB LEIB *approaches from off stage.)*

LEIB: Excuse me, gentlemen. I would be honored to carry such information.

BENYA: Reb Arye Leib, an excellent man for the job. This is what I want you to do. Tell Tartakovsky there's a man in town who sympathizes with his terrible plight and wishes to retrieve his money. With interest. Tell him the man will appear at his door tonight at precisely nine p.m. He will wear a big fur coat and go by the name of . . . a friend in the night. Have you got that all?

LEIB: Down to the last syllable. I have an excellent ear for a story.

BENYA: Then go to your work, Reb Leib and remember when you do, you are helping to create the new and modern age of man.

Scene 6

Lights up on JEW-AND-A-HALF *sitting, inconsolable, in an armchair.* LEIB *appears next to him and speaks to audience.*

LEIB: What is more pitiful a sight, my friends, than a grown man grieving over loss. And what is so great as the power of a few small words whispered softly into an ear *(*LEIB *bends over and whispers to* JEW-AND-A-HALF *who becomes jubilant)* that a man, hearing them, can take hope again and put an end to deep despair. Whether the words are true or not, the hearer never wants to know. And so, who was I to do anything more than whisper a message and be on my way. Meanwhile, as Tartakovsky jumps for joy within, a hat, a coat, and a black mustache, wrapped in the Russian moon, are making their way across the square to a rendezvous with miracles.

*(*BENYA *in his red car, dressed in a wig, a hat and a fur coat, moves to where* JEW-AND-A-HALF *is sitting, then standing and anxiously pacing.* JEW-AND-A-HALF *begins speaking before* BENYA *arrives in his disguise.)*

JEW-AND-A-HALF: Oh, God! Oh, God! The ways of fate are wonderful and strange. Here alone, in my darkest hour, a friend has come without a name, like a blessing from above. I will go to synagogue this week for sure. Amen! Amen! Amen!

(Slowly, a figure wrapped in a huge fur coat walks in. His head is dropped, a black armband around one sleeve. The figure coughs and JEW-AND-A-HALF *wheels around.)*

JEW-AND-A-HALF: Mysterious stranger. Are you? Are you the friend in the night?

BENYA: Yes, Mr. Sufferer. A friend till the end.

JEW-AND-A-HALF: Come in, miraculous comrade. I could fall on my knees and kiss the knuckles of your hand for what you have done for me. Please. Please. Do not be a stranger in my home. Sit down and let me tell you how I've suffered. Such a thing he has done, the hoodlum. The dog. To steal from the rich is a crime against God. To steal from the poor is not so bad. How can you miss what you never had. But to steal from a rich man's purse is to leave him helpless before the world. A fool, an imbecile in rags. What will I do without my money? How will I live if I'm not rich? Once you get used to silk, you itch to death in wool. This is a fact of life. I tell you, my friend. Before your message reached my ears, life had no meaning for me at all. None, none at all.

(There is a scream from above, a wailing cry.)

That sound. Like sirens in the night. That is the weeping of unhappy Tante Peyse, the aunt of dead Joseph. Your good deed will turn her tears to smiles before long. Come, come my friend. Take off your coat and stay awhile. I wish to look straight into the face of revenge.

*(*JEW-AND-A-HALF *helps* BENYA *with his coat.* BENYA *whips out a bouquet of flowers, presents them to* JEW-AND-A-HALF, *and bows as his regular self.)*

BENYA: Good evening to you, Jew-and-a-half. We have business to discuss. You'll put these flowers in water, I trust. They are the first and least thing I could do for unfortunate Tante Peyse.

JEW-AND-A-HALF: Imposter! Hooligan! Son of a whore! Now I'm going to kill you for sure.

(Throws down flowers and takes a step towards BENYA.*)*

BENYA: It would be unhealthy for you to proceed. Ten armed men are waiting outside. They are in deep mourning like me and would not like to fight. These flowers should not be thrown on the ground. They bruise easily.

JEW-AND-A-HALF: What do you want with me now? Haven't you taken enough?

BENYA: There are still details to clarify, my friend. We must have a short, sweet meeting. I am a sorry man, Jew-and-a-half. With the blood of the clerk still on my conscience.

JEW-AND-A-HALF: A fine trick you thought up. Killing live people. But you won't get away so easy, Mr. Benya Krik. I'll get my money back.

BENYA: But I have gotten away, Jew-and-a-half. And now you'll listen to me. All night long I have been weeping for the dead Joseph while you have been weeping only for your money which you'll never see.

JEW-AND-A-HALF: Don't say that, Benya Krik. I want my money back. I need my money back. Half my earnings in the future will be yours. Guaranteed. Just give me back what you have taken. If only the shiny jewels.

BENYA: I'm afraid that would be impossible, Mr. Jew-and-a-half. I have already disposed of your money.

JEW-AND-A-HALF: Disposed? What do you mean, disposed?

BENYA: The poultry workers' orphans home is richer tonight thanks to the generosity of Benya Krik. Half your money I gave to them. In memory of Joseph Muginstein.

JEW-AND-A-HALF: Half my money. To smelly orphans?

BENYA: They're naming a wing after me. The Krik Pavillion, it will be called.

JEW-AND-A-HALF: With my money, they name wings after you?

BENYA: A fitting memorial to Joseph, don't you think?

JEW-AND-A-HALF: The rest. What did you do with the rest?

BENYA: The Import Square Synagogue will have a nice new roof. Compliments of Benya Krik. A small plaque will go up to honor my generosity . . . Simple gold with scrolls on the side. In memory of Muginstein, the perished.

JEW-AND-A-HALF: Is there anything left, Mr. Torturer? Or have you thrown it all away?

BENYA: What is left will pay expenses for the funeral of Joseph Muginstein. Believe me, Tartakovsky, they will be talking about Joseph's final ride when the name of the Tsar is remembered by no one on the earth. I myself will ride in the first car tossing golden coins to the crowd. You should thank me today, Jew-and-a-half. Without my help, you would never have honored the memory of your clerk in so generous a manner.

JEW-AND-A-HALF: You win your bitter victory today, Mr. Benya Krik. But everyone's luck must change. And yours will too. You can't push and push and not get pushed in return. I have friends in places. I have ways to retrieve what is mine.

BENYA: A man without money has power nowhere. You are a thing of the past, my friend. Benya Krik is a thing of the future. You'll never catch me again.

JEW-AND-A-HALF: We'll see. Benya Krik. We'll see. Now it would give me pleasure if you left my premises. Our business is at an end.

BENYA: One more item we have to discuss, then I'll be on my way.

JEW-AND-A-HALF: One more item and I'll be in the poorhouse for sure.

BENYA: My brains shivered an hour ago when I heard you intend to pay Tante Peyse a thousand rubles for a settlement. In what safe have you locked away your heart?

JEW-AND-A-HALF: Give me back my money, I'll pay her more. You kill a man and expect me to pay expenses?

BENYA: Joseph Muginstein was not killed by me, Tartakovsky, nor did he die yesterday, as you say. Joseph Muginstein died seven years ago,, when he first entered your employ. You killed the soul of the clerk with hard work and low wages. You refused to treat him like a man, Jew-and-a-half, and his spirit got sicker by the day. You loaded his shoulders with sacks of grain until he walked like a broken branch. Next time you shave yourself, look in the mirror and don't look away from what you see. Just look hard and deep into your fat murderer's face and think, Tartakovsky, think. *(Another cry from above.)* Ten thousand down and a pension till she dies. And may she live to a hundred and twenty. Sign here *(unfurls a document)* or we'll adjourn to my limousine.

JEW-AND-A-HALF: This is blackmail, Benya Krik. Extortion too.

BENYA: This is giving the people their due, Tartakovsky. Nothing more than that.

JEW-AND-A-HALF: I'll take a loan for 2,500. That's all I can afford.

BENYA: Seven years, he worked for you. Seven years he suffered.

JEW-AND-A-HALF: Five thousand down and fifty a month. That's all.

(Another wail from above.)

BENYA: Don't those woman's cries play on your heartstrings even a simple tune? You wouldn't want her wailing out her lungs in the square.

JEW-AND-A-HALF: *(Shouts upstairs)* Shut up you crazy woman. You're a worse robber than he is.

BENYA: Ten thousand down, Tartakovsky. If she keeps it up, you'll pay more.

JEW-AND-A-HALF: All right. All right. I'll pay. But believe me, Benya Krik. When the people learn what you've done to me, they'll string you up by your toes in the square.

BENYA: On the contrary, my friend. When the people find out where your money has gone and who has done the giving, they'll lift me on their shoulders and march me through the streets with dances and songs. They'll know in their hearts that the old have fallen and that the new age has begun. And that will be only the beginning. Only the beginning.

(Another wail from above. BENYA *picks up the bouquet and shouts to the voice above.)*

BENYA: Tante Peysa. Bereaved old woman with lungs of steel. If you need my life to make you happy, come and take it. But everyone makes mistakes in this life. God included. He could have put the Jews in Brazil, where there are mountains and lakes and a person can walk naked in the streets. Instead, he put us here, to live tormented in Hell. Have no fear old woman. Benya Krik will ease the burdens of your heart. You'll have ten thousand down and fifty a week till you drop. *(The wails begin to subside)* Your nephew Joseph will have a first-class funeral. A suprise of my own I promise as well. Guaranteed to make you sleep easy on your pillow of tears. No need to cry anymore, old woman. In the new age to come, Benya Krik will provide. *(The wails subside. As* BENYA *continues to speak, a low, slow drumbeat is heard behind. It continues through his speech.)* You have made a sad old lady happier today. There is still some good in your soul. I shall now make preparations for the sorry day to come. Make sure I see you there, with your long face on, when the sun comes up white in the sky. Until then. *(Wraps himself in his big fur coat, puts on his hat and wig)* I bid you . . . adieu.

Scene 7

Lights fade on BENYA *and* JEW-AND-A-HALF. *At center of stage is* REB LEIB *with a prayer book in his hand. The drumbeat is louder now. And continues while he speaks. As he speaks, a small procession moves down the theater aisle*—ROOK *and* LEVKA *carry the casket, followed by* TARTAKOVSKY, DEVORAH. *As* LEIB *speaks they move on to the stage and place the casket at his feet. Behind the procession is* BENYA *and* LYUBKA *riding in* BENYA'S *car. Another casket sticks out the back of the car.* BENYA *and* LYUBKA *come on to the stage just after the others. The drumbeat continues all through.*

LEIB: The funeral of Joseph Muginstein. What was it like? Not like any funeral you've ever seen. This I can say for sure. Hundreds of people turned out that day. Thousands of people it seemed. Weaving like a black snake of mourning through the streets of the salty town. And behind them all, in his bright red car, Benya Krik, the provider, with Lyubka by his side, waved to the mourning crowd. And when poor Joseph was nearly in the ground, the provider provided one surprise more. The surprise that made him the king.

(BENYA *steps forward.)*

BENYA: I have in mind to make a brief funeral oration. We are here today, my friends, to pay our last respects to a valiant laborer who perished for the sake of rubles, who died for the greed of his employer who today stands shamefaced among us. Poor Joseph Muginstein. What did he get out of life? Nothing worth mentioning. What did he pay for what he got? Plenty . . . and through the nose. How did he spend his ink-smudged days? Counting other men's money. Why did he die? So that people could take a lesson from his passing. Who did he die for? The whole working class. Friends, the living and dying of Joseph Muginstein is a reminder to all the suffering workers of the town. Clerks. Assistants. Market boys. Tailors. Don't sit meek like birds on a bough and wait for something to happen. Be bold. Be brave, dream some dreams and life can be something you never thought it could be. An adventure. A holiday. A festival. When a Cossack stares down at you through his beard, stare back at him and don't blink your eyes. Show him there's no fear in your heart and you'll be free, my friends. Free. If you're afraid to do it now, that's all right. Watch Benya Krik and you'll see how its done. And now, my friends, before we lay poor Joseph to rest, one small detail remains. I believe it only proper for the murderer to be buried beside his victim, joined in death as they were, so briefly, in life.

(He makes a signal and he and ROOK *carry the other coffin from the car and lay it down next to* JOSEPH'S.*)*

So I ask you to accompany to his last resting place, one unknown to you but, like Joseph, already deceased. One trigger-pulling Savka Butkis. And now, my friends, with justice done and the sun overhead, I bid you all . . . good day.

*(*BENYA *freezes in the position he is in at the end of the speech.* LEIB *steps out and speaks to the audience.)*

LEIB: As soon as these words came out from his lips there was a silence everywhere around. And then, like the sound of a sacred horn, a voice cried out high and loud. Some say it came from the back of the crowd. Some say it came from above. Nobody knows quite from where it came but everyone remembers what it said.

VOICE *(offstage):* A king. A king I tell you. This Benya Krik is a king.

LEIB: And that was how it was said in Odessa. And on that day, with casket at his feet, Benya Krik began his amazing reign.

(Lights fade.)

Act II

Scene 1

REB LEIB *stands alone at the apron of the stage. Behind him there is a doorframe and in front of the door,* BENYA'S *red car.*

LEIB: There are times in life when events in the air change the course of a person's days. And when they do, a man is transformed from a man to something more. This is what happened to Benya Krik after he buried poor Joseph in his grave. In every shop on the square, word got around of the king's miraculous deeds. People in the streets talked over tea of the courage of Benya Krik. Old men with bent backs scratched their beards in wonder that such boldness could come from a Jew. And the king himself? What did he do with his fame? He used it as smart men do, to make himself more famous still. *(pause)* But first, he took some relaxation in the house of Lyubka Schneiveis on the square. Three days he stayed within her walls without once coming out for air. On the fourth day, a crowd began to gather, waiting for the king to emerge. They waited all night under a starry sky but the king did not appear. Then, like a visitation from above, at the break of the fifth morning's light, Benya the King appeared at the door and made a declaration. A new age in Odessa had begun.

*(*BENYA *emerges and speaks to audience.)*

BENYA: I am weary, my friends, but I am happy too. While resting within from my courageous deeds, some thoughts I have thought in my head. Since under the Cossacks' rule there is no justice for a Jew in Odessa, I, Benya Krik, will sit as judge in the

Court of the People's Griefs. Every Friday at ten o'clock you may bring your troubles here to me and, like King Solomon, I will be wise and fair and true. And now, to show you that justice can be done, the Court of the People's Griefs will convene. *(He throws an orange cloak around him, takes out a gavel, and sits down like a judge in his car.)*

Reb Leib, who knows all the troubles of the town, tell me the first case of the day.

LEIB: *(As* LEIB *speaks two men enter. One wears a black coat and a strange hat on his head. The other, who holds a handkerchief to his nose, is contorted, seemingly in pain. He can barely walk and he is constantly moaning his discomfort. They enter as* LEIB *introduces them.)* This is Solomon Gunner, a healer of warts and boils of the neck. And this unfortunate gentleman *(he points to the contorted man)*

CONTORTED MAN: Oh, such pain. Such pain.

LEIB: is the farmer Chaim Blit who sought assistance with a raging boil on the premises of Gunner six weeks past. He paid the charmer a fifty-ruble note and now wants his money back. Plus damages in cash for suffering.

CHAIM BLIT: I have suffered. God knows I have suffered.

BENYA: An interesting case. A serious problem here exists. *(To* BLIT.*)* My suffering friend, tell me your troubles.

BLIT: Such pain, I have Mr. Justice Giver. Such terrible pain. Nothing but troubles are plaguing me since I saw this cossack of chants and charms. Look at my nose, Mr. Benya the King.

(He takes the handkerchief away and shows his nose close up to BENYA.*)*

Like a turnip after it's cooked. And that's just the beginning. I have pains in my neck. Up and down my arms. My eyes tear in my soup at night and I can't make love to my wife.

BENYA: All from a boil on the nose?

BLIT: Not from the boil. From the cure. He would have done more, but I ran out of the house into the street.

BENYA *(to* GUNNER*)*: What do you have to say in defense?

GUNNER: I can't work miracles, Mr. Justice Maker. I applied to his proboscis a plaster of mustard seed, cow's urine, pine oil and matzo meal, a cure passed on to me by a great Rabbi in Minsk. It worked for many, it didn't work for him.

BLIT: It smelled worse than cows after a rain. And it burned like the fires of hell.

GUNNER: You should have seen the boil I was dealing with. As big as the testicle of a horse. I used everything I knew. Even the chant of the Shamuses of the Chelm Synagogue. There are some boils, that even a charmer can't reduce.

BLIT: He made my nose into a bleeding rag. He ruined my life. Money is all that can make me better. Oh, the pain. The pain.

BENYA *(Intervening. To* GUNNER*)*: You have to admit the man's nose looks worse now than when you began your treatment.

GUNNER: It was bad then, it is bad now. You must understand my position. People come to me for a wart or a boil and think they'll leave looking like a singer in the café. When they look the same as before, they blame it all on me. One boil, more or less, does not make a man.

BENYA: A wise thought, my friend. You are obviously a learned fellow. But you are also a liar and a crook.

GUNNER: I beg your pardon?

BENYA: A robber of the meek and the sick. Recite for me the Shamuses' chant of the Chelm Synagogue.

GUNNER: Right here? Right now?

BENYA: There is no better place.

GUNNER: It is a secret chant. Not to be sung in public.

BENYA: Sing the chant, my friend, or I'll break your arm in two.

GUNNER: All right. All right. But it's against my principles to do so.

Boils on the neck and boils on the nose,
Lick the fingers, lick the toes,
Turn the muscles of the arm,
Three times round, apply the balm.
There. That's all I shall reveal.

BENYA: Very strange, my friend. Three years ago this March, I had a wart removed from my right ring finger by great Reb Goldcorn of Chelm. He sang the chant in my ear for an hour. It sounded nothing like that. You have been trying to pull cloth over eyes and you know it. You will return the money you have extorted from farmer Blit plus fifty rubles fine for false testimony. That is the verdict of the Court of the People's Griefs.

BLIT: Oh, Mr. Benya the King. You are as great a man as they say. Thank you so much. So much. *(He goes over and kisses*

BENYA'S *hand. Then he straightens up as though nothing is wrong.)* I am beginning to feel better already just hearing the verdict from your lips.

BENYA: The verdict isn't over yet, my friend. You are a maker-up of injuries to your person and will pay as well. For the next six weeks, every man and woman with a boil or a wart will come to your house for hot water and words of comfort. I want you to see suffering, farmer Blit, so you will not counterfeit it again. Here is fifty rubles apiece for your troubles. May that be a balm on my decisions of the day. *(To audience)* And now, fellow citizens of Odessa, with justice done and sentences made, I declare the Court of the People's Griefs . . . adjourned.

(Lights down on BENYA. LEIB *speaks as Scene 2 begins.)*

Scene 2

LEIB: Every week, like Solomon of old, Benya Krik heard the people's woes. And every week he gave them money when the case was through. In the morning when he walked the streets, people followed by his side. Women tried to kiss his lips. Babies to hold his hands. They say those he touched were transformed on the spot. Even the sick they say he healed, so mighty was the gangster's hand. And yes, my friends, even Ephraim Rook, the one-eyed partner of Benya Krik, was touched by the magic of the King. Come . . .

(We see ROOK *at another part of the stage. He wears a scarlet suit and a pinky ring. He primps in an invisible mirror.)*

I'll show you what I mean.

*(*ROOK *stands there primping a second when* BENYA KRIK, *dressed to the teeth, bursts in.)*

BENYA: Good morning, partner Rook. How are you feeling this sunshiny day?

ROOK: *(He rushes to him and kisses him forcefully):* Kiss me first on the lips, Benya Krik. Then we'll talk. This philosophy of yours is a thing of magic. Today, I walked at twelve o'clock, head high through the square, and even waved at the chief of police. And he waved back at me. With his gloves still on. And that was only the start, Benya Krik. After that, everything happened just like you said it would. I didn't have to do a thing. *(He is telling a story.)*

For twenty years on Tuesday night I have eaten dinner in the restaurant of Misha Kimmel. Chicken boiled and kasha on the side. Also a glass of tea. For twenty years, alone in the corner, no one has even given me a look. Then, last night, with my suit on my back, I'm sitting like always at the table, when a beautiful woman walks up to me. A vision she was. From the sky.

(A BEAUTIFUL WOMAN *stands there.)*

BEAUTIFUL WOMAN: Do you mind if I join you, Monsieur Rook. I am all alone in the night.

ROOK: Her lips were wet as cabbages in the rain and her breasts breathed white beneath her dress.

BEAUTIFUL WOMAN: You are the famous Ephraim Rook, are you not? The partner of Benya the King? I like the cut of your suit.

ROOK: This she said to me, Benya. To me. I could not deny her a seat at my table. And she, for her part, could deny me nothing either. I didn't even have to pay. Not even a ruble for soap. And later. Later . . .

BEAUTIFUL WOMAN: We'll meet again, Ephraim darling. I can't find another with style like you. Good night.

*(*WOMAN *exits.)*

ROOK: I'm telling you, Benya, I didn't know if I was awake or dreaming. *(Pause)* You have been a messiah to me, Benya Krik. A transformer of olden ways. I will do anything you say.

BENYA: Good, partner. Because there is plenty more we have to do.

ROOK: If it gets me women I'll do it. No questions asked.

BENYA: That's the spirit, partner. Tell me. Have you ever thought of milk?

ROOK: Milk? When I was a baby, I thought of milk all the time.

BENYA: Start thinking of it again. We're becoming dairy men.

ROOK: Dairy men? What are you talking about?

BENYA: Answer me this, Rook. How many milk cows are there in Russia?

ROOK: What do I know about cows?

BENYA: Millions maybe. And how many babies? Millions too. Now all these babies, to grow up big and strong, need milk to drink. Follow me so far?

*(*ROOK *nods, confused.)*

So, it seems to me, that the man who has his hand on the udders of the cows of Russia stands to have his hand on a lot of money. Simple is simple. The more you pull, the more money pours into the till. I have just the person in mind to take over.

ROOK: Really? Who's that?

BENYA: Zender Eichbaum. Owner of sixty milkcows, all save one. First we move in on his farm, then we expand operations. Buy new property, force old farmers out. It is an evergrowing operation. I have written the robbery note already.

ROOK: Not another note, Benya. To play the pipe, you need more tunes than one.

BENYA: I've got plenty of tunes in my head, partner. But a note has become my trademark in the town. "Dear Zender Eichbaum, owner of sixty milkcows, all save one.

(As he continues his speech we see, at another part of the stage, a YOUNG WOMAN *wearing a white shift dress. She is pretty and also has an air of toughness about her. She is sitting at an imaginary mirror, making herself up. This continues as* BENYA *reads.)*

Have the goodness to deposit, tomorrow morning under the steps of your milking shed, the sum of 20,000 rubles. If you fail to reply, something unheard-of will happen to your milkcows and you will be the talk of Odessa for years to come. Yours with abiding admiration, Benya the King." If he refuses to comply, we move in like a fox on a chicken. Soon every baby in Odessa will drink a toast to Krik and Rook morning and night. Our picture will be on all milk cans.

ROOK: I don't know about this, Benya. Eichbaum's a crook, like us. There's got to be loyalty somewhere.

BENYA: There is loyalty until necessity overwhelms it, Rook. Eichbaum is the man for me.

ROOK: But not for me, Benya. We've made enough enemies already in the town. Tartakovsky hasn't forgotten what you've done. He calls it the night of the great humiliation. He's talking to everyone who'll listen, the chief of police included. He won't stop until he's paid you back. Crime for crime.

BENYA: Stop worrying about Tartakovsky, Rook. His is a thing of the aging past. But you and I, my friend, we are the wave of the future. Stick with me, Ephraim Rook, and you'll have more women than you ever dreamed there were. And they'll do whatever you want them to.

ROOK: They will, Benya Krik? I don't know how many nights like that I can take.

BENYA: Don't be silly, Ephraim Rook. You can take more and more and more after that. In the new age of man, there's no end to the things you can take. With the sun shining bright on your head. I intend to get everything there is to get, partner. With you or without you. Understand?

ROOK: I understand, Benya Krik, I understand.

BENYA: Good, Ephraim Rook. Because before I'm through, they'll call you Rook the Rake. And me? They'll have to call me, Benya the Great.

(He waves the robbery note above his head and freezes. LEIB *takes the note from his hand, walks across stage, and places it on a desk near a* YOUNG WOMAN *who is seated behind a mirror.* YOUNG WOMAN *becomes animated.)*

LEIB: The note was passed from hand to hand, but there was no reply. Not because Eichbaum was a stubborn man, but because he was not in town. And so it happened that one cloudy night, Benya the King, impatient for gain, paid a visit to Eichbaum's farm. But more was to happen that cloudy night than anyone would think. For when Benya Krik moved in with knives to teach a lesson in life, he came away with more than blood and money. He came away . . . with a wife.

SCENE 3

LEIB *exits. The* YOUNG WOMAN *sits alone. A second later,* BENYA *bursts through the door with a bloody knife in his hands. She seems terrified.*

TSILYA: Hey! Hey! What's going on around here?

BENYA: Good evening to you, mademoiselle. Where is Zender Eichbaum? I have urgent words for him.

TSILYA: What are you doing here? Get out! Get out!

BENYA: Listen to the night air a second and what will you hear? The death moos of fifty cows, stabbed to death by my men. Zender Eichbaum has crossed swords with Benya Krik and now he pays in dead cows.

TSILYA: Robber! Thief! Pimple on the face the earth! Tell your hoodlums to leave or I'll put my foot up their behinds and do a dance.

BENYA: Angry words, mademoiselle. What air do you breathe to talk to Benya the King this way?

TSILYA: I'm Zender Eichbaum's daughter and may God piss on your head for your acts. Help! Help!

BENYA: You're not a shy girl, Zender Eichbaum's daughter. But your mouth blows like a foghorn at sea. *(Puts his hand on her mouth.)* You need to learn restraint. Speak to me like a lady to a gentleman and I'll release my hand. You have a first name, I assume?

TSILYA: Tsilya's my name. And what do you have against my father?

BENYA: Nothing personal. I sent your father a note. He did not answer. Now he suffers the consequences.

TSILYA: He didn't answer because he wasn't here. You night-crawling piece of slime.

BENYA: You've got a clever head, Tsilya Eichbaum, and a nice pair of breasts. Just the combination I need. I have a plan that will make you smile again.

TSILYA: What can you do to make this right, you robber of fathers in the night?

BENYA: Simple is simple. Right now, your father needs a man with money in his pants and influence in the town to make good his losses.

TSILYA: And such a man is you?

BENYA: An excellent deduction, Tsilya. I will restore your father to his former wealth and double his holdings in a month. When he dies he will have a grave in the suburban cemetary, right near the gate. *(Pause. He looks at her longingly.)* You have beautiful eyes. Tsilya. Very beautiful eyes.

TSILYA: Tell me later about my eyes. Talk to me now about money.

BENYA: But they turn colors when the light is right. Like pebbles under the sea.

TSILYA: What else can you do for my father?

BENYA: Everything. I'll do everything. He'll be a partner to me. He will run his business without interference. I will pick up profits Tuesday and Friday. All this your father will have, with one slight condition.

TSILYA: With men like you there's always a condition. What is it?

BENYA: That you agree to be my wife.

TSILYA: The wife of a gangster of the night? Are you crazy?

BENYA: You are talking to Benya the King. The gangster's gangster. I'll make you happy, Tsilya. That I know how to do. You have beautiful hair. Deep and beautiful hair.

TSILYA: And I also have a lover. Almost a husband.

BENYA: Tell me his name and I'll cut him up like an onion. Such teeth, Tsilya. Such fine white teeth.

TSILYA: He's a sailor. Out at sea. And he'd crack your skull like a hazel nut if he saw you look at me.

BENYA: A sailor at sea? What a story. What a joke. Zender Eichbaum's daughter engaged to a sailor.

TSILYA: And what's wrong with a sailor?

BENYA: Nothing. If you want to be poor all your life, go and marry your sailor. If you like the smell of fish on a lover's lips, the touch of his leather hands on your breasts, who am I to deny you?

TSILYA: And you can offer me more, I suppose?

BENYA: What can't I offer, you should have asked. Close your eyes, Tsilya. And imagine the things I will tell you now. They will all be yours. Are your beautiful eyes closed?

TSILYA: They're closed. They're closed. Hurry up.

BENYA: You are rich, Tsilya. The richest woman in all of Russia. When the snow falls heavy in gray December, you have sable coats to warm your neck. When the sun shines hot in the August days, the black sea waters wash the heat away. Flowers are cut fresh on your bedstand so you sleep with lovely smells in your nose. You're the Queen of the Moldavanka, Tsilya. When you walk down the street, merchants toss flower petals at your feet and scrape the ground before you with their beards. You drink champagne at night under the rising moon and sing songs of love to the stars. And for your husband you have no sailor, or clerk, or grubby market boy but Benya the King himself, who knows the way to a woman's heart. What do you say to that?

TSILYA: Will you write that down and sign your name?

BENYA: What will you say if I do?

TSILYA: Show it to me in black and white and . . . a deal's a deal.

BENYA: I'll have papers delivered to you in the morning. Sealed tight with red wax.

TSILYA: They better have everything in them. I'm going to check every word.

BENYA: You drive a hard bargain, Tsilya Eichbaum.

TSILYA: A person can't be too careful. Especially with gangsters. I want a lot, Benya Krik. More then you think.

BENYA: You'll have it all and then more, Tsilya. Just one more thing I need now.

TSILYA: One more thing is one too many.

BENYA: One little thing to make another happy. This you can't deny.

TSILYA: Ask me. We'll see what I can deny.

BENYA: I have a sister, Devorah is her name. A sturdy girl who's too old to be single anymore. You have a cousin who works as a tailor in the square. Jonah Butman, am I correct?

TSILYA: How do you know that?

BENYA: I know everything, Tsilya. I'm Benya the King. Now, Devorah needs a husband and your Jonah needs his shirts washed now and again. It's a perfect match.

TSILYA: Impossible. He's engaged. Almost married.

BENYA: Then unengage him. Dress him up in a fancy suit and we'll have a double wedding. More than a wedding, a coronation, that's what it will be. A people's coronation in the center of the square. You inspire me, Tsilya, to greater and greater deeds. Now I shall kiss my bride-to-be.

Brian Kale and Ellen Newman in the JRT production of *Benya the King*.

TSILYA: Not so fast, Mr. Wet Lips. No kisses till the wedding's done. Sample merchandise now, you may return it later. My hand will do until there's a ring on my finger. And it had better be a big one.

BENYA: You'll blind half the town when the sun shines right, Tsilya. I'm going out now and stealing a house. If it doesn't suit your needs, I'll steal another. And another after that, until my Tsilya is cozy and happy and warm.

(Lights down on BENYA *and* TSILYA *and up on* LEIB. *He sits on the arm of a chair at a long table. In the center of the table is a centerpiece of flowers. Three places are set. As he speaks,* BENYA, LEVKA *and* DEVORAH *enter and take places at the table.* LEVKA *is wearing a stark black suit and looking uncomfortable.* DEVORAH *wears a lovely dress.* BENYA *pours three glasses of milk from a pitcher and the three sit silently as* LEIB *speaks.)*

SCENE 4

LEIB: There's a place in Odessa, where the trolley line ends, where the city turns country for a while. There the grass grows green on the ground and flowers bloom fragrant on the trees. And there in a house that he called Krik's Domain, on the eve of his wedding day, the King of Odessa ate a last family meal and had dessert with an old, old friend.

*(*LEIB *puts a towel over his arm and assumes the role of a waiter. He brings in huge dishes of food from time to time.)*

DEVORAH: How do I look, Benya? In my new dress.
BENYA: Beautiful, Devorah. Like a princess in a storybook.
DEVORAH: You really think so, Benya? Really?
BENYA: Of course I do. And you'll have a meal fit for a princess too. The best food I could smuggle off the ships. This Jonah Butman. He's okay?
DEVORAH: He has a good man's eyes, and he loves me. I can tell when he talks.
BENYA: He'd better love you if he knows what's good for him. My sister's going to be happy all her days.
(Music comes in. Dance music.)
Listen, sister, to the music they're playing. Come and dance with Benya the King.

(They dance together. LEVKA *looks on disapprovingly.)*

DEVORAH: It's like flying, Benya. Just like flying through the air.
BENYA: Higher and higher, Devorah. There's no one to stop how high you can go.
DEVORAH: You made it happen, Benya. You did it all.

*(*LEVKA *coughs to interrupt.* BENYA *notices him. They stop dancing.)*

BENYA: Come, Levka. You can dance too. Just get on your feet and try.

LEVKA: I'll sit here by myself if you don't mind.

BENYA: Your disposition has improved, brother. A regular live wire you've become.

LEVKA: The houses of gangsters make me uneasy. I'd rather be in an honest man's home.

BENYA: An honest man's home he says, with that sad-dog look in his eyes. Do me a favor, brother. Enjoy yourself. Just for a night. I promise you won't die from smiling.

LEVKA: I don't feel happy surrounded by stolen goods.

BENYA: You'll feel better after you eat. Guaranteed.

(He rings bell and LEIB *comes in carrying a platter filled with meat.)*

First we eat, then I'll show you my house.

DEVORAH: It's beautiful, Benya. Just beautiful. Like a dream with carpets and walls.

LEVKA: My business is growing, Benya. Faster every day.

BENYA: I'm happy to hear it, brother. A toast to your business. *(He lifts a glass of milk and drinks a toast.)* I only drink milk these days. It helps my business grow.

LEVKA: Three carts are hauling now. Twelve hours a day.

BENYA: I'm impressed. Very impressed.

LEVKA: You can still come back. I'm offering you a chance for an honest life. A married man needs dignity in the town.

BENYA: Come back? To what, Levka. Hauling scrap? Lugging junk? Like my father before me? I've gone too far to go back to that. I'll leave taking orders to you.

LEVKA: I'm a respectable businessman. That means something, doesn't it?

BENYA: It means you wear black coats and have no fun. That's not my kind of business.

LEVKA: You're only interested in prancing like a stallion through the streets making a mockery of the name of Krik.

BENYA: Your vision's too narrow, Levka. You should be proud to have a famous brother like me. There are benefits in such things.

DEVORAH: I'm proud, Benya. Very proud. You should hear the things they say about you on the square. They say you're the greatest Jew since King David and no giant is too big for you to slay.

BENYA: Your sister's a sensible girl, Levka. You should take a lesson from her.

LEVKA: They should look up to me. To me. I'm respectable. I've never done a wrong thing in my days. My shop is always clean. So tell me, brother. Why do they only laugh at me in the square? Why? Why?

BENYA: Because you don't dream, brother. You don't dream and you never will.

DEVORAH: Oh, Benya. You talk so beautiful. So very beautiful.

LEVKA: He talks nonsense and makes the family into fools. A man must have dignity in the town to live right. I will not be humiliated by this gangster dream-talk anymore. I am leaving right now.

DEVORAH: Please, Levka. Not on the night before the wedding.

BENYA: Shake hands, brother. For Devorah's sake.

LEVKA: I refuse to shake the hand of a gangster.

BENYA: In that case, I refuse to shake the hand of a drudge. It's been a pleasure having dinner with you, brother. Make sure you're in the square when the birds begin to chirp. I wouldn't want you to miss the celebration.

LEVKA: I'll be there. I'll be there. For the respect of the family, I'll do anything. Goodnight, Devorah.

(LEVKA *exits.* BENYA *is livid with rage.)*

BENYA: Who does he think he is, that long-faced prude of a brother of mine. I'll show him what Benya the King can do. I'll show them all what Benya the King can do.

DEVORAH: Don't listen to Levka, Benya. He's scared of shadows and doesn't mean what he says. It's wonderful what you do. Wonderful and exciting.

BENYA: It's nothing to what I'm going to do, Devorah. And I can't wait to see the look in Levka's eyes when I do it.

DEVORAH: What are you saying, Benya. What are you going to do?

BENYA: Something, Devorah. Something soon and so great that they'll never forget the name of Benya Krik. Never. But don't you worry Devorah. Just dream of honeymoons tonight, you hear? It won't be long now.

DEVORAH: I won't sleep at all, Benya. I'll stay up all night by the window sill and watch the sun rise over the trees. Big as a balloon, right over the trees.

(She exits. BENYA *sits in a chair as music plays and* LEIB *comes forward and speaks.)*

LEIB: What thoughts the king thought as he sat in his chair, no one will know for sure. Perhaps he was thinking of deeds to do or splendid days to come. Or of his bride sleeping quiet as a child in her father's house near the square. Or perhaps another was in his mind. One he had meant to see for days but had not found the time. One who, with a street coat on and a tear in her eye, stood silently at his door. *(*LYUBKA *is seen, looking at* BENYA.*)*

LYUBKA: There's a person here to see Benya the King. May she come in?

BENYA: Lyubka.

LYUBKA: You don't come to see me anymore, so I have to come to you.

BENYA: You're hurt, Lyubka. I can see it in your eyes.

LYUBKA: It's all right, Benya. Next-day bridegrooms don't have time for old friends. Lyubka understands.

BENYA: You think I can forget you just like that.

LYUBKA: The first young girl who comes along. Just like I told you. You already forgot my name and address.

BENYA: Don't be crazy, Lyubka. I've had arrangements to make, things to do. But I'll be back in your big purple bed tomorrow night just like always.

LYUBKA: You're getting married tomorrow. Did you forget that too?

BENYA: You think a little thing like a wedding can spoil a nice relationship like ours? Don't be a silly goose. You can't get rid of Benya Krik so fast.

LYUBKA: Sorry, Benya. This time you can't have it your own way. Marry Tsilya milk cow tomorrow and say goodbye to me.

BENYA: Have a heart, Lyubka. We can work things out. Like always. Yes?

LYUBKA: No, Benya. Things are different for me now. You're a man now and I need you more than a few nights a week in the shadows. It hurts to work something out.

BENYA: I wouldn't hurt you for anything in the world, Lyubka. You took me in when I had no place to go. You gave me a chance to make plans.

LYUBKA: If you care so much, tell Tsilya milk cow to take a walk.

BENYA: I can't, Lyubka.

LYUBKA: Why not? You're not going to tell me you're in love with that little baby with a big fat mouth?

BENYA: I wouldn't say I love her, Lyubka. She's a pretty girl with a cunning head and I need her. Very much. She makes me try for more. I need her but I want you. All the time. And I think I can have both.

LYUBKA: I've got news for you, Benya. You can't. And that's that. Even the famous Benya the King has to have some feelings in his heart for a woman like me. Marry your Tsilya Eichbaum and don't come around to my house when you get bored at dawn. My doors will be closed up tight.

BENYA: You want me to marry you, Lyubka. Is that what you're saying?

LYUBKA: Is that such a crazy idea?

BENYA: Come on, Lyubka. You're a sophisticated woman of the town. A woman who demands variety and style and far more men than one. If we were married, you'd be tired of me in a week. It's a law of nature. I know it, Lyubka. And inside, you know it too. *(pause)* Listen, Lyubka. I need a wife with a pretty face to hold my arm as I walk through the square. But at night, when longings arise, then I need a woman with hips and breasts and the smell of the earth in her hair. And you're the only woman who'll do. Remember, Lyubka. Under every great man lies a great mistress. What do you say?

LYUBKA: Your way or nothing, just like always, Benya? Is that the way it is?

BENYA: That's the way, Lyubka. Now, what do you say?

LYUBKA: You don't give me a choice, do you Benya? I can't let you go, so you'll have your way. But don't ask me to make excuses when the dawn sun shines. That you'll have to do for yourself.

BENYA: Oh, my sweet, lovely Lyubka. I knew you'd never let me down. What fun we're going to have. What wonderful fun. A toast. To Benya the King and Lyubka the Whore. Many happy returns on the night.

(They drink.)

LYUBKA: You should be proud of yourself, Benya. Very proud. You're a hero and this is your greatest night. Yes?

BENYA: No, Lyubka. Not a hero yet. But soon. Soon.

LYUBKA: What do you mean, not yet? If not yet, then when?

BENYA: I have a plan in my head to make myself a real hero in the town. A hero even I can believe in. And you will see it soon enough, Lyubka. Soon enough, everyone will see.

LYUBKA: Be careful what you do, Benya. There are rumors in the square. They say the police and Tartakovsky have a plot to do you in. Right under the canopy.

BENYA: You think I don't know that, Lyubka? I know what they're thinking before they even think it. Benya Krik has a thousand ears. I'll have some surprises for the police when they come, don't you worry about that. Just come to my wedding, Lyubka. First we'll drink to my blushing bride and then, when night shadows come, I'll visit you in your big purple bed. In that way everyone will be happy and I'll be happy . . . twice.

SCENE 5

Lights down on BENYA *and* LYUBKA, *up on* REB LEIB *at another part of the stage. Music under. A procession of wedding guests begins as* LEIB *speaks. He ends up on a canopy which has been created behind him.*

LEIB: What happened that day in the center of the square? How did the King survive the threats of the raiding police? Watch, my friends, and you will see another miracle take place. Right before your open eyes.

(Music up and the procession makes its way down the aisles of the theatre and to the canopy. BENYA, TSILYA, DEVORAH *and* JONAH BUTMAN, *in a cardboard car longer than* BENYA'S *first and second. This one is almost a limo. Also,* LEVKA, LYUBKA, ROOK *and, last of all,* JEW-AND-A-HALF, *looking agitated and concerned. When they all reach the canopy, the music ends and* LEIB *speaks.)*

LEIB: Devorah Krik, loving and devoted sister, will you take Jonah Butman, who cares for you with his soul, to be your husband as long as his feet shall walk?

DEVORAH: I will. I will.

LEIB: Jonah Butman. Do you take Devorah Krik, lovely as she is, to be yours as long as she cares to be?

JONAH: Yes. Yes. Anything you say.

LEIB: Benya Krik, famous citizen of Odessa, King of the Moldavanka, respected businessman and person of the world, beloved through all of Russia and beyond, will you take Tsilya Eichbaum, with skin white as milk, to be your wife as long as your luck holds out?

BENYA: The pleasure is mine.

LEIB: Tsilya Eichbaum, fortunate woman, will you take Benya the King, who stands next to you with his heart pounding in his suit, to be your husband as long as his luck holds out?

TSILYA: It's a deal.

LEIB: In that case the world will call you, Jonah and Devorah, man and wife. And you, Benya and Tsilya, King and Queen. You may now plant kisses on the lips of your brides and break the stepping glass.

*(*LEIB *places a glass on the ground. Before* BENYA *can step down, we notice a strange light above. It grows brighter quickly.* DEVORAH *is the first to notice and speak.)*

DEVORAH: Look, Benya, look in the sky. There's a light. A yellow light.

BENYA: So there is. So there is. My dear Reb Leib. Kindly investigate the glow.

LEIB: Of course, Benya the King. Of course.

*(*LEIB *leaves.* BENYA *speaks to the audience.)*

BENYA: Have no fear, my friends. I am sure it is nothing but a spark and a glow.

*(*LEIB *rushes back in and whispers in* BENYA'S *ear.* BENYA *speaks.)*

BENYA: Friends and comrades, the festivities of my nuptials have been marred by a tragic act of God. The Market Street police station, a treasured landmark in the town, is no more. Destroyed by burning flames even as we stood here sharing our joy. But have no fears, citizens of the town. Do not cry too hard on your good clothes. In my pocket *(he takes out a wad of bills and holds them in the air)* is the sum of ten thousand rubles, cash. Tomorrow morning I will give them in person to his majesty, the Chief of Police, so a new police station, greater than the one we loved, can rise anew from the ashes of the old. After all, my friends, what is a town without its policemen? And what is a policeman without a police station? All is well again, my friends. Do not fear sparks in the night. Stay. Stay.

Take a partner in your arms and dance, my friends, dance. First I will break the stepping glass, and then, let celebrations begin.

(Music begins. Lively dance music. DEVORAH *dances with* JONAH. LYUBKA *dances with* ROOK. BENYA *takes* TSILYA *in his arms and dances.)*

LEIB: You have been to weddings before, I know. But never have you seen one like Benya the King's. Things occurred that night, my friends, that have never occurred, before or since, on the streets around Import Square. What kinds of things, you ask? Take a look for yourself.
(He turns to the cast which has been dancing slowly behind and, suddenly, they come to life. Dancing first, then piling up presents in front of BENYA. *During it all,* LEIB *dances round and round with an older woman. He breaks off his dancing and addresses the audience again.)*
And the greatest thing that happened that night? The thing I'll never forget, is that I, Reb Arye Leib, a widower thirty years, danced three times the waltz with Rivka Gold and kissed her twice. On the lips. And where was the King during the great revelry night? Before the dancing was even through he returned soft and quiet to Krik's Domain to get close to his blushing bride.

(While LEIB *speaks, the dancers leave the stage, couple by couple.* BENYA *and* TSILYA *are the last to leave. As* LEIB'S *speech is ending,* BENYA *and* TSILYA *dance to the other side of the stage where there is a couch. They sit down, exhausted, and the music stops.)*

SCENE 6

BENYA: I've bought myself a police station, Tsilya. Tomorrow a firehouse. After that, who knows? Maybe the city hall. So, tell me my wife. What did you think of the wedding?

TSILYA: It was all right.

BENYA: All right? It was the greatest wedding the town has ever seen.

TSILYA: I heard once, in St. Petersberg, a man bought a whole ship for his wife and they sailed away after the wedding for a honeymoon. That's what I call a real wedding. But I liked the rings, Benya. Especially the gold ones.

BENYA: You'll have all the rings you want, Tsilya. And one day, boats bigger than any the world has seen. Because your husband is Benya the King. Now come, my Tsilya. It's time to mingle our thoughts in bed. Then I'll tell you all the lovely things you'll have.

TSILYA: Sorry, Benya the King. We must discuss business before we adjourn to other chambers.

BENYA: Pleasure first, business later. Let's go.

TSILYA: Business first or nothing later. I've been thinking things over. Talking with my father.

BENYA: That old man's like a bear sticking his nose into trees.

TSILYA: He's my business adviser and investment helper.

BENYA: We'll bring a pad and pen to bed. We'll do the figuring there.

TSILYA: First we make a deal, then we fool around. That's the businesslike way. I like you. I like you a lot. Even that night when you came with your knife, I thought you were handsome and smart. But I must protect my investments.

BENYA: What do you have to protect? Benya the King protects everything.

TSILYA: The way I see it, being a gangster's wife is not a sound investment. What would happen if, one day, your head was in one place and your body in another? Where would that leave me?

BENYA: A rich widow crying bitter tears. Now come upstairs.

TSILYA: Not till there's a will written down. With provisions for after death benefits. Cash and assets too.

BENYA: What a time to talk about wills. Who's going to die so fast?

TSILYA: With a gangster like you, who can tell? A flash of a knife and that's the end. It could happen anytime. If it does, I want all the milk cows for my father.

BENYA: Impossible. I have other people to consider.

TSILYA: Then I think it will be impossible for me to climb the stairs to our wedding chamber. I have such pains in my legs. And my head is spinning like a crazy dancer.

BENYA: All right. All right. All the cows will go to him. But only when I croak. Everything's settled then, right? Now let's go.

TSILYA: One more thing, Benya the King. If you don't mind.

BENYA: I mind. I mind. I want what I want, Tsilya. You'll have to learn that fast.

TSILYA: And I need what I need. That you'll have to learn too. I told you I wanted lots of things, Benya the King. If you're really the king you say you are, you'll get them for me. All.

BENYA: What do you need now?

TSILYA: I want a settlement for life in case you leave. Plus a house. Agreed?

BENYA: What has your father been teaching you. That I'm as rich as the Tsar?

TSILYA: I won't be left weeping and poor if you decide to fish in other waters. These are simple precautions.

BENYA: You're a woman to inspire confidence, Tsilya. This I must say. A man could think you were hoping I'd leave or die.

TSILYA: A man could think that. But a woman couldn't. Collateral. That's all I ask. Collateral on an important loan. You will do that for me, won't you Benya?

BENYA: You are fooling now with powerful forces, Tsilya. The forces inside a man. It would not be wise to play any more. I will sign the forms you wish me to sign. I will even bring them to a lawyer tonight. But come upstairs with me now, hear? This is your husband speaking.

TSILYA: Of course, my husband. I wouldn't dream of disobeying you. Not after you've been so kind. *(Whips out a long piece of paper.)* Just sign right here, and we'll go to our pleasure.

BENYA: I'll call for the lawyers after we make love. Then I'll sign on the line. Come, my Tsilya, with skin white as milk. I will hold you tight in my longing arms and tell you a plan you will not believe.

TSILYA: Don't just tell me, Benya. Show me. Do something bold and brave and daring, just for me. Something to show me you're really the king you say you are.

BENYA: I'll do more than you ever thought a man could do, Tsilya. I've got a plan in my head you would not believe.

TSILYA: I hope it's a plan for making money. That's the kind that makes a house a home.

(They go off together. REB LEIB *enters.)*

SCENE 7

LEIB: Late that night, between kisses and groans, Benya the King whispered his plan to his bride. So bold was the deed he had in mind that Tsilya the Queen, right then and there, added fifty a month to the settlement. And on the morning after his wedding night, with love still sleepy in his eyes, Benya the King shared his plan with his partner Rook and took a step across the line.

(Lights down on LEIB, *up on* BENYA *and* ROOK. ROOK *is dressed more gaudily than before.* BENYA *is wild with excitement.)*

BENYA: I'm glad I found you so early, partner. I have to talk about a plan.

ROOK: *(Lifts a glass of milk and drinks it):* Easy does it, Benya Krik. There's time later to talk of plans. First let me make a toast. To Benya Krik, the king of all Odessa. Here's to how he changed the life of the lucky Ephraim Rook. You have a dancing look in your eyes, partner. What is going on inside your head.

BENYA: I am going to do a great deed, Rook. I worked it out last night. It cannot fail.

ROOK: Tell me what it is, Benya. Maybe the new Moses has come to town. The new Moses in an orange suit.

BENYA: You won't be making jokes when you hear what I have to say. Every Wednesday at exactly noon, the coach from Minsk rides through the square. You have seen it, yes?

ROOK: Of course I have. The strongbox with the Tsar's taxes are inside. Two armed Cossacks sit on board.

BENYA: Tomorrow at noon I, Benya the King, will steal the strongbox of the mighty Tsar from beneath the noses of his Cossack guards. I'll do it all in broad daylight and I won't even carry a gun.

ROOK: This is not a good idea, Benya. This time you're going too far.

BENYA: Don't be silly, Rook. Where is there to go if not too far? I've got it all worked out right here. I'm going to become a hero.

ROOK: Listen to me now, Benya, and don't be a fool. Let someone else be a hero. Don't push the Cossacks farther than they'll let you go.

BENYA: You think I'm afraid of Cossacks? I can outthink them in my sleep. Before they know I'm there I'll be gone. With the money under my coat. The people will see me do it, Rook, and they'll throw their hats in the air for joy. And, after that, they'll never be fearful again. The act I do will take the fear from their hearts for good.

ROOK: Don't be foolish, Benya. The people will always be fearful. Because that's what people are. You can't change that. The police will arrest you on the spot. The Cossacks will beat in your brains. Then they'll close us down. Take our money away. Then the girls won't come around anymore. You can't do this, Benya. Terrible things will happen. I know.

BENYA: Wonderful things will happen, partner, incredible things. I will give back the money I steal only after the Tsar visits me in person and guarantees the rights of Jews in the town. Nothing less will do. This is going to be the greatest crime in the history of Russia.

ROOK: Listen to me, Benya. To the Cossack guards there is no such thing as Benya the King. Once they start swinging their clubs, they don't know when to stop.

BENYA: I won't kiss their saddles like my father. They're going to respect me, Rook. I'll make them respect me.

ROOK: A Cossack never respected a Jew and a Cossack never will. Do something smaller if there's something you have to do. This is too much. Even for Benya the King.

BENYA: Nothing smaller will do, partner Rook. I have to do this.

ROOK: If you do it, it will be on your own. Don't tell them I helped you. Please, Benya Krik. Please.

BENYA: You're scared, Ephraim Rook. Your hands are trembling even now.

ROOK: I'm not young, Benya Krik. I've seen what the Cossacks can do to a man, and I leave bravery to others.

BENYA: Well, I'm young, partner. There are things I want to change and no Cossack guard will stand in my way.

ROOK: Do what you have to do, Benya. But remember my words. Don Quixote they'll call you before they call you Moses. I know the ways of the world.

BENYA: The world can be changed, Ephraim Rook. With imagination and will. The world can be changed.

ROOK: Maybe it can, Benya. But not in Odessa. And not by a Jew.

BENYA: We'll see, Ephraim Rook. We'll see. Tomorrow at noon, alone in the sun, I'll show you what a man without fear can do.

ROOK: Good luck, Benya Krik. And be careful. Please, be careful.

(They hug and BENYA *exits.)*

SCENE 8

*Slowly, from both sides of the stage, the cast enters—*TSILYA, LYUBKA, LEVKA, DEVORAH, *and* LEIB. *They form a line with* LEIB *in the center.*

LEIB: The sun went down and the sun came up on the day of the greatest deed and, like people waiting for battle news, the court of the King stood in fear. The red car. Sunlight dancing. The silent square.

TSILYA: You said I'd be happy, Benya. You promised.

LEVKA: Now we'll see what dreams can do against the Tsar.

DEVORAH: You can do it, Benya. If anyone can, it's you.

LEIB: A soft breeze blows. A brown dog barks. He waits alone in the street.

ROOK: Reach too high and they cut you down. I've seen it happen before.

LYUBKA: Like a man, Benya. Do it like a man and show them what you are.

TSILYA: What will I do if they put him in jail? I should have asked for more than I did. On the auction block of life, there's always a higher bid.

LEIB: The coach is coming. I hear its wheels on the ground.

DEVORAH: I love you, Benya. Be brave and run fast.

LEVKA: Now they'll look up to me. To me.

TSILYA: Fifty thousand. That would have covered me well. Fifty thousand I should have asked.

LEIB: He's up to the coach. He's climbing aboard.

LYUBKA: Take it in your hand and get away.

ROOK: Please, Benya Krik. Make another miracle today.

DEVORAH: If they shoot bullets at your head, let them be like drops of rain. Come home. Please come home.

LEIB: He has taken the box of the Tsar in his hands. He's waving it for the people to see.

LYUBKA: Run, Benya, run.

DEVORAH: Like a deer, Benya. Like a deer in the woods.

LEIB: He is standing in the square. The strongbox is still in his hands. He has not moved. The Cossacks are coming closer. They are lifting their clubs in the air.

LYUBKA: Run, Benya, run. Run.

(Suddenly, we see BENYA*, at one side of the stage, head bowed, in handcuffs. The people on stage turn and look at him.)*

DEVORAH: Oh, God. No. No.

*(*BENYA *is pushed, violently on stage by a large, bearded* COSSACK *who immediately speaks.)*

COSSACK: Jews. Here is your famous Benya Krik who committed the crime of getting caught. Benya the King they call you, yes? Benya the King who thought he could steal from the Tsar. *(He slaps* BENYA *hard across the face.* BENYA *doesn't move.)* That is what a Cossack thinks of Benya the King. *(He pushes* BENYA *over toward the others.)* We have no time to waste punishing foolish Jews. We leave you in the hands of one of your own who sells grain to feed our horses. Ruven Tartakovsky *(*JEW-AND-A-HALF *walks out proudly from behind the* COSSACK.*)* will be your judge. He promises to take good care of you. *(*COSSACK *turns to* TARTAKOVSKY.*)* Tell us fast the verdict of the day, Tartakovsky. Your happiness is also at stake. *(Addresses the group.)* Goodbye, Jews. Take a lesson from your Benya the King.

*(*COSSACK *exits.* JEW-AND-A-HALF, *victorious, moves over to* BENYA.*))*

JEW-AND-A-HALF: So, Benya Krik. The day of judgment has come. Now you will suffer hard for your sins as I have suffered for mine. Now, my friends, the world will be safe again . . . for commerce. *(He unfurls a document and clears his throat.)* These are the crimes you have committed against the people and myself.

Turning the rich into beggars and fools. Putting ideas into people's heads. Expanding operations without doubt and fear. And last and worst . . . trying to rob from other than Jews. Such crimes deserve punishments of the greatest kind, punishments fit for a king. And such punishments you shall have, Benya Krik. Such punishments you shall have. And now, before I pass sentence on your head, I must ask if there are Jews with further charges to make.

LEVKA: I have charges to speak.

DEVORAH: No, Levka. No.

LEVKA: I said, I have charges to speak.

JEW-AND-A-HALF: Excellent, Levka Krik. So great are the crimes of Benya the Terrible that even his own brother must speak. Go on, my friend. What are the charges you make?

LEVKA: Playing the fool in the public square. Dreaming too much and working too little. Wearing orange suits. Turning a sister into a fool. Making people look up to him and not at all at me. These crimes against dignity he has done. Despite my warnings and frowns.

JEW-AND-A-HALF: An inspiring recitation, Levka Krik. Now we'll get on with the sentencing.

LEVKA: I have a suggestion for sentencing. One that will fit the punishment to the crime.

JEW-AND-A-HALF: In that case, let me hear. I am a respecter of family ties.

LEVKA *(He takes out a broom from behind his back and holds it in front of* BENYA.*)*: I am handing you now a sweeping broom, brother. You will work in my shop until you pay back Tartakovsky all the money that is his.

JEW-AND-A-HALF: All the money! A splendid idea. With interest. Five percent.

LEVKA: And until such time as you are judged a respectable citizen once again. Do you agree with my sentence, Tartakovsky?

JEW-AND-A-HALF: Agree? At five percent interest it is wonderful. You are an impressive fellow, Levka Krik. You have a fine head, and a keen instinct for punishment. The sentence is passed. The king is dead. Justice is done in Odessa.

BENYA: I have something to say. And I believe I have the right to say it.

JEW-AND-A-HALF: Go ahead. Go ahead. But make it quick. I have to tell the Cossacks the verdict.

BENYA: I have stood here in silence, gentlemen, feeling sorry and ashamed for the spectacle that has taken place before my eyes. Something greater than your money and my brother's dignity is at stake here today, gentlemen. And neither of you even know it.

JEW-AND-A-HALF: I said make it quick, Benya Krik. The Cossacks are waiting.

BENYA: Yes, Tartakovsky. Your friends the Cossacks are waiting. Your friends who make you forget who you are.

JEW-AND-A-HALF: I know who I am, Benya Krik. And I know what you are too.

BENYA: I am a Jew, Tartakovsky. And so are you. When that Cossack slapped my face, he slapped your face as well. But you didn't feel a thing, did you? When a Cossack slaps and you feel nothing, you put yourself at his mercy for life. Do you know that?

LEVKA: Watch out for him, Tartakovsky. He's a worm who'll wiggle out of anything.

BENYA: Don't talk to me about worms, brother, I know a worm when I see one.

JEW-AND-A-HALF: I have known the Cossacks for years, Benya Krik. The Cossacks are my friends.

BENYA: Don't fool yourself. A Cossack is like a crazy horse. You never know which way he'll turn. Or when. But when he does, he kicks you so hard you feel the pain for years. I hope they like the sentence you bring them. If not, they may turn today. I've seen what they do to fearful Jews who fail to make them happy. It is not a pleasant sight.

JEW-AND-A-HALF: What do you mean, Benya Krik? What are you saying?

BENYA: You know what I'm saying, Tartakovsky, you have a choice here today. A choice for your dignity. Pass my brother's sentence to the Cossacks or join together with me and do something, so you can feel like a man the rest of your days.

LEVKA: Don't let him get away with this, Tartakovsky. A man like my brother is trouble. He must be taught to be respectable . . . like me.

BENYA: Fearful and terrified, you mean. You can't teach me to be like that.

LEVKA: I will teach you what it means to be respectable. That's what I will teach you.

LYUBKA: Levka Krik. Your cruelty here is forcing me to speak.

LEVKA: What do you have to say?

LYUBKA: Tell them, respectable Levka Krik, where and in whose bed you can be found on Tuesday's at nine o'clock?

LEVKA: That's none of their business.

DEVORAH: You told me you went to a meeting. With the Board of Trade.

LYUBKA: He goes to meetings, but not with Boards of Trade. He meets body to body with sweet-fingered Linda Gruber, an expert pleaser of the needs of men. Isn't that right, black-coated Levka Krik?

DEVORAH: I didn't know that Levka. That makes me feel better about you.

JEW-AND-A-HALF: Is it true what she says, Levka Krik? Tell me honestly. Your sentence is at stake.

LEVKA: It's a lie. A lie. I have to go back to my shop. Goodbye. *(He exits.)*

JEW-AND-A-HALF: Such a world this is that the longest faces have the biggest secrets to hide. I must revise my thinking. And fast. The Cossacks are tapping their sticks in the street. If they hear I've been fooled by this Levka Krik, they won't trust me anymore. And then maybe they'll turn, like you said, Benya Krik. You must help me. Please. What do I do now?

BENYA: So now you turn to me, Tartakovsky, and not to your Cossack friends. Fortunately, I have more compassion than them. I have a plan in my head for us both. I resume my activities and you get back your money tomorrow.

JEW-AND-A-HALF: Tomorrow? At five percent?

BENYA: At twenty percent. Plus a thousand ruble bonus for your suffering.

JEW-AND-A-HALF: Twenty percent and a bonus too?

BENYA: That's just the beginning, Tartakovsky. Listen to reason and work together and you and I can be stronger than all the Cossacks in the town. All the Cossacks in Russia. Just know who you are and Cossacks disappear into thin air. Like smoke.

JEW-AND-A-HALF: But a sentence. I need a sentence or they'll beat me purple.

BENYA: Tell them I am going to work for you. As your clerk in place of Muginstein. Tell them you will hire a man to watch over me and whip me if I don't do right. Tell them you'll pay me nothing and make sure I reform my ways. They'll believe you because punishing is what they like to do. And after they believe you, we can begin making plans. Together. Do you agree?

JEW-AND-A-HALF: I agree. I agree. I'm scared. But I agree.

BENYA: You won't be scared for long, my friend. Stand up to them once and you'll hold up your head proud in the streets. There are great things in our future, Tartakovsky. My mind is beginning to work. Go tell the Cossacks your sentence and remember . . . you don't have to fear them anymore. When you return, I'll begin my rehabilitation. And what a rehabilitation it will be. Come, my wife, and we will celebrate the day the Jews stopped being afraid. What do you say to that?

TSILYA: You're a king, Benya Krik. Just like you said you were.

BENYA: And I've got plans and schemes for every person in the town. Today is just the beginning. The end isn't even in sight.

DEVORAH: That's right, Benya. That's right. No one can put an end to Benya the King.

ROOK: I should have known you could do it. I'll never doubt you again.

BENYA: Next time, you'll do it too, partner. Next time, hand in hand we'll show them what we can do.

(TARTAKOVSKY *enters, and extends his hand to* BENYA.)

JEW-AND-A-HALF: It is done, Benya Krik. It is done.

DEVORAH: What a day this has been. What a wonderful day.

BENYA *(Puts his arm around* LYUBKA): One arm around you. Just as always. Lyubka. Yes?

LYUBKA: Just as always, Benya. Proud and sad and happy too. Just as always. Tell me. Has it happened? Are you a hero yet?.

BENYA: Am I am hero yet? Almost, Lyubka. Almost . . . but not quite.

(The company freezes as REB LEIB *comes forward and addresses the audience.)*

LEIB: So justice that day was done in Odessa and the reign of the King went on. What did he do and how long did it last, you want to know? That I cannot tell you, my friends. But if you want answers to deep questions in your minds, this is what I advise you to do. Sit down in your chair tonight. Close your eyes tight. Put worries out of your head. And imagine, my friends . . . Imagine.

(Music up and lights slowly fade.)

36

by

NORMAN LESSING

Norman Lessing, *36.*

NORMAN LESSING'S first love was the theatre but the realities of life led him to television and film. He, his wife, Betty, and three of his five daughters settled in Santa Monica where Mr. Lessing wrote over three hundred television dramas and a number of motion pictures. In addition, he concentrated on his hobbies, tennis and chess. Mr. Lessing is co-author of *The World of Chess* and has won the Senior Championship of the National and American Open Tournaments a record half-dozen times.

With *36* he returned to the theatre and provided the Jewish Repertory Theatre with its first big popular success. It opened at the start of a hot New York summer and received what are known in the trade as "money reviews." Richard F. Shepard in the *New York Times* wrote, "It is a breezy, funny play with crisp dialogue and good humorous performances by its cast of six. . . . The theatre is air-conditioned and, as one of the characters might say, believe me, there are worse ways to spend time on a hot night."

The initial limited run was happily extended through Labor Day and *36* recently repeated its success with a production at the Jewish Community Center of Cleveland.

36 was first produced by the Jewish Repertory Theatre in June 1980 with the following cast:

MENDEL	Harold Guskin
NACHMAN	Charles Carshon
PITZIK	Richard DeFabees
JOE	Joe Ponazecki
RABBI	William Wise
MARY	Sherry Rooney

Directed by Marc Daniels
Visual consultant: Samuel Leve
Sets by Jay Klein
Costumes by Jessica Fasman
Lighting by William Hladik

Time: The Present.
Place: Cincinnati, Ohio

ACT I

Scene 1. A Reform Temple.
Scene 2. About two hours later.

ACT II

Scene 1. Joe and Mary's apartment.
Five months later.
Scene 2. The Temple.
A short time later.

Act I

Scene 1

The stage is dark. Light slowly suffuses a rectangular area. Represented is "The Window of Heaven," a stained glass impression of exaggeratedly fleecy clouds stabbed with shafts of light. It is a cyclorama used for lighting effects over the stage of a Jewish Reform temple. From the darkness below, we hear the garbled chanting of prayer, abruptly dominated by MENDEL'S *poignant outcry.*

MENDEL'S VOICE: *Riboinu scheloilum, Riboinu scheloilum, Riboinu scheloilum . . .*

(Light fades in below, to reveal the corresponding portion of the temple's stage. Three Hasidim are grouped around a table laden with well-worn, ancient books of the Torah. MENDEL *rises, lifts his arms toward the Window, his voice loud and clear, like a Cantor's.)*

MENDEL: O Master of the Universe, pay attention, please! We want to sing you a *dudele. . . .*

PITZIK: A *dudele,* a *dudele!*

(All three are wearing the traditional Hasidic street costume, long black overcoats reaching to the floor, and wide-brimmed black bowlers. When they divest themselves of their outer garments, they will be dressed in black silk caftans and black silk skull caps called yarmulkes. MENDEL *has a closely cropped black beard.* NACHMAN, *the eldest, has a long white beard.* PITZIK, *the youngest, is beardless. All three have curly earlocks which cascade down their cheeks.*

At stage rear, are ornate, richly decorated Gothic arches, flanking a gold-latticed doorway, emblazoned with a golden star of David, behind which is the cupboard housing the Torah scrolls. MENDEL'S *arms are upraised as he sings. The other two clap hands, silently at first, then with increasing volume, rocking and swaying to the rhythm. As the song progresses and enthusiasm grows, they join in certain phrases, particularly the "Du, Du, Du!")*

MENDEL: Where can we find You? And where can we not find You? Wherever we go, You are, and wherever we stand, You are.

ALL: Du, Du, Du! Du, Du, Du, Du, Du, Du!

MENDEL: If we prosper, it's because of You, and if, God forbid, we have trouble, *Oy!* it's still You.

ALL: You are, You were, You will be.

(The three Hasidim start moving around the table in a postured, stylized Hasidic dance, singing in gutteral exclamations.)

THE THREE HASIDIM:

Du, Du, Du! Du, Du, Du!
Dudu, dudu, dudum, dudu, du,
Dirra, dirra, dirra-du,
Duddee, dudum, dudum, du,
Dirra-dirra, duddel, duddel, du - Ai!
Duddel, duddel, duddel, duddel, Du!

(Light slowly spreads to reveal details of the scene. The Window of Heaven cyclorama is a complicated mechanism for special lighting effects. At the moment, it is out of order and being repaired. A ladder is positioned directly below it. On the ladder, JOE, *dressed in electrician's coveralls and wearing a tool-belt, is working on a mass of jumbled wires protruding from the bottom of the Window.*
As the Hasidim reach an ecstatic peak, there is a bright blue flash from the Window, accompanied by a loud snapping sound.)

JOE: Goddammit!
(The Window responds with an angry rumble. The Hasidim stop dead at the height of their song, then scurry like mice to

take their seats around the table. They bury their heads in their books, but glance up covertly from time to time.)

Sonuvabitch!

(The Window rumbles. Fitful blue flashes chase each other behind the scrim. JOE *looks up.)*

Okay, okay, simmer down.

*(*JOE *hefts the jumbled wires in his hand.)*

Goddamn spaghetti!

(The Window rumbles mildly. JOE *takes a rubber-handled screwdriver from his tool-belt, and with great care, starts separating the wires. The screwdriver touches an exposed wire. A loud snap and flash! The screwdriver comes clattering down on the floor near the table.)*

Owwwww!!!

(He shakes his hand and blows on it, looks up angrily at the Window.)

You mother!

PITZIK: Mother?

JOE: Where's the goddammed tape?

*(*JOE *exits to get tape.* PITZIK *ventures from the table to retrieve the fallen screw-driver.)*

PITZIK: What is this thing?

MENDEL: A screwdriver.

PITZIK: It's purpose?

MENDEL: To drive screws.

NACHMAN: Observe how marvelous a piece of work is the human hand! The Great Rambam has enumerated twenty distinct and separate parts, each with its own special function—to hold, to let go, to strike, to bless, the long finger to point with, the fat finger for logic. . . .

MENDEL: But not one finger to drive a screw with.

NACHMAN: For this the Holy One, blessed be He, has given Man a brain, to invent tools. . . .

MENDEL: Excuse me, but it seems a terribly roundabout way to do things. Now if I had been there to offer the Ancient One, blessed be His Name, a humble piece of advice, I would have suggested to make each finger different, each with a practical use. The thumb a hammer, this one a file, this a chisel, the little one an ice-pick, and this crooked one—what then?—a corkscrew to pull the corks from wine bottles. . . .

NACHMAN: And then some day, with God's help, you would find a bride, and you would fondle her with such a hand? You would do this to a nice Jewish girl?

MENDEL: No . . . maybe not.

PITZIK: How does it work?

MENDEL: Here, I'll show you!

(He snatches the screwdriver from PITZIK'S *hand, looks around for something to demonstrate on.* PITZIK *squats down beside him, as* NACHMAN *walks over, bends down to watch also.* MENDEL *starts unscrewing the table leg.)*

MENDEL: For a simple job like this, not one thing in the human hand is suitable. If you stuck your nail in, it would break.

PITZIK: May I try?

MENDEL: Try.

(They exchange places. PITZIK *works the screwdriver. He is ecstatic.)*

PITZIK: Wonder of wonders!

MENDEL: To Pitzik, everything is a miracle.

NACHMAN: He's right.

MENDEL: The other way! Turn the other way! Your leg will fall off!

PITZIK: My leg?

MENDEL: The table leg, O calf of the world!

*(*RABBI DORFMAN, *a well-dressed youngish forty, enters briskly, rubbing his hands. He wears neither hat nor skull cap.* MENDEL *bristles noticeably.* PITZIK, *abashed, sets the screwdriver on the table, returns to his book.)*

RABBI: Good morning, boys, good morning!

NACHMAN: Good morning and a good year, Rabbi.

RABBI: How goes it, how goes it?

NACHMAN: Fine. Fine.

RABBI: Boys, I'll have to move you out tomorrow. In the morning, we're giving prizes for the Little League and in the afternoon, the Ladies' Auxiliary needs the stage for a rehearsal. So only for one day, if you'll be so kind, you'll use the basement—the ping-pong room.

PITZIK: Ping-pong?

RABBI: It's a game. Like tennis, only smaller.

PITZIK: Tennis?

RABBI: You'll see, you'll see when you get there.

MENDEL: You play this game of ping-pong, Rabbi?

RABBI: I play, I play. Lately I've become pretty good, if I must say it myself.

MENDEL: I'll spot you five points.

RABBI: You'll spot me?

MENDEL: For money.

RABBI: Uh-uh! My father, may he enjoy eternal peace, once told me, "Manfred, never fool around with a *Hasid,* they'll make a jelly out of you." Now golf, golf is another story.

MENDEL: Stuck is stuck. How's about a five-dollar nassau?

RABBI *(laughs, wags a finger):* Never mind, never mind!

*(*JOE *re-enters.)*

Oh, Mr. Electrician!

JOE: The name's Walski. Joe.

RABBI: How do you do? I'm Dr. Manfred Dorfman. We conversed on the phone. Could I see you a minute, please?

JOE: Sure, you're paying for the time.

RABBI: Okay, okay, it won't take long. You're in my parking space. It has my name on it—Dr. Manfred Dorfman. You'll have to move your truck.

(The RABBI *and* JOE *exit.)*

MENDEL: Doc-tor Man-fred Dorf-man!

NACHMAN: Ai, Mendel, Mendel. . . .

MENDEL: Big shot! Just because he's a Reform rabbi!

NACHMAN: What do you want from his life?

MENDEL: *DOCTOR* Dorfman!

NACHMAN: So he has a degree, what's wrong?

MENDEL: Why only doctor, why not a general?

NACHMAN: He's a nice man, he lets us use his Temple.

MENDEL: What should he do? Throw us out on the street like dogs?

PITZIK: If my father knew I was in a Reform Temple, he would jump out of his grave.

MENDEL: Don't tell him.

PITZIK: I keep asking myself, what am I doing here? I say to myself, Pitzik, what are you doing in a Reform Temple?

NACHMAN: What should we be doing? Studying Torah, as always.

PITZIK: But why here, *Rebbe?* What was wrong with our own *shul* in Brooklyn?

MENDEL: It's good to travel.

PITZIK: Why?

MENDEL: Why not?

NACHMAN: We should tell him, Mendel.

MENDEL: Tell him nothing. Pitzik can't keep a secret.

PITZIK: Mendel is right, *Rebbe.* If it's a secret, better not tell me.

NACHMAN: This much, you have a right to know. We're not here by accident. A Voice ordered me to go to this city.

PITZIK: A Voice?

NACHMAN: A Voice.

PITZIK: A Voice ordered you to come here to Sitsin . . . Sincit. . . .

MENDEL: Cincinnati.

PITZIK: I can't even pronounce it.

MENDEL: Don't worry. The Voice is smarter than you.

PITZIK: Did the Voice order you to bring me and Mendel?

NACHMAN: No.

PITZIK: Then why did you?

NACHMAN: I was afraid to go alone.

PITZIK: You were afraid?

NACHMAN: I was afraid.

PITZIK: Now I'm afraid.

NACHMAN: There's nothing to be afraid of.

PITZIK: But you're afraid.

NACHMAN: Yes.

*(*JOE *leads the* RABBI *back to a lectern near the window.* NACHMAN *motions* MENDEL *and* PITZIK *back to their books. They pretend to be absorbed, but from time to time,* NACHMAN *and* MENDEL *sneak glances upward.)*

JOE: Your board's shot and you got a few bugs in the dims, but right here's your main trouble, this—uh—watchamuhcallit. . . .

RABBI: Window of Heaven. (JOE *looks at him)* Symbolically speaking. . . .

JOE: Uh-huh. Well, anyway, the idea is to sneak in some indirect lighting, right?

RABBI: Right.

JOE: You don't want no ashcans hanging from the ceiling.

RABBI: Ashcans?

JOE: Giant spots—you don't want those. This ain't no burlesque house, right?

RABBI: I'm aware of that.

JOE: So what happens? You spend a pile of dough to create a nice peaceful atmosphere, where the customers can relax, grab a little shut-eye maybe, then you reach the end of a big sermon and you hit all the switches and push the brights up as high as they'll go, like your speech has flooded the joint with light.

RABBI: It's an effect. . . .

JOE: Don't I know it? It's the same in my wife's church, and she's Catholic.

RABBI: You're not?

JOE: My wife's got enough religion for a regiment, what do they need me for? The thing is, Rabbi, when you apply maximum juice to everything all at one and the same time, your loop just naturally burns up, the fuses melt, and all hell breaks loose.

(Rumblings and flashes from the Window.)

Only static electricity, nothing to be scared of.

RABBI: You're sure?

JOE: Worst it can give you is a shock. Anyway, I can fix up your electrical system good as new, only if you keep right on doing the same thing, sooner or later the same thing's gonna happen—something's gotta blow! So try and keep it down a little, huh? Everything don't have to be The Last Supper. Excuse me.

RABBI: It's all right.

JOE: We'll need a new rheostat, a couple of arms, and a good juiced-up jenny. . . .

RABBI: Jenny?

JOE: Generator, your auxiliary's just about gone. A new jenny runs into money.

RABBI: How much?

JOE: I got a rebuilt one home can handle the job. I'll pick it up on my lunch break so's to save you travel time.
RABBI: A second-hand jenny for a big Temple like this? You think she'll work out?
JOE: She's got new teasers and tremblers, a brand-new exciter, and a real sensitive vibrator on her coil. What more do you want?

(He exits. The RABBI *shrugs, follows.)*

NACHMAN: He's not Catholic.
MENDEL: Proving?
NACHMAN: Nothing.

(JOE *enters from right.* PITZIK *has his back to him.* MENDEL *and* NACHMAN *pretend to be completely absorbed, sinking their noses into their prayer books and chanting louder than ever.* PITZIK, *infected by their enthusiasm, raises his voice too.* JOE *hesitates to interfere, finally taps* PITZIK *on the shoulder.)*

JOE: Hi.
PITZIK: Hi. . . .
JOE: Pardon me for interrupting.
MENDEL: Interrupting what?
JOE: Your number, or whatever. . . . You see my screwdriver?
PITZIK: Your screwdriver? . . . Oh, the screwdriver . . . yes, yes. *(He rummages frantically among the books and finds the screwdriver.)*
Thank you, thank you!
JOE: You're welcome. What are you thanking me for?
PITZIK: I . . . I. . . .
MENDEL: Pitzik always gives thanks.
JOE: Why?
MENDEL: Why not?

(JOE *walks away, shaking his head. Abruptly,* NACHMAN *and* MENDEL *start a curious colloquy, plainly enacted to spear* JOE'S *attention.* JOE *stops, oddly transfixed, at a darkened portion of the platform, the upper part of his body caught in a patch of light. He does not turn around, but the tilt of his head indicates he is listening closely.)*

NACHMAN: O, Master of the Universe, Why is it forbidden to look upon Thy face?

MENDEL: The face of God is the face of Man. In God's image was Man created.

NACHMAN: Yet each man has a different face, Which, then, does God resemble?

MENDEL: It is Man who must resemble God. God existed before Man.

NACHMAN: As it is written, In five days did He create the Heavens and the Earth, And Man only on the sixth.

MENDEL: It follows, therefore, if God created Man, The new must resemble the old. . . .

JOE: Excuse me. . . .

NACHMAN: Man resemble God? What *hutzpa!* Who among us can say, He is like unto God?

*(*JOE *turns and slowly approaches them. They watch with a curious concentration, conscious of his trance-like behavior.* JOE *tries to break the spell with a short, embarrassed laugh.)*

JOE: Excuse me, fella, I don't like to barge in but I couldn't help overhearing. How can you say, God looks this way or that way? You can't see Him, and even if you did, you'd only be seeing Him with human eyes. To know what He really looks like, you'd have to see Him with God's eyes. Anyway, it's all baloney because there's no reason why God can't change His looks? He can do anything, right? He's everywhere, right? Some people see a funny-shaped cloud and think they're seeing God. Others see Him like an IBM computer. My wife claims she once saw Him in a drop of rain. Wild, huh? But not half as wild as expecting God to look like Joe Blow from Kokomo—that's a lot of crap!

NACHMAN: Golden words!

MENDEL: A head like iron!

PITZIK: Ah-uh. . . .

NACHMAN: Let us try another question. . . .

MENDEL: A riddle! Ask him a riddle!

NACHMAN: All right, let be a riddle. . . .

JOE: Ask any riddle you like, the answer is Man.

NACHMAN: Ahhh. . . .

MENDEL: Profound!

PITZIK: Light of the world!

JOE: Nothing to it, fellas. I just happen to dig the game.

MENDEL: He digs the game.

NACHMAN: Slowly, slowly . . . we must make sure. One more test, this test will decide. . . .

JOE: Test?

NACHMAN: Listen carefully. *Lamed Vov.* Those syllables, do they mean anything to you?

JOE: Nope.

NACHMAN: The sound, it conveys nothing?

JOE: Not a goddamn thing!

NACHMAN: Let your mind run free. *Lamed Vov.* What does it suggest? *Lamed Vov.*

JOE: A number?

MENDEL: A number, a number! In Hebrew, it means thirty-six.

JOE: Okay by me.

NACHMAN: A number, but more than a number! A sign and a charm, a blessed symbol against destruction! It represents the exalted and venerated body of *tzaddikim*. . . .

JOE: Come again?

MENDEL: Holy men. . . . *Tzaddikim!*

NACHMAN: The thirty-six hidden saints, the righteous ones, the *Lamed-Vov-Tzaddikim* we call *Lamedvovniks,* for whose blessed sake God spares the human race. You understand what I'm saying?

JOE: Sure, sure. . . .

NACHMAN: Good! Then perhaps you can also explain why God chose a number like thirty-six? Why not a nice round number like fifty or a hundred?

JOE: That the whole question?

NACHMAN: Mmmmm. . . .

JOE: Why not a nice round number?

NACHMAN: Mmmm. . . .

MENDEL: *Nu?*

NACHMAN: Electrician, shed some light!

JOE: You want a nice round number, huh?

NACHMAN: Mmmm . . . mmmm. . . .

JOE: Well, you can't find a nicer, rounder number than three. It's got a shape like my wife's behind, and six—I don't have to tell you what six looks like. But that ain't the reason he picked thirty-six, and it's not because there's thirty-six hours in a day and a half, which is half of three, which is half of six, which is half of the twelve months of the year, which multiplied by the same three equals thirty-six, thereby completing the circle . . . no, it's nothing like that, there has to be a more logical reason. . . .

PITZIK: The thirty-six days of the month!

MENDEL: Quiet, Pitzik!

JOE: The answer's simple. Thirty-six is the kind of number you reach at the bargaining table.

NACHMAN: Does God have to bargain?

JOE: Even General Motors has to bargain. Where there's God, there's anti-God, right? Call it the Loyal Opposition. . . . Okay, suppose God opens up the session with a nice round number like fifty. Say, he wants a panel of fifty saints. "Fifty saints!" screams the Opposition, "You gotta be kidding! You expect fifty saints to kick the bucket all at one and the same time? What do you want, that stupid old Earth to last forever?"

"Make it forty-five," says God.

"A dozen's plenty."

"Don't be a smart-ass! Tell you what I'm gonna do, just to avoid a long drawn-out hassle, I'll lower the ante to forty."

"Twenty-five and not one saint more!"

"Forty."

"Thirty."

"Forty. That's my final offer, take it or leave it."

"Thirty."

"Forty."

"Thirty."

So they end up splitting the difference.

MENDEL: That makes thirty-five, you're one saint short.

JOE: He's God, for crying out loud! He's gotta have some edge!

NACHMAN: The wisdom of Solomon!

MENDEL: Pearls, pearls!

PITZIK: Words with wings!

JOE: What gives? What's the gimmick?

MENDEL: No gimmicks!

JOE: I have a funny feeling this whole thing's been planned.

NACHMAN: Everything is planned, my son, but not by us. It is time to reveal, a Voice ordered me to come to this city.

JOE: Huh? What voice?

NACHMAN: I was instructed to seek out a *Lamedvovnik.*

JOE: You were?

MENDEL: It's true! One of the holy thirty-six!

PITZIK: Him?

JOE: Me? Boy, have you got a wrong number! I'm not even Jewish, for Christ sake!

MENDEL: You're sure?

JOE: Sure, I'm sure! I was raised by a Polack named Walski. He made me go to church every other Sunday.

MENDEL: He was not your father?

JOE: Hell, no! He used to beat the crap out of me.

MENDEL: Why?

JOE: Why not?

MENDEL: Because you were Jewish maybe.

JOE: Because he was drunk, and no maybes about it! He got stinking drunk every single day. I couldn't wait to get out of there!

NACHMAN: "For ye were strangers in the land of Egypt."

JOE: Not Egypt, Poland! I'll tell you something else. I didn't just run away. I laid the old man out with a shovel first. How does that grab you? Some *Lamed*-whajuhmuhcallit!

NACHMAN: *Vovnik.*

JOE: A plain working stiff is all I am.

NACHMAN: All the *Lamedvovniks* were working men.

MENDEL: What did you expect them to be, millionaires?

JOE: They're not? Then you can keep the job!

MENDEL: What makes you so positive you're not Jewish?

JOE: I can tell, for Christ sake!

PITZIK: Are you afraid of dogs?

JOE: Look, I'm married to a red-hot Irish Catholic, Mary O'Brien Walski!

PITZIK: A *shiksa?* . . .

NACHMAN: It does not matter.

JOE: The hell it don't!

NACHMAN: The beloved of God can do anything he wishes. King David desired Bathsheba, so he had her husband killed in battle and took her.

JOE: You saying I can make any dame I got a yen for?

NACHMAN: If that is your wish.

JOE: Just my luck! To be stuck on that dumb Irish broad! Aw, knock it off, fellas! I ain't no King David.

NACHMAN: My son, when I told you a *Lamedvovnik* can do anything he wishes, it was not altogether true. All the ordinary sins are forgiven him, he can steal, murder, even marry a *shiksa,* but there is one thing he cannot do. He cannot hear an error of Torah without correcting it.

JOE: I don't know what Torah is.

NACHMAN: It is not necessary for you to know. Your wisdom comes from God. We arranged our dispute on purpose in order to test you.

JOE: I was only playing a game.

MENDEL: We, also.

JOE: Can't you get it through your head? I'm not Jewish. I don't know what I am.

PITZIK: If you don't know, why not be Jewish?

MENDEL: Quiet, Pitzik!

NACHMAN: Let him speak, Mendel. Maybe he's got something.

MENDEL: Maybe, maybe! We can't live by maybes. We need proof.

JOE: You guys are serious, for Christ sake! I'm mixed up with a bunch of loonies. Goddamn!

(There is an unusually loud rumble from the Window.)

JOE: It's beginning to get me, I swear. Where's the can?

NACHMAN: Can?

JOE: The men's room, the toilet!

MENDEL: The second door.

*(*JOE *exits.* NACHMAN *jerks his head for* MENDEL *to follow.)*

NACHMAN: Go with.

MENDEL: Wait, I'll show you!

(He exits swiftly.)

NACHMAN: You go too.

PITZIK: I already went.

NACHMAN: It is written in the Talmud, two witnesses are better.

(It penetrates. PITZIK *hurries out after them. Left alone,* NACHMAN *paces like an anxious father, from time to time casting quick glances in their direction. Offstage, we hear* PITZIK'S *shrill, excited voice.)*

PITZIK: *(offstage):* Oh, wonder of wonders!

(The beam of light from the Window becomes suddenly intensified. In its cone, the old man raises his arms in gratitude and exaltation. Blackout.)

SCENE 2

Light fades in. The THREE HASIDIM *go through the motions of studying, but their excitement is evident.* NACHMAN *and* MENDEL *whisper together conspiratorially, break off as the* RABBI *enters.*

RABBI: Hello, hello, the electrician's not back? Two hours for lunch! What is he, a banker?

NACHMAN: God will forgive him.

RABBI: God. . . .

MENDEL: The Rabbi has heard of Him?

RABBI: Go on, go on, give me needles, you can't make me mad. The truth is, I envy you fellows your simple faith.

MENDEL: Our simple faith? Explain to me, please, how it's different from your high-class faith?

RABBI: My faith, Mendel? It isn't high-class, it isn't low-class. The truth, I'm not sure it exists.

MENDEL: Shame on you, a rabbi!

RABBI: Rabbi, Rabbi! I'm not a rabbi, I'm an emcee. You think this is a synagogue? It's a social club. Once a week, the women come to show off their dresses and the men their donations. It's like a theater benefit.

NACHMAN: What's so terrible? We also put on a little theater for God.

RABBI: Who said it's terrible? We're big with the theatricals. So far this season we had *Medea* and *The Three Little Foxes.* Next week, we're playing *Peter Pan.*

PITZIK: That's like ping-pong?

MENDEL: So tell me already, what's your Christmas show?

RABBI: Hoo-hoo. Big joke.

MENDEL: No joke. When people have an atheist for a rabbi. . . .

NACHMAN: Sha, sha, Mendel! Such talk makes me very angry. It's—what can I tell you—it's . . . not *nice.* So the Rabbi has a few doubts. . . . Should a man command his brain to stop thinking?

MENDEL: About certain things, I commanded it to stop thinking long ago.

NACHMAN: Then it's possible you're making a small mistake. If everything in the Torah is so clear, why do our scholars engage in endless disputation? Doubt is a dark cellar, but it is necessary to dig the cellar before one lays the foundation, and only on such a foundation can the house of faith be built.

MENDEL: All right, all right! Let him live in a cellar!

RABBI: You're calling this a cellar?

NACHMAN: Don't let Mendel aggravate you, Rabbi. He's a little jealous because you raise more money for your *shul* than we do. But what is there to quarrel about, children? Don't we all serve the same God?

RABBI: The truth, Reb Nachman? I no longer know. I don't know what to believe any more.

NACHMAN: You don't believe in God?

RABBI: I told you, I no longer know.

NACHMAN: Don't you want to believe in him?

RABBI: Naturally I want to. What person doesn't want to?

NACHMAN: Then why don't you?

MENDEL: Who's stopping you?

RABBI: That's the trouble nowadays, nobody stops you.

PITZIK: If nobody stops you. . . .

MENDEL: Quiet, Pitzik!

NACHMAN: Let him, Mendel. What were you going to say, Pitzik?

PITZIK: I forgot. . . .

NACHMAN: It will come back to you. Maybe you can tell the Rabbi why you believe in God.

PITZIK: Because. . . .

MENDEL: That's a reason? Because?

PITZIK: Because I . . . can't live without Him.

NACHMAN: Ahhh. . . .

MENDEL: It is written: One may learn from a fool.

NACHMAN: Spoken like a sage, Pitzik. How can any person find the strength to go on living without believing?

RABBI: Then I must have the strength of Samson, or . . . who knows? . . . maybe I'm not living.

NACHMAN: It's for you to decide, Rabbi.

(JOE enters. He carries a white paper bag stained with fat spots. The bag has a blue Star of David on it, the imprimatur of Cohen's Kosher Delicatessen.)

PITZIK: Hi.

RABBI: Good morning, good morning! I hope you enjoyed your siesta. All right, you get paid by the hour, it's not costing me money, but it's costing me time. The Window has to be ready Thursday, Thursday's the dress rehearsal.

JOE: Dress rehearsal?

RABBI: For *Peter Pan, Peter Pan!*

PITZIK: It's like ping-pong.

MENDEL: *Oy,* Pitzik!

JOE: It'll be ready, Rabbi. I . . . I had to pick up the jenny.

RABBI: So long it takes? You're only a few blocks away.

JOE: It's a big job to load. Why don't you take a look at 'er? She's outside on the truck.

RABBI: What do I know about jennies?

JOE: You can tell. I need your okay before unloading.

RABBI: Okay, okay. You're coming?

JOE: Be with you in a minute.

RABBI: All right, all right, I ought to check my messages anyhow.

(He shrugs, exits.)

JOE: Boyohboyohboy! . . . You guys got me all mixed up . . . I go home, guess what my wife's got for lunch? Lox and bagels!

PITZIK: Aaaah!

JOE: I couldn't eat a thing. Here, I brought it for you. It's strictly kosher. From Cohen's Kosher Delicatessen.

NACHMAN: Thank you. It's very nice on your part. But today is our fast day.

JOE: Then eat it tomorrow, what do I care! Cohen's deli is pretty far away. I ask my wife what she's doing there? She went to see Dr. Feinstein.

NACHMAN: Ts, ts, it's not serious?

JOE: Serious! She's going to have a baby!

PITZIK: Aaaaaaah!

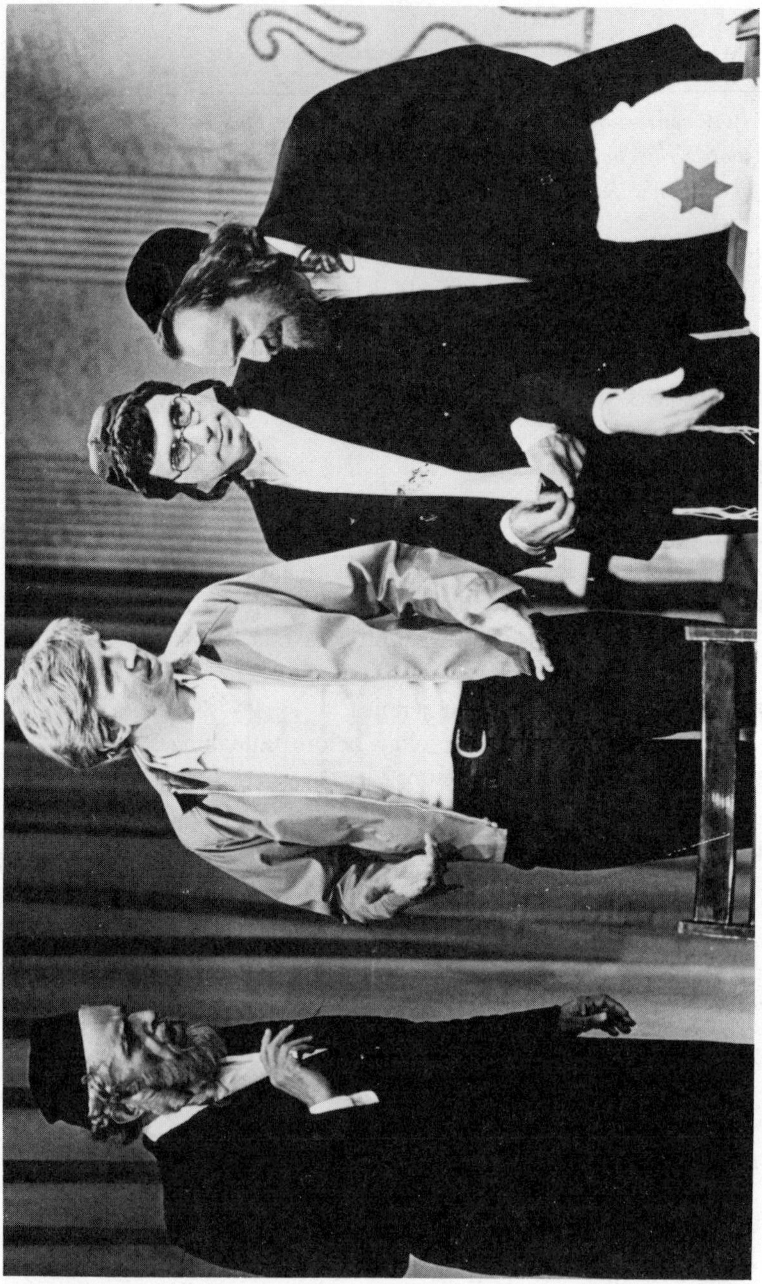

Charles Carshon, Joe Ponazecki, Richard DeFabees, and Harold Guskin in the JRT production of *36*.

MENDEL: What "Aaaaaaah?" It's already a miracle by you? People go to bed, they have sex. . . .

JOE: Ten years we've been going to bed! We had sex night and day! All we ever wanted was a kid. And now . . . just like that! . . . What's going on around here?

NACHMAN: My son, after you left, we telephoned our archives in the East and gave them the name of your stepfather Walski. From this, they were able to trace your true parentage to the revered *Lamedvovnik* Yitzhok Halevy, may his light shine forever!

JOE: How could they trace anything? Not even that sonuvabitch Walski knew my father. He got me from the priests.

NACHMAN: At the time of the Warsaw Ghetto, a group of Catholic priests arranged to help your father escape, but Yitzhok Halevy, may his name be blessed, chose to perish with his flock in the ovens of Auschwitz. In order to perpetuate the holy line, he persuaded his pregnant wife to escape in his place. She died shortly after you were born and the priests cared for you until it became their turn to run for their lives. Then and only then did they give you up for adoption to the peasant Walski.

JOE: It's hard to believe.

NACHMAN: Belief will come later. For now, we ask only that you join with us.

JOE: What's that supposed to mean?

NACHMAN: Only that you celebrate God as we do, with joy and singing and laughter.

MENDEL: You dig the game.

JOE: Fun and games, huh?

MENDEL: Games and fun.

JOE: The games and riddles, that part's okay, but this saint business . . . I'll be honest with you, it throws me higher than a kite.

PITZIK: So high?

JOE: Even if this Yitzhok character was my father, what does that make me? I won't be the first son who didn't measure up to his old man.

MENDEL: You'll measure, you'll measure.

NACHMAN: All the *Lamedvovniks* were humble. Your father before you and his father before him, as your son will be after you.

MENDEL: It should only happen a boy!

JOE: I don't know . . . it scares me . . .

PITZIK: There's nothing to be afraid of.

JOE: I guess not. Only one thing we better get up front, I'm not the religious type.

NACHMAN: It does not matter. We ask only that you join us.

JOE: We'll sit around and discuss?

MENDEL: We'll discuss.

JOE: I'll study, like you guys, and I'll learn! I'll learn everything there is to learn!

PITZIK: Oh, boy, is he Jewish!

RABBI: *(offstage):* Walski!

JOE: Do I tell him?

MENDEL: Tell him nothing!

JOE: But he's the Rabbi.

MENDEL: What rabbi, he's a doctor!

NACHMAN: A *Lamedvovnik,* my son, must be a saint in secret.

JOE: I told my wife. Wrong move, huh?

NACHMAN: It is done.

MENDEL: Stuck is stuck.

NACHMAN: You can only instruct her to keep your secret.

MENDEL: A woman? . . .

RABBI: *(offstage):* Walski!

JOE: Coming Rabbi.

RABBI: I don't like the looks of this jenny.

JOE: How d'y like that? No faith.

RABBI *(entering):* Walski!

JOE: Coming, Rabbi!

(He hurries off with the RABBI.*)*

MENDEL: Lox and bagels! How can one doubt he's a saint?

PITZIK: May I smell?

MENDEL: Smell.

(He hands the bag to PITZIK, *who sniffs greedily.* NACHMAN *takes the bag from* PITZIK, *plunks it down firmly on the table.)*

NACHMAN: Today we fast.

MENDEL: Who suggested otherwise?

(They attempt to concentrate, but it isn't easy. From time to time, they lift hungry eyes to the bag. Even NACHMAN *is not immune.)*

NACHMAN: The greater the temptation, the greater the *mitzvah.* Come, children, back to *Midrash.*

MENDEL: On the other hand, Reb Nachman, we are not fanatics. If food is in danger of spoiling, surely there is a codicil in the Law which permits it to be consumed. What's so terrible if a fast is postponed for one day?

NACHMAN: There is no danger of spoilage. The fish is smoked. The bagels will not turn sour.

PITZIK: May I ask something, Rebbe?

NACHMAN: Ask, Pitzik.

PITZIK: A *Lamedvovnik* brings us a present—it's from a holy man, it must be respected. Do we have the right to say, no, we won't eat it now, when he wants, we'll eat it when we want? It may be a sin, God forbid! I have this bad feeling inside of me.

NACHMAN: Is it an empty feeling?

PITZIK: You have it also?

NACHMAN: There is only one way to handle temptation. Put it on ice.

(He moves resolutely toward the wings. MARY *comes hurrying down the audience aisle.)*

MARY: Hey, Mister! Just a minute, I want to talk to you!

(She climbs the steps to the stage. The effort leaves her breathless for a moment, and she leans against the abutment to rest. MARY *is a handsome voluptuous woman, with wild, auburn hair reaching to her shoulders.)*

Give me a second to catch my breath, huh? I'm going to have a baby.

NACHMAN: *Mazel Tov.*

MARY: So you're the guys who've been bothering my Joe! He told me about you. Do me a favor, huh? Stop filling his head with crazy notions. He's crazy enough as it is.

MENDEL: Lady. . . .

MARY: What's the big idea, what are you trying to pull? You could be arrested for what you're doing. . . . Who gave you that—

Joe give it to you? He didn't have time to eat, he said, he was going to eat on the job, he said. A lot he cares about me and my condition! Dragging myself all the way down to Cohen's for lox, bagels, and cream cheese!

PITZIK: *Oy,* with cream cheese. . . .

MARY: What do you want from him, for God's sake? He's not even religious. For years I've been after him. . . .

MENDEL: Lady. . . .

MARY: Leave him alone! That's all I ask, just leave him alone!

MENDEL: All right already!

MARY: This is our first chance to be happy. We're just getting our heads above water, we got a kid on the way. . . .

MENDEL: Lady, listen! Once I also had a son. . . .

PITZIK: You, Mendel?

MENDEL: Me, me! What's wrong with me? . . . After my wife ran away, I did everything for him. I cleaned the house, I cooked, I washed dishes, it made no difference, he still hated me. So I went to the Social Worker. "Your son resents you," She said. "What, resents? He hates me."

"Be a pal to him," she said.

Nu, go raise children! I went home, I was a pal. But all the time he kept looking at me funny. In the end, he says, "What's eating you, Pop?" Hear an expression! What's eating me! "Idiot!" I hollered, "I'm being a pal!" You know what he said? "I don't need no pals, I got too many pals." The next day, he left home and I never saw him again. Not even on Yom Kippur.

PITZIK: I'm sorry, Mendel.

MENDEL: Who asked you to be sorry?

MARY: Excuse me, but . . . what has this got to do with me?

MENDEL: You think you're the only one with troubles? Have some respect.

MARY: Oh! I didn't mean to be disrespectful in your Temple.

MENDEL: It's not our Temple!

PITZIK: God forbid!

MARY: I apologize.

NACHMAN: You don't have to apologize.

MARY *(holds out bag):* You can have this . . .

NACHMAN: No, but we thank you.

MARY: I want you to have it, I really do! I was upset. . . .

I have nothing against you people, honest! I mean, even Father Ignatius has nothing against you any more. I'm sure you meant well, but you made a mistake, it could happen to anyone. Joe Walski, a saint, sweet Jesus have mercy! If I only told you some of the things he's gone and done!

NACHMAN: He can do anything he wishes.

MARY: We have different ideas about saints in our religion.

NACHMAN: All religions are alike.

MARY: How can you say that? You don't believe in the Saviour.

NACHMAN: Oh, we do, we do!

MENDEL: Only our timetable is different.

MARY: I know you people hate the Gentiles, I can't say I blame you. . . .

NACHMAN: Why should we hate them? They introduced our Bible to the world.

MENDEL: They forgive us, we forgive them. Past is past.

PITZIK: *O-mayn!* Peace and love, love and peace.

MENDEL: Quiet, Pitzik! Don't start a pogrom.

MARY: Please . . . I don't want to hurt your feelings, but you're so strange . . . I mean, you're like . . . like beings from outer space. How could my Joe be part of anything you're part of? And on top of that, to elevate him to the sainthood! Don't make me laugh!

NACHMAN: Laugh, laugh, my daugther.

MARY: How did he ever get into this?

NACHMAN: We made an error in Torah and he corrected us.

MARY: Torah, what's that?

NACHMAN: Torah is God's truth, my child. He had no choice.

MARY: He had a choice! He could have kept his big nose out of it!

MENDEL: Already anti-Semitic.

NACHMAN: Your husband is the only surviving son of the martyred saint Yitzhok Halevy.

MARY: Oh, come on!

NACHMAN: It has been verified by priests of your own religion.

MARY: What do they know about Jewish saints?

NACHMAN: They sheltered Yitzhok's wife who was then big with Joseph. After she gave birth, she clung to life only long enough to make sure he was circumcised.

MARY: That don't mean a thing! Not these days . . . plenty of guys . . . Gentiles I mean . . . lots of Gentiles are circumcised.

MENDEL: Not in Poland!

NACHMAN: The priests kept a record of Joseph because they realized his importance. After the war, they notified the Lublin rabbi, who notified the Williamsburg rabbi in Brooklyn. Many years later when a committee was organized to bring Passover *matzohs* to Poland, they tried to find out what happend to the son of Yitzhok Halevy. They discovered that Joseph had killed his stepfather and run away.

MARY: Killed?

ALL: Mmmm . . . mmmm. . . .

MARY: My Joe!

ALL: Mmmmm . . . mmmm. . . .

MARY: That's a lie!

NACHMAN: It is written in the record.

MARY: Joe would have told me.

MENDEL: Why? Would it make you happy?

MARY: He couldn't carry such a terrible sin on his conscience without confessing.

NACHMAN: He confessed to us.

MENDEL: Anyhow, it wasn't such a sin.

MARY: No sin to kill?

MENDEL: The stepfather used him like a slave, so Joe killed for his freedom. Better than King David, who killed for a woman!

MARY: Lies, all lies!

NACHMAN: We would not deceive you, my daughter.

MARY: Stop calling me your daughter.

NACHMAN: The Torah does not shut out those of another faith.

PITZIK: You saw God in a drop of rain. What did he look like?

*(*PITZIK'S *innocent statement has an unnerving effect.* MARY *stares. A long pause.)*

MARY: Oh, my God! What's gonna happen to him?

MENDEL: What can happen to a saint?

MARY: I know what happens to saints! Oh, Holy Mother of God!

PITZIK: Mother?

MARY: Please . . . I beg of you . . . let him go! Let him go before it's too late!

NACHMAN: Why do you cry? He will experience the greatest glory which can come to a man.

MARY: No, no! No, no. no!
NACHMAN: You can share it with him.
MARY: I don't want to, I don't want to!

(She collapses, weeping, into a chair. They watch helplessly. MENDEL *sighs.)*

MENDEL: How can a person stand all this on an empty stomach?
PITZIK: Maybe she's hungry.
NACHMAN: Let her cry, let her cry.

*(*JOE *rushes in excitedly.)*

JOE: Hey, fellas, I got a brand new angle! Even supposing we could see God with God's eyes, how could we describe what He looks like in human speech? Human speech is only good for . . .
(A wail from MARY.*)*
Mary! . . . What are you doing here?
(She sobs.)
Honey, what's wrong, what happened?
(Her sobs grow louder. JOE *looks suspiciously from her to the others.)*
These guys make a pass at you?

(The HASIDIM *react. Blackout.)*

Act II

Scene 1

Illuminated is a section of stage representing the kitchen of the WALSKI *(Now the* HALEVY*) home.* MARY *and the* RABBI *sit side by side at the kitchen table, which is littered with tracts and books.* MARY, *noticeably larger, wears a shawl over her head.*

RABBI: Enough! Enough for one morning, it's time for your constitutional. Oh . . . have you read the books I left you?

MARY: Which ones?

RABBI: Steinberg's *Basic Judaism* and *A Manual for Proselytes.*

MARY: Some of it. Frankly, Rabbi, I'm not much of a reader.

RABBI: I'm not forcing you, you understand. I only want you to be aware of all the problems. You're leaving a majority religion for a minority one, that's not easy. Once more, it's my duty to ask you, do you still wish to be confirmed in the Jewish faith?

MARY: I answered that twice already.

RABBI: Answer it again. Our rabbis laid down a rule: "Three times you must return." But if the proselyte continues to press, we're forced to accept.

MARY: You make me feel like I've got bad breath or something.

RABBI: It's only a formality.

MARY: All right, I'm pressing.

RABBI: Here we are. . . .

(The RABBI *takes the Certificate of Conversion out of his jacket pocket.)*

MARY: Not another!

RABBI: The first two were your Application and your Record of Instruction. This is the actual Certificate of Conversion. Because you're pregnant, we're allowed to speed things up a bit in accordance with the principle of "laidoso bikdusho," so that your child may be born in the Jewish faith. You must sign this and have it witnessed by two impartial witnesses.

MARY: Sounds important.

RABBI: Hoo-hoo-hooo! Without this, you can't get buried in a Jewish cemetery.

MARY: Rabbi, I certainly appreciate all the trouble you've gone to.

RABBI: It's my job.

MARY: Except. . . .

RABBI: Yes?

MARY: Can I get you something? A glass of tea?

RABBI: A glass of tea? No, thank you. You have a question?

MARY: Well, you're a Reform rabbi. . . . There are two other denominations, the Conservatives and the Orthodoxes.

RABBI: The Orthodox. I'm glad to see you've been studying up.

MARY: Joe explained it to me. Please understand, Rabbi, it's nothing against you personally, but Joe decided it might be better if I joined up with the Orthodoxes.

RABBI: I see. Why Orthodox?

MARY: Well, I'm Catholic. . . .

RABBI: Not for long. As soon as you sign this, you're automatically excommunicated.

MARY: Oh, sweet Jesus, save me!

RABBI: You see, you see! Now it comes out! You're still clinging to your old faith!

MARY: I didn't mean it, Rabbi, honest! It's just a habit.

RABBI: I warned you! I told you, you had to get rid of every last vestige. Well, it's no skin off my nose. You want to be Orthodox, go get your instruction from an Orthodox rabbi!

MARY: Couldn't I just get to be Jewish first?

RABBI: I'd only be misleading you. The Orthodox requirements are much more demanding.

MARY: You wouldn't mislead me. Joe explained everything.

RABBI: Joe, Joe! Since when is he such an authority?

MARY: He knows, Rabbi, he knows. Look, Rabbi. . . .

(She lifts the shawl from her head. Her hair is cropped quite close, though not actually unbecoming.)

RABBI: My God, what have you done?

MARY: I didn't do it right, I know. Joe told me you're supposed to shave it all off, I just didn't have the heart. Still it's close enough so I can wear a . . . a . . . what do you call it?—that wig they wear?

RABBI: A *sheitel,* a *sheitel!* But good God, Mary, Jewish women don't do this sort of thing any more. Did Elizabeth Taylor shave her head? Next thing, you'll be going to *mikveh.*

MARY: *Mikveh* . . . That's the ritual bath-house. . . . What's wrong with taking a bath?

RABBI: Nothing, not a solitary thing! Only today we have bathtubs in every home. It's not necessary to make a public ceremony out of it.

MARY: I don't mind.

RABBI: It's simply not necessary. Like those two sets of dishes. I never told you you had to do that.

MARY: One for meat, one for dairy. I though all Jewish people did.

RABBI: Not in my congregation.

MARY: The Orthodoxes think you should.

RABBI: The Orthodoxes. . . . The Orthodox think a lot of things. They think women are an inferior class. In my Temple, women are equal to men.

MARY: I don't want to be equal, I want to be Jewish.

RABBI: You can be just as Jewish without becoming a . . . a . . . I'm sorry, I don't know why I'm arguing with you. You have a perfect right to do anything you want.

MARY: Then you'll convert me?

RABBI: I suppose it's all right . . . *(consults Conversion Certificate)* It says here, ". . . with the expressed desire of joining the Jewish religion and accepting the principles, doctrines, and institutes of Judaism." I guess it's okay to enlist now and choose your own branch of the service later.

MARY: Thank you, thank you.

RABBI: You're welcome, you're welcome. Did you discuss this with anyone besides Joe?

MARY: Only you.

RABBI: No one else?

MARY: Who else knows about such things? Except, maybe, Father Ignatius.

RABBI: Who?

MARY: My confessor. I feel kind of bad about him, I haven't told him a thing.

RABBI: You no longer have to.

MARY: I feel bad about it. If I don't show up again, he might think I got run over or something.

RABBI: That wouldn't be Father Ignatius O'Flaherty, by any chance?

MARY: You know him?

RABBI: Do I know Iggy!

MARY: Iggy?

RABBI: He calls me Manny, we're very good friends. From the Little League. Don't worry, I'll tell him.

MARY: Won't he be angry?

RABBI: Why should he be angry? Last year, he bagged three from my congregation. When it comes to conversions, he's got me beat a mile. Baseball, that's another story. Our team won the Inter-Parochial World Series three seasons in a row. Even though Iggy had his kids crossing themselves like crazy every time they came to bat.

MARY: What's wrong with that?

RABBI: Not wrong, not wrong, only . . . it does seem like trying to take advantage.

MARY: Can't your kids do the same thing? I mean, they can make some kind of a sign, can't they?

RABBI: For instance?

MARY: I don't know . . . a Jewish star? . . .

RABBI: Mary, we Jews don't believe in bothering God for small favors. We don't pray to shoot a ball through a hoop or hit a home run. We save our prayers for something big—like ulcers.

MARY: I want to pray for something big.

RABBI: The baby? The baby's small.

MARY: It's more than that . . .

RABBI: You're expecting twins? Tell me, I'll throw in a prayer too.

MARY: Pray for Joe, Rabbi.

RABBI: For Joe?

MARY: Pray for him, Rabbi! Promise me you'll pray for him!

RABBI: For whatever my prayer is worth, I promise. Only, why are you so worried about Joe?

MARY: Oh, Rabbi, Rabbi . . .

RABBI: He's not sick, God forbid!

MARY: He's strong as a bull.

RABBI: Knock wood. Mentally? He spends an awful lot of time in Temple. . . .

MARY: There's nothing wrong with him mentally. Mentally he's stronger than ever.

RABBI: I see, I see. He's certainly changed in the last few months.

MARY: You have no idea!

RABBI: What made him change so much? Why did he become so religious all of a sudden? Mary, I want to know what's happening! There's something funny. First questions first: Why did you decide to become Jewish? That's the most important thing I'm supposed to ask you.

MARY: I already told you.

RABBI: You told me and you didn't tell me. I want the truth, Mary, the whole truth!

MARY: My husband's Jewish. I love him.

RABBI: So you love him! Fine, fine! And you found out he's Jewish. So what? There's plenty of mixed marriages. You were a devout practicing Catholic, you didn't have to give it up. Did Joe decide that too?

MARY: He didn't have to.

RABBI: No? You decided by yourself?

MARY: It was the only thing I could do.

RABBI: Why? Mary, as your Examiner in these proceedings, I insist upon a complete and truthful answer. Unless you comply, there can be no question of your confirmation.

MARY: I can't!

RABBI: What do you mean, can't? You can't keep secrets from your rabbi at a time like this. Would you keep a secret from your Priest?

MARY: It's not my secret.

RABBI: Not yours, then whose?

MARY: Joe's, the boys. . . .

RABBI: The boys, the boys! I knew there were mixed up in it. I tell you, I'm getting sick and tired of those crazy *Hasidim!* Mary, I positively demand that you tell me everything. I can't let you convert to Judaism under some crazy false impression.

MARY: I swore I wouldn't tell, Rabbi, please don't make me!

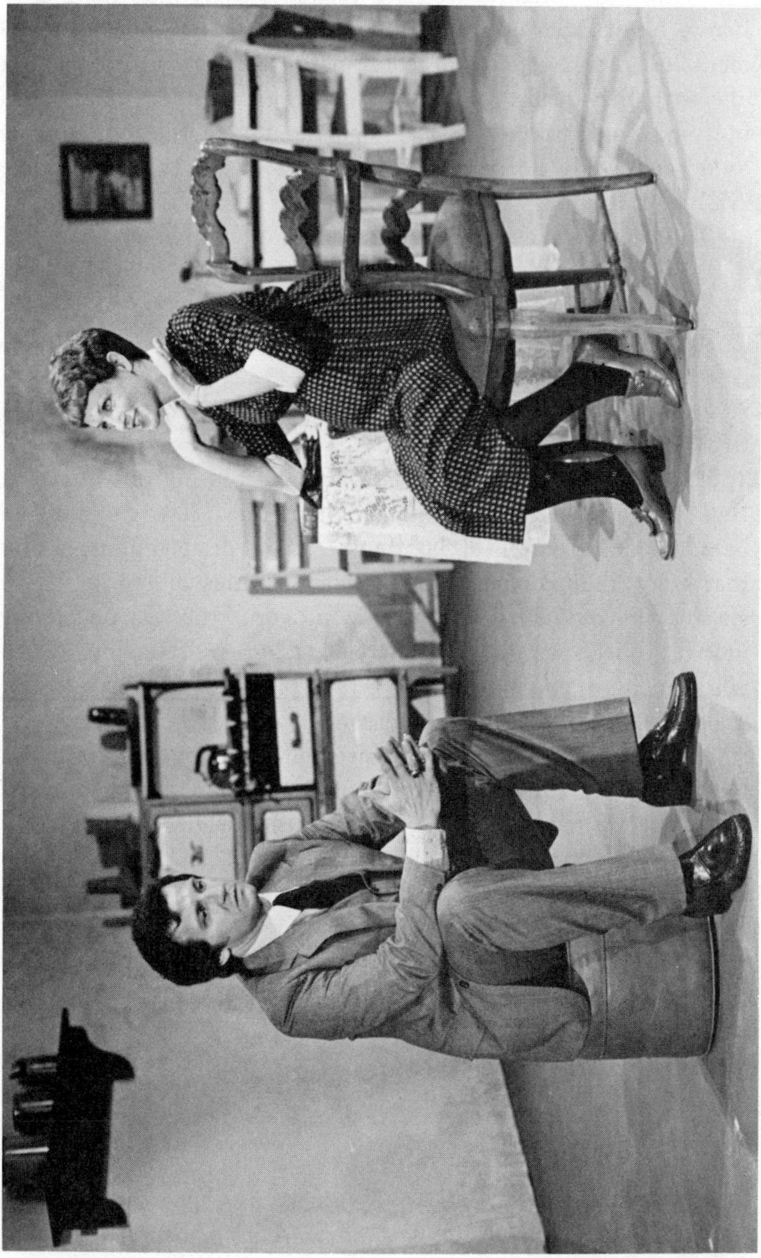

William Wise and Sherry Rooney in the JRT production of *36*.

RABBI: So important it was that they made you swear? In our religion, we don't swear lightly. And we don't make anyone else swear. Mary, once you've embraced our faith, we don't require any confessions. But before, we have to know everything there is to know. Now listen carefully, I'm going to make a solemn statement. On the eve of your confirmation, I hereby declare that any oath they made you take, all vows made under duress, are null and void. I free you of all blame, I take the guilt on my own head. Only no secrets, I order you to tell me the truth!

MARY: I can't.

RABBI: Okay, okay. I'll get you the name of another rabbi, an Orthodox one. Maybe you'll make out better with him.

MARY: Please, please don't leave me!

RABBI: Who's leaving you? You make me sound like a playboy. I'm getting you another rabbi, that's all.

MARY: I don't want another rabbi, I want you! I can't go through this all over again.

RABBI: Mary, I'm not a terribly strict man, and I'm not unreasonable. But I do have a sense of moral obligation. That you want to be Orthodox—well, I'll be frank—it's a disappointment. But that's not the problem. The problem is, this is too serious a step to let you take without knowing your true and underlying motive. To leave your church, to abandon the faith into which you were born, you must have a very strong reason. It is absolutely imperative that I know this reason.

MARY: If I tell . . . will you promise not to tell them I told? I mean, I really think it's something you should know, I really do. I'm surprised they didn't tell you themselves.

RABBI: Tell me what?

MARY: About my Joe.

RABBI: What about your Joe?

MARY: He's a *Lamedvovnik.*

RABBI: A what?

MARY: A *Lamedvovnik,* a saint.

RABBI: *Oy gevald!* Who told you?

MARY: They did.

RABBI: The boys?

MARY: Uh-huh.

RABBI: *Hasidim, Hasidim!* God in Heaven, why did you sic them on me, what have I done to deserve it? I know what I did, I took them in, I let them stay! Morgan was right. I'm going straight up to him and I'm going to tell him, "Morgan, you were right!"

MARY: Who's Morgan?

RABBI: Mr. Howard P. Morgan is Chairman of the Board of Trustees of my Temple, and, as it happens, a very intelligent man. He begged me to kick them out, but I was too stupid to listen. Mary, you can't possibly grasp all the implications, you haven't the faintest notion . . . These fellows are nuts! They belong to a bygone age, they have no place in this century. When I first saw them, it was like looking at old, faded pictures of ancient Jewish history. That's why I tolerated them, because I'm a sickly, sentimental slob!

MARY: I don't understand . . . what did they do?

RABBI: They didn't do a thing, not a single, solitary thing! They ruined me, that's all! I'll be the joke of the Reform Movement, the laughing stock of the Rabbinate! *Oy,* Papa, Papa, to be made into a jelly by these mystical superstitious morons!

MARY: You mustn't say things like that!

RABBI: You ain't heard nothing yet! Wait! Wait till I get back to Temple, then you'll hear! Mary, forget this conversion business. You've been swindled, taken in, the same as me. Your Joe is nothing, nothing but a good electrician, but believe me, that's a whole lot. For a man to be skilled in his trade is the greatest blessing.

MARY: My Joe's a saint!

RABBI: Mary, my poor pregnant pupil, you know better. Go back to Father Ignatius, Mary, tell him the whole story, let him absolve you. And tell him I apologize, I'm sorry.

(He tears the Conversion Certificate in half, throws the pieces on the table.)

MARY: Rabbi!

RABBI: Dr. Dorfman to you. Dr. Manfred Dorfman. Goodbye, Mrs. Walski.

MARY: Don't leave me!

RABBI: Go back to Father Ignatius, Mary! That's where you belong. God pity me, I thought I was getting even. In baseball, in baseball, I'll beat him!

(He storms out. MARY, *dazed, eyes the torn Certificate. Her fingers move up to touch her close-cropped head. Blackout.)*

SCENE 2

Light fades in on platform of temple. The Window of Heaven has been repaired. The THREE HASIDIM *and* JOE, *are grouped around the table.* JOE *wears a black suit of shiny material and a black skull cap. His sideburns are in ringlets like the* HASIDIM'S, *and almost as long.*

NACHMAN: *Mo-loch, me-lech, yim-lock,* God is here, there, everywhere. Hallowed and magnified be His name!

JOE: *O-mayn.*

MENDEL: *O-mayn.*

PITZIK: *O-mayn.*

MENDEL: What are you waiting for, Pitzik, a trolley car? The *o-mayn* should come in quick like Yussel's.

JOE: Don't be rough on the kid, he's up against the fastest *o-mayn* in the West. You were saying, *Rebbe?*

NACHMAN: The Holy One, blessed be He, took Adam's thirteenth rib and from it he fashioned a mate, called Woman because she came out of Man. But why did God choose a rib for this purpose? Why didn't he take something from . . . from Adam's mouth, for instance?

JOE: Easy. He didn't want her to gossip.

NACHMAN: One of his ears?

JOE: And have her listening behind doors?

NACHMAN: A slice of brain?

JOE: Would make her vain.

MENDEL: *O-mayn.*

PITZIK: *O-mayn.*

NACHMAN: Why not an eye?

JOE: He didn't want her to pry.

NACHMAN: Since Adam was not circumcised, why not utilize this unnecessary bit of foreskin?

JOE: It would make her lustful.

NACHMAN: A fingernail?

JOE: Too sharp.

NACHMAN: A vein?

JOE: Too plain.

MENDEL: *O-mayn.*

PITZIK: *O-mayn.*

NACHMAN: Since woman was intended as a helpmate, why not a hand?

JOE: She'd be a meddler.

NACHMAN: Only one finger?

JOE: The same.

NACHMAN: Why?

JOE: She'd stick it in every pie.

MENDEL: Ai-yi-yi!

NACHMAN: The feet?

JOE: She'd run from man to man.

NACHMAN: The heart?

JOE: Not smart. Why teach her jealousy?

NACHMAN: Therefore the Holy One, in His all-encompassing wisdom, chose the rib, a hidden part. . . .

JOE: So that Woman too should be shy and modest and keep her desire hidden.

MENDEL: And in spite of all these precautions, Woman turned out to be vain, jealous, false, a gossip, a busybody, and a bitter carping nag!

PITZIK: *O-mayn.*

MENDEL: Not so fast, Pitzik, let a person finish. And when it comes to lust, there's not a man alive who can satisfy her.

JOE: Don't condemn lust, Mendel. Without lust, there'd be no children.

MENDEL: Who's condemning? Wasn't I married myself? Once a week, like clockwork, I devoted a full fifteen minutes to my wife.

JOE: Fifteen minutes?

MENDEL: The last fourteen apologizing.

PITZIK: *O-mayn.*

MENDEL: Sha. . . .

NACHMAN: The Holy One, blessed be His Name, created Evil as well as Good. For without Evil, why would a man seek to rival his neighbor, and how much work would be accomplished in the world? At one time, the Will to Evil was captured and held prisoner for three days, and for three days not a new-laid egg could be found in the land of Israel.

MENDEL: No eggs, no eggs! . . . Cock-a-doodle-doo! . . .

(Starts to chant, claps his hands.)

Du, Du, Du, Du, Duddel-duddel, duddel-duddel, Du! No eggs, no eggs! Ai-yi-yi-yi-yi! Dirra-dirra, duddel-duddel, *Du!* . . .

*(*JOE, NACHMAN *and* PITZIK *join in the* "dudele," *chanting, clapping hands, swaying rhythmically in Hasidic dance poses. The sound of a door is heard slamming loudly, as if in anger.* JOE *stops abruptly.)*

JOE: It's the rabbi! He's coming from my wife. I'd just as soon not see him now.

MENDEL: Because she wants to be Orthodox? It's such a sin?

NACHMAN: Stay, Joseph. Perhaps, by some miracle, we may even convert the rabbi.

JOE: If it's all the same to you, Rebbe, I'd rather not.

(He exits hurriedly, left, as the RABBI *enters from the other side.)*

RABBI: Reb Nachman, Reb Nachman, I'd like a word with you. You're all here? Good, good!

MENDEL: Where else would we be?

RABBI: Where you would be, I don't know, and where you're going to be, I don't know and I don't care, as long as it's not here.

NACHMAN: What is it, Rabbi? What's your complaint.

RABBI: Me complain? Heaven prevent me from doing anything so foolish! If I do, you'll come back with an answer. I'll reply to the answer and you'll answer the reply. You'll swamp me with proverbs, you'll drown me in parables, and I—idiot that I am!—I'll end up enjoying it and forget what I came for. You speak beautifully, I don't deny it.

NACHMAN: May God strike me dumb before I speak beautifully!

RABBI: Excuse me, Reb Nachman, I must be blunt. When you fellows first came, I didn't expect you to stay more than a few days, a week at most. Well, it stretched out to months, and frankly . . . well, there are three good reasons I think you should terminate your visit. First, the Board of Trustees, they want you out. . . . Second. . . .

NACHMAN: Back in the terrible days of the Inquisition, the King of Portugal demanded a large sum of money from the Jews. . . .

RABBI: You're starting with the stories?

NACHMAN: The Representative of the Jewish Community met with the King and told him there were three good reasons why the Jews could not meet his demand. First, they had no money. . . .

RABBI: Well?

NACHMAN: The King didn't need the other two reasons.

RABBI: I see, I see. Well, whether you need them or not, I want you to know. That's my curse, I'm an honest man, and an honest man makes a rotten witness. He's not satisfied to make a simple point, he has to go on explaining, and by the time he's through, the jury is ready to send him to the electric chair.

MENDEL: *Nu,* so talk yourself into the electric chair!

RABBI: To begin with, I'm Reform, you're Orthodox. But Orthodox of the Orthodox! You make the rest of the orthodoxes look like Episcopalians. All right, that's your privilege. You're entitled to your ideas, I'm entitled to mine. But when you come into a Reform Temple and put your ideas into action, that's a horse of an entirely different complexion.

NACHMAN: How have we done this, Rabbi?

RABBI: You know how, I don't have to tell you. So I'll tell you! You took a plain ordinary electrician and turned him into a saint. You made a *tzaddik* out of him, this ignorant laborer!

MENDEL: Now he's anti-labor. . . .

NACHMAN: All the *Lamedvovniks* were working people.

RABBI: A *Lamedvovnik,* of all things!

NACHMAN: Not of all things. A *Lamedvovnik* among men.

RABBI: That *bubba mysa,* that old grandmother story! No, honestly, it's too much! To maintain seriously in this day and age that God spares the world on account of thirty-six privileged characters, the sainted Joe Walski and thirty-five helpers . . . even for *Hasidim,* this has to be the most ignorant, the most insane superstition!

MENDEL: How about God—he's also a superstition?

RABBI: Now listen, Mendel . . .

NACHMAN: Don't mind him, Rabbi.

RABBI: How can I mind anything? After a thing like this happens in my own Temple!

NACHMAN: Then if you don't mind, let me ask you one question. Which is easier for you to believe in, God or a good man?

RABBI: You're taking advantage! Once I confided something, and now you're taking advantage!

NACHMAN: I'm concerned about you, my son.

RABBI: It's not wrong to have doubts, you said so yourself.

NACHMAN: Not wrong, not right. For a rabbi with a congregation, a little inconvenient.

MENDEL: Not a Reform rabbi.

RABBI: Reform, Orthodox, what's the difference? Can a man stop thinking? Can he shut his eyes to the advancements of science?

NACHMAN: Einstein was a religious man.

RABBI: Never mind Einstein, let's talk about Darwin and the theory of Evolution! The Bible says God created the world in five days and man on the sixth. . . .

NACHMAN: The Bible is right.

RABBI: But Charles Darwin says man evolved from lower forms of life and the process took millions of years—*billions!*

NACHMAN: He's right too.

RABBI: How can they both be right?

NACHMAN: They're right, you're right, and I'm right. It may well be that life on Earth has been destroyed many times by fire and flood. Skeletons of fish have been found on top of the highest mountains of the Himalayas, and deep in the bowels of the Earth are many sandy layers with the bones of ancient animals, but even more significant are the layers between, layers which are coal black and hold no bones at all, marking the periods when all living creatures were consumed in the conflagration.

RABBI: How does all this support the Bible?

MENDEL: If the Rabbi will read the seventh chapter of Genesis, he may find out we had a flood.

RABBI: I know all about the flood, and about Sodom and Gomorrah too, but where does it say that all life was wiped out by fire?

NACHMAN: It is written in the *Midrash* that the Eternal One, blessed be He, created many worlds and destroyed nine hundred and seventy-four generations before He found one which pleased Him. The Bible relates how often He threatened to destroy the life He had created. Let us imagine that once, just once, He carried out his threat. Who would be left to record it? We cannot discount the possibility that God did destroy all life on Earth, at least once, and further punished Man by only allowing him to come back very slowly, starting as a monkey.

RABBI: Congratulations! Very ingenious! Only the Bible happens to be written in a certain chronological sequence—Noah begat Ham and Ham begat Cush and Cush begat Nimrod, and so on and so forth, and to keep track of all this begatting, all the bigamy and incest, the wars and murders and all the other wonderful events, we have our Jewish calendar, according to which the whole history of the Universe, starting with the first day of Creation, totals less than six thousand years. How does this fit in with your marvelous hypothesis?

NACHMAN: I never claimed it was perfect.

RABBI: Thank you, thank you very much.

NACHMAN: I was simply stating a theory, like the scientific ones which are always being changed and replaced. I only wanted to show we're closer to the scientists than you think.

PITZIK: Only our timetable is different.

RABBI: Reb Nachman, I must make one thing very clear. . . . Your arguments fail to convince me . . . they don't convince me at all. . . .

NACHMAN: The soul of man is a dark abyss. Faith is a big jump to take, but one can only cross the abyss by taking this jump.

RABBI: If you're a goat, maybe.

NACHMAN: You have hardened your heart against belief.

RABBI: I don't believe with my heart, I believe with my mind.

MENDEL: Your mind, your mind! . . . Excuse me.

(He exits abruptly.)

NACHMAN: Poor Mendel! He's been upset ever since we came to a Reform Temple.

RABBI: Good! Then he won't mind leaving.

NACHMAN: One asks, why were we ordered here? To find a *Lamedvovnik,* yes, but why in a Reform Temple?

RABBI: Frankly, Reb Nachman, I don't know and I don't care.

NACHMAN: Perhaps it was so we might be able to help you, my son.

RABBI: God forbid! You're helping me right out of a job!

NACHMAN: The Earth burns as it turns, our house is on fire. Shall we end up as another black layer beneath the surface? Only by faith may such a calamity be averted. Everywhere, people are beginning to understand this, everywhere they search for something to believe in.

RABBI: Believe in what? Zen Buddhism, Vitamin C, the Cincinnati Reds?

NACHMAN: Better anything than no faith at all. When a man believes in nothing, he becomes a vacuum and who knows what dark and terrible things may rush in to fill the void?

RABBI: And how does one get this faith, *Rebbe,* by pushing a button? Just throw a quarter in the slot and pick it up like a Hershey bar?

NACHMAN: What would it take to make you believe? A miracle, perhaps?

RABBI: Miracles no longer happen.

NACHMAN: How dull for a man not to see miracles all around him!

RABBI: All right, have it your way, I'm dull.

NACHMAN: I meant, how dull for you.

RABBI: I know what you meant.

NACHMAN: Forgive me, my son. What kind of a miracle would you like? The good old-fashioned kind like they have in the Bible? Shall I change my walking stick into a snake or make wine from water? Believe me, modern magicians do much better.

RABBI: Then do better.

NACHMAN: What? Suggest something. Pitzik believes in God. You want him to fly to Heaven for you?

RABBI: *(mimicking* MENDEL*):* Why not?

NACHMAN: Pitzik!

PITZIK: Yes, *Rebbe?*

NACHMAN: Fly to Heaven for the Rabbi.

PITZIK: To Heaven?

NACHMAN: Heaven.

PITZIK: Me?

NACHMAN: You.

PITZIK: Right now?

NACHMAN: Now.

PITZIK: I'm afraid.

NACHMAN: Don't be afraid.

PITZIK: I'm too young.

NACHMAN: I'm too old.
PITZIK: Must it be now?
NACHMAN: Yes, Pitzik.
PITZIK: It's your fault.
RABBI: Mine?
PITZIK: Goodbye, *Rebbe.* Goodbye, Rabbi.

*(*NACHMAN *rises with a sigh, moves to dimmers at stage right and brings down the lights. The* RABBI *follows a few steps, watches in amazement.)*

RABBI: Why are you dimming the lights?
NACHMAN: God's radiance is enough.

(Meanwhile, PITZIK *takes advantage of the diversion to scurry off stage left.)*

PITZIK: Goooood-byyyye! . . . . .

(At this signal, a shadow figure of PITZIK *rises in the air and flies off into the wings, right. The* RABBI *turns just in time to see the figure, apparently* PITZIK, *take off. His mouth falls open in amazement.)*

RABBI: I'm going crazy.
NACHMAN: That's a good sign.
RABBI: You saw it too?
NACHMAN: I ordered it. *(He casually brings the dimmers up again.)* Don't let it upset you, my son. Think how an Atheist must feel when he wakes up to find himself in the Hall of Judgment.

(The RABBI *is stunned.* MENDEL *reappears, rubbing the dampness out of his hands, looks back over his shoulder at the flying figure offstage.)*

MENDEL: Was that Pitzik who just flew past? I thought so. Well, the Rabbi wants us to leave. . . .
RABBI: Wait! I must have time to think.
NACHMAN: Think, think, my son.

(The RABBI *moves to the darkened fringe of the stage.* MENDEL*'s expression is owlish as he turns to* NACHMAN.)

MENDEL: On top of the highest mountain in the Himalayas? The skeleton of a fish?
NACHMAN: It's true.
MENDEL: Proving?
NACHMAN: What does it prove to you?
MENDEL: A Jew was there. He ate a herring.

*(*NACHMAN *covers his mouth to conceal his mirth. There is a commotion, stage right.* JOE *enters, pulling* MARY *after him. She appears to be under a spell. No shawl covers her shorn head, and her eyes are wild.)*

JOE: *Rebbe, Rebbe,* help me!
RABBI: What happened? What's wrong?
JOE: I got home . . . she didn't know me! She kept shouting all kinds of crazy things in a high crazy voice.
NACHMAN: A high crazy voice?
MENDEL: It's Lilith! Lilith, the Howling One! She specializes in pregnant women.
NACHMAN: Not so quick, Mendel. Put her. . . . *(*JOE *helps* MARY *into a chair.)*
JOE: The house looked like a cyclone tore through it. The dishes we just bought, two brand new sets. . . .
MENDEL: She broke them?
JOE: Worse, she mixed them up—the meat with the dairy, the dairy with the meat!
NACHMAN: Did she drop a hint, any possible reason. . . .
JOE: Nothing! She just raved! I found this on the table . . . her Certificate of Conversion. She tore it up.
RABBI: No . . . it was me! I tore it up!
JOE: You?
RABBI: I refused to convert her, I was angry. . . .
MENDEL: Because she wanted to be Orthodox? Shame! Shame on you!
RABBI: That had nothing to do with it!
JOE: Why did you tear it?
NACHMAN: Shhh . . . Calmly, children, calmly.

MENDEL: It's all the Rabbi's fault!

RABBI: Mine?

MENDEL: If he made her Jewish, she would have been sealed against demons.

NACHMAN: Not necessarily.

MENDEL: Consider, *Rebbe,* today is Wednesday. Lilith's power reaches its zenith on Wednesdays. And his wife is still a *shiksa, ai-yi-yi-yi-yi!*

NACHMAN: Who's the Howling One, you or Lilith?

MENDEL: He makes jokes! I tell him it's Lilith and he makes jokes, may God protect us!

NACHMAN: Slowly, Mendel, slowly. It's not hard to make sure. She-demon Lilith, whom some call Mayalleleth, I invoke the names of the three angels whom God sent to drown you and who spared your life, the angels Sensoi, Sansenoi, and Sammangelof, to whom you are sworn in eternal obedience, and by their authority and with their sanction, I command you to leave the body of this woman!

(They watch MARY *closely. There is no change.)*

It's not Lilith. Did the voice howl?

JOE: No.

NACHMAN: Was it the voice of a woman?

JOE: I thought it was Mary. I figured she sounded funny, being hysterical and all. But . . . now that you mention it, I think it sounded more like a young boy.

NACHMAN: A young boy?

JOE: It sounded like.

MENDEL: Then why don't he say something?

JOE: He talked a blue streak before. He only clammed up when we got here.

MENDEL: It's all clear to me now! It's a *dybbuk!* He thinks you brought him to the Temple to exorcise him, so he's afraid to speak. It's a *dybbuk,* a *dybbuk* has entered her body. *Oy, vey, vey, vey! Vey, vey!*

NACHMAN: Stop carrying on, Mendel. There are *dybbuks* and *dybbuks.*

(To MARY.*)*

Dybbuk, if you are a *dybbuk,* what are you called? I order you to reveal yourself!

(No answer.)

Dybbuk, if you resist me, I will summon a *minyan* of ten men in ten white robes. You will be exorcised with seven black candles and seven rams' horns and seven sacred scrolls taken from the Holy Ark, and your soul will know no peace from now till the end of time. I command you to reveal your name!

(The DYBBUK*'s voice, boyish and querulous, issues from* MARY*'s lips, though her eyes are closed and her expression barely changes.)*

MARY (DYBBUK): I won't do it!
NACHMAN: You won't?
MARY (DYBBUK): You can't make me!
NACHMAN: I can't?
MARY (DYBBUK): You can't! It's none of your business. Even if I told you my name, you wouldn't know me.
NACHMAN: I wouldn't? Are you sure?
MARY (DYBBUK): Yaaaaa, sure, sure, sure!
NACHMAN: Your voice is familiar. Keep talking. *Dybbuk,* don't try to resist me, I warn you!
MARY (DYBBUK): I'm not resisting you, I don't know what to say.
NACHMAN: Say anything. Say, *"Shema Yisroel Adoshem Elakeynu."*
MARY (DYBBUK): Stop it, stop it! Stop it, stop it, stop it!
NACHMAN: Is it so hard to repeat a simple prayer?
MARY (DYBBUK): It's not fair, not fair! You know you're not playing fair!
NACHMAN: Tell me, *Dybbuk,* have you ever been in Poland?
(No answer.)
Are you acquainted with the small *shtetl* of Sheliba, near the Wista River, between the towns of Opatasu and Ostrowiec?
(No answer.)
Your silence speaks louder than words. *Dybbuk,* I know you! Your name is Essig!
(A convulsive movement from the Dybbuk.)
A-hah! . . . Rabbi!
MENDEL: You mean it, *Rebbe?* You really know him?
NACHMAN: Hmf, hmf, hmf, do I know him! From the old country! . . . When I was a young man in Sheliba, they married me off to a woman named Layamalka. A woman, did I say? A wild animal, a raging beast! Like the Angel of the Erelim, she had seventy thousand heads, each head with seventy thousand mouths,

each mouth with seventy thousand tongues, each tongue a dagger in my side! She wouldn't let me go to the House of Study, she wouldn't even let me go to the toilet in peace. She would stand outside in the snow, in the most freezing weather, and scream insults through the moon crescent. . . .

MENDEL: *Vey is mir!*

NACHMAN: I stood it for a year, then one day while she was busy cursing out a passing beggar, I took my *tallis* and *tefilin,* a few crusts of bread, and sneaked out the back door. I walked maybe a mile when I spied, by the side of the road, a little man wearing a long black coat which reached to the ground and a black hat with a brim as wide as he was tall. I could only see a small part of his face which was covered with a greenish fur. What can I tell you? He looked like a poison mushroom. "Good day to you, Nachman," he says to me.

I spit out quick three times, poo, poo, poo! "You know me?"

"Know you? Why shouldn't I know you? I'm your demon. My name is Essig."

RABBI: A real demon?

NACHMAN: Darwin doesn't mention them? In Sheliba, the average person had hundreds of demons and Holy Men had thousands, some tens of thousands. Me, I was so poor, I was lucky to have one. Besides, with a wife like mine, who needed them? "So you're my demon," I said, "so what are you doing here?"

"Waiting for you."

"Waiting for me! You're supposed to be with me."

"Have pity," he said. "I couldn't stand your wife Layamalka a moment longer. The truth is, I ran away over two months ago."

"What do you want from me?"

"I'm sorry for you, I want to help."

"You want to help, so help."

MENDEL: You took the word of a demon?

NACHMAN: It was good as gold. Don't we all serve the same God? We made up that he would enter the body of a maiden, and I would be the only one who could exorcise him. It went like butter. Immediately, I was promoted to a Holy Man and given a place by the East Wall of the Synagogue. You think it made a difference to my wife? Just the opposite.

MENDEL: May she have boils like *matzoh* balls!

NACHMAN: *O-mayn!*

MENDEL: May she grow like an onion with her head in the ground!

NACHMAN: *O-mayn.* Finally our holy *Rebbe,* may he enjoy his stay in Paradise, took pity on me. "Nachman, my poor afflicted one," he said, "I'll give you a divorce with pleasure. But you'll never get rid of that *schlock* Layamalka, not until you leave Poland."

MENDEL: May she give birth to a crocodile!

NACHMAN: *O-mayn.*

MENDEL: May she live a hundred and twenty years and spend a hundred and nineteen in jail!

NACHMAN: *O-mayn.* "Leave," I cried, "where would I go, *Rebbe,* what would become of me?" "It's no big thing to be a holy man here," said the *Rebbe,* "Holy men are the chief industry in Sheliba. Go to America, where there's no competition." So I took his advice. But who ever thought that my little Essig would squeeze into the same overcrowded steerage?

MENDEL: All these years he never bothered you?

NACHMAN: Not until now.

MENDEL: I'll go collect a *minyan.*

NACHMAN: Wait . . . wait, Mendel. One must first ask, why did this demon invade the citadel of the child? Upon whose orders?

MENDEL: Does a demon need orders? A demon's a demon, he took a notion. . . .

NACHMAN: He would not dare such a thing unless he was directed by an authority far greater than his own. . . . And it was I who provided him with the opportunity . . . I, in my sinful pride!

MENDEL: You, *Rebbe?*

NACHMAN: Worm of the Earth that I am, I took it upon myself to conceal the whole truth. For this have the forces of evil descended upon us!

MENDEL: *Rebbe. . . .*

NACHMAN: May God grant it is not too late to make amends! Joseph! *(*JOE *approaches reluctantly, sensing something ominous in* NACHMAN*'s manner.)*

The time has come to reveal something to you, something I've told no one, not even Mendel. The fact is, I was not sent to Cincinnati just to seek out a *Lamedvovnik.* It was that, but much more. . . . The Voice which ordered me here also made sure to inform me that the *Lamedvovnik* I found would be the last!

JOE: The last?

NACHMAN: The last.

JOE: What are you trying to say, *Rebbe?* That if I die, the Earth dies? Fini, boom, the works!

NACHMAN: When that day comes, Joseph—and God willing it should be a long way off—your son will be ready to succeed you.

JOE: What son? The kid won't be born for three months.

NACHMAN: All the more reason to guard him!

JOE: Guard? . . . You saying the kid's a target?

NACHMAN: Mighty forces are arrayed against you. You are vulnerable and now . . . the child is vulnerable.

JOE: Just because I'm a *Lamedvovnik?*

NACHMAN: Because you are the last.

JOE: Then why didn't you tell me all this in the first place?

MENDEL: Excuse me, *Rebbe* . . . it's possible you misunderstood. The Voice probably meant the last in this country or the last in Cincinnati. . . .

NACHMAN: Not the last in Cincinnati, not the last in Hong Kong, China, or Hoboken, New Jersey . . . the last *Lamedvovnik* left on Earth!

MENDEL: How may this be? Does it not stand written that of *Lamedvovniks,* there must be thirty-six in every generation?

NACHMAN: Thirty-five died.

MENDEL: How is it possible? . . .

NACHMAN: How is death possible? Is that your question?

MENDEL: But thirty-five . . . it's a large number.

NACHMAN: Six million is larger.

JOE: Look, I don't know what's going on here. . . . I was willing to play at being a *Lamedvovnik,* but forget it, not now!—Not when it threatens Mary and the baby!

NACHMAN: Before you ever saw the light of day, your life was forfeit. Ask yourself why you were spared? Why were you not left to perish in your mother's womb?

JOE: You tell me, *Rebbe.*

NACHMAN: Because you are the holy descendant of a holy line, because it lies in your power to perpetuate that line. It was for this that the Ancient One, blessed be He, caused your wife to become pregnant.

JOE: And I had nothing to do with it, I suppose.

NACHMAN: Hear me out, Joseph. For most of his life a *Lamedvovnik* lives like other men. He dwells among the lowly in order that he may understand them and share their joys and sorrows. One asks, why does the beloved of God subject himself to earthly trials when his place is already reserved in Paradise.

JOE: I don't know from Paradise. In the beginning, it was all fun and games, I was happy to join you—happier than I've ever been in my life. Every morning on my way to temple, I watched the sky lighten up over my head like a pink pearl, and every morning I said, "How beautiful the world!"

NACHMAN: There are other worlds even more beautiful.

JOE: Not for me, *Rebbe.* For you maybe, and Mendel and Pitzik. Big believers, all of you!

MENDEL: Why do we waste time, *Rebbe?* Shouldn't we be busy trying to exorcise the demon?

JOE: Yeah, yeah. . . .

NACHMAN: Consider, Mendel. If we succeed, what is to prevent other and more terrible demons from entering the child's abode? As long as there is even a small crack in the fortress. . . .

JOE: Meaning me, Reb Nachman? Can you command a person to have faith.

NACHMAN: I never tried to force you, Joseph.

JOE: No? What are you doing now?

NACHMAN: We need your help if we are to help your wife and child. Only you can plead our cause.

JOE: What are you talking about? What cause?

NACHMAN: The world hangs by a hair, the Executioner of the Human Race is ready. Daily, Samael presses for our destruction.

JOE: Who?

MENDEL: Samael . . . Satan by the *goyim.*

JOE: I don't believe in him either.

NACHMAN: Pretend, Joseph . . . play one more game with us.

JOE: Back to that, eh?

NACHMAN: Belief will come later.

JOE: Stop feeding me that line! If I play your *cockamamey* game, it's only to help her, but spare me the commercials! Okay, what do you want me to do?

NACHMAN: You love this world so much? Give God one good reason to spare it.

JOE: If I bump into Him, I'll tell Him.

NACHMAN: Tell Him now! In this game, Joseph, imagine yourself standing before the All-Powerful Judge. Mendel will play the Prosecuting Angel.

MENDEL: Me, play Samael! I hate him like poison! How can you suggest such a thing?

JOE: It's only a game.

(The Window of Heaven starts to sputter, emits blue flashes. The RABBI, *concerned, turns to* JOE.)

RABBI: Static electricity?
(The sputtering and flashes stop, and the Window becomes very bright. The RABBI *is even more alarmed.)*
What's happening?

JOE: Just a short—it gets bright first . . . before it burns out.

NACHMAN: Talk to Him.

JOE: Why can't you?

NACHMAN: I am not one of the great ones, Joseph. I am only a messenger.

JOE: You're a Western Union boy? You, *Rebbe?* All right, I'll talk to Him. *(Moves up to the Window.)* Master of the Universe, this is me, Joe Halevy speaking. Joseph Halevy of Cincinnati, Ohio, U.S.A., son of the revered Lamedvovnik Yitzhok Halevy of Warsaw and Auschwitz. Lord of Creation, it's time for a showdown!

(The Window sputters angrily. NACHMAN *winces, the* RABBI *watches, intrigued.* MENDEL, *in his role as Samael, puts on a show of indignation.)*

MENDEL: Such a pisk! A showdown, the man wants! If I was Your Honor, I'd give him a showdown—right in the *gadkes!*

JOE: Watch it, Counselor, your prejudice is showing.

MENDEL: What prejudice, it's a simple business proposition. Your Honor, You never got anything but aggravation from this miserable planet, it's strictly a loser. So do like any smart business man, liquidate and move on to greener pastures.

JOE: You'll never find no greener pasture!
(Up to the lights.)

How long has it been since You last walked the Earth, Lord? How long since You walked the sandy shore by night with the white surf curling around Your toes and the salt wind biting Your whiskers? I could remind you of a few things, Lord—the stars You strung out like baby spots, the sun and the planets . . . why, You threw a switch and started the whole damn circuit humming, that was a job, Lord!

MENDEL: Who do you think you're talking to, Eb-eh-leh, Beb-eh-leh? Flattery will get you no place, just stick to the facts.

JOE: Facts, I'll give you facts! Apples and apple strudel, baseball and beer, Beethoven and the Beatles, old books, boat whistles in the night, bagels and belly lox, and I'm only up to the B's! There's breathing, breathing in and breathing out, and my wife's beautiful bare bottom, warm under the covers. . . .

MENDEL: Your Honor, this is irrelevant, immaterial, and just plain dirty. *Feh,* Your Honor!

JOE: Your Honor, how beautiful the world, how divine the gift of life, how wonderful is Man! Your Honor, I beg You, don't blow the works!

MENDEL: Ts, ts, ts! It's a pity I left my hanky in the wash, I could cry a whole river. Man, he says! and wonderful yet! Wonderful wars, wonderful massacres, wonderful inquisitions, and wonderful tortures! And now they have a wonderful bomb to speed everything up. And in case the fuse don't work, they poisoned the air and the water too. Take my advice and wipe them out, You'll be doing them a big favor, Your Honor.

JOE: Your Honor, I lived my life on Earth and found it good, even though You saw fit to curse the ground for our sake and made us eat of it in sorrow all the days of our lives . . . *(an aside to* NACHMAN*)* Genesis. . . . Don't get me wrong, Your Honor, I'm not complaining. I managed to scratch out my daily allotment of bread from that hard ground and reaped my fair share of acid indigestion, thank You, Lord. I lived among the lowly as You commanded and took part in their small joys and endless fears. We shivered before Your lightning and shook at the sound of Your thunder. We saw the end of the world in every sunset, the burning mountains and the blood-red seas, and right above us the shadow of Your mighty hand, long black fingers streaking the sky. . . . Oh, You never let us forget who held the fly-swatter!

MENDEL: Use it, Papa, use it!

JOE: Give us a chance, Lord, a chance to crawl out from under the shadow of our fear, one more chance!

MENDEL: You're not listening! He ain't heard a word I said!

JOE: I heard, Sam . . . every word . . . the wars, the massacres, the inquisitions, and the torture . . . it's all true, all of it! *(Looks up at the Window.)* And with all that, we still love You, God. Ain't it a scream?

(Abruptly, the light in the window goes out, signifying the case is closed. JOE *blinks, looks around.* MENDEL *steps back and out of his role as Prosecutor, a pleased smile on his lips.* NACHMAN *too is pleased but strives to maintain a solemn decorum as he announces:)*

NACHMAN: The game is over. Essig!

(He motions for MARY (ESSIG) *to approach. She shuffles toward him sullenly, eyes downcast.)*

You heard the *Lamedvovnik.*

MARY (DYBBUK): So what!

NACHMAN: Essig, my dear little demon, to you I owe everything, my divorce, my reputation, my American citizenship. Don't make me punish you.

MARY (DYBBUK): Then why don't you leave me alone as I left you alone? I'm comfortable here, I've found a nice home. Let me live in peace.

NACHMAN: I'm sorry, Essig, I must dispossess you.

MARY (DYBBUK): I won't go!

NACHMAN: Remember what you promised me in Sheliba, that I would have the power to exorcise you.

MARY (DYBBUK): What *hutzpa!* Because I once did you a favor? The promise was for one time only, and anyway, this is another country.

NACHMAN: Demon Essig, I command you to leave the body of Mary Walski, wife of the *Lamedvovnik* Joseph ben Yitzhok Halevy.

MARY (DYBBUK): You called her Walski! She's still a *shiksa!*

NACHMAN: Whatever she may be, she carries the *Lamedvovnik's* unborn child. There is no room for both of you.

MARY (DYBBUK): A lot you know! There's plenty of room.

MENDEL: Should I get the black candles?

NACHMAN: It may not be necessary. Demon, I invoke the signet ring of King Solomon upon which is engraved the *Shem Hameforash,* the Ineffable Name of God, and by virtue of the power the Wise King holds over your master Ashmodai and all the hosts of demons, I order you to leave the body of this woman or suffer anathema and excommunication from your own kind and all the Powers of Darkness!

MARY (DYBBUK): No! No, no, no, no, no!

NACHMAN: Unhappy Essig, you force me to do this. Up until now, I felt compassion for you, but now you leave me no choice. Because you have willfully disobeyed my command, you have brought this doom upon yourself. Miserable Demon, I am sending my ex-wife Layamalka after you!

(From MARY*'s mouth issues a horrible scream.* ESSIG*'s last despairing cry.* MARY*'s body shudders, strains, and becomes suddenly relaxed. She opens her eyes and looks around. There are two more heartbreaking wails from* ESSIG, *fading as he flies off into the darkness. The men follow the sound with their eyes.)*

MARY: . . . How did I get here? . . . Joe!

JOE: I believe, *Rebbe,* I believe!

NACHMAN: Compassionate Father, we thank you. The living God we praise, exalt, adore, He was, He is, He will be evermore!

JOE AND MENDEL: *O-mayn!*

NACHMAN: *O-mayn.* Now we may leave with a light heart.

RABBI: Leave? How can you leave now? I insist that you stay.

NACHMAN: But the trustees. . . .

RABBI: It's for their own good. Let them remember they once were Jews!

JOE AND MENDEL: *O-mayn!*

MARY: What about me, Rabbi? Will you make me a Jew?

RABBI: Will I make you a Jew! Father Iggy won't recognize you. Who would have suspected—a genuine Lamedvovnik in my congregation! It's a first for Cincinnati.

*(*PITZIK *enters.)*

PITZIK: I enjoy flying. I think I'll become an astronaut.

NACHMAN: Pitzik, Pitzik, I told you to fly to Heaven.

PITZIK: I'm sorry, Rebbe, I tried.

MENDEL: He couldn't get into orbit.

RABBI: Pitzik, my dear friend, I'm overjoyed to see you. I don't understand it, but I'm overjoyed.

MENDEL: You understood it when they played *Peter Pan.*

RABBI: You wore the flying harness. . . . *(turns to* MENDEL*)* and you operated him. . . .

(MENDEL *smiles, nods.)*

RABBI: Ohhhhh . . . You tricked me, *Rebbe!*

NACHMAN: I watched you during the play. When Peter Pan cried out, "Do you believe in fairies? Clap your hands, if you believe!" the whole audience went wild with applause, and you, Rabbi, you clapped louder than all the rest.

RABBI: It's part of the plot. If we don't, Tinker Bell dies.

NACHMAN: It's the same with God. Neither Pitzik nor Peter Pan can really fly. The miracle is that they can walk. But suppose Pitzik stepped to the front of the stage and asked, "Do you believe in God?," would you still clap your hands?

RABBI: Yes, *Rebbe.*

NACHMAN: Then I did not trick you.

RABBI: No, *Rebbe.*

JOE: See what a wonderful thing faith is! Not even the truth can shake it!

MENDEL: *O-mayn!*

PITZIK: *O-mayn!*

NACHMAN: Still, I think we should go. Trouble with the trustees you don't need.

RABBI: *Rebbenu* darling, I handled them before without faith. With, I'm a thousand times stronger.

MENDEL and JOE: *O-mayn!*

PITZIK: *O-mayn!*

NACHMAN: Faith is like fine-tempered steel. The hotter the crucible, the harder it becomes.

THE OTHERS: *O-mayn!*

JOE: It's like an electric bulb. The more resistance, the brighter the light.

THE OTHERS: (MARY *tentatively joins in.) O-mayn!*

MENDEL: It's like a rug. The more you beat it, the better.

THE OTHERS: *(with* MARY*) O-mayn!*
MARY: Faith is like having a baby . . . you get out a lot more than you put in.
THE OTHERS: *O-mayn!*
JOE: Like potato chips. The more you eat, the more you want.
THE OTHERS: *O-mayn!*
PITZIK: It's like flying. . . .
MENDEL: Why flying?
PITZIK: Why not?
RABBI: He's right, he's right, it's exactly like flying! *O-mayn, o-mayn!*
THE OTHERS: *O-mayn!*
RABBI: Faith is everything you say and more, a thousand times more! Come, children, let us sing a *dudele* to the Lord!
PITZIK: A *dudele,* a *dudele!*

*(*MENDEL *raises his arms toward the Window, as he leads them. They sing and dance.)*

ALL: *Duddel-duddel, du, du, duddel-duddel, du,*
Dirra-dirra, dirra-dirra, diddel-dum-du,
Dum du diddel, dum du diddel, dirra, dirra, dirra, du,
Dirra, dirra, dirra, dirra, du!

(The dance becomes completely abandoned, the syllables more and more guttural. They immerse themselves completely, oblivious to everything else.)

RABBI: Lights, lights! This is a celebration.

(He moves to the dimmer panel in the lectern, pushes the lever all the way up. All the lights go up, possibly including the house lights. Light streams down in a golden cone from the Window of Heaven. NACHMAN *bathes himself in its glow.)*

NACHMAN: The *shekhina,* the *shekhina!* The radiance of God surrounds us!

(The Window of Heaven starts acting up, the light fluctuating, now dim, now strong. A stern powerful Voice seems to emanate from it.)

THE VOICE: Rabbi, Rabbi! . . . Stop trying to flood the joint with light, something's gotta blow!

(The RABBI *stops dead in the middle of a dance step, downstage center, stares dumbfounded at the audience. The others go right on with their dancing and chanting. None of them have heard. The light from the Window continues to fluctuate in rhythm with the words.)*

RABBI: Pitzik, you heard?
PITZIK: Who can hear?
RABBI: Mendel! I heard a Voice!
MENDEL: You too, Rabbi? *Mazel Tov, Mazel Tov!*

(He pulls him into the dance. The RABBI, *overcome with the wonder of it all, allows himself to be swept along. The dancing and singing, cries and Hasidic gestures reach a peak of exaltation. The curtain falls.)*

Elephants

A play in two acts by

DAVID RUSH

For Becky, B.J. and Fran—
with my love

David Rush, *Elephants.*

DAVID RUSH'S play, *Beethoven/Karl,* was done in New York at Playwrights Horizons and the Manhattan Theatre Club, and at theatres in Texas and Wisconsin. His civil war piece, *Leander Stillwell,* was seen at the Mark Taper Forum, and a bicentennial play, *Calls Out Billy Morgan,* was written on commission for Tufts University. Rush has worked extensively on musicals, collaborating with Errol Pearlman on *The King of New London* and *Happy Hour,* both of which have been produced in Chicago.

Elephants was a courageous choice for the Jewish Repertory Theatre. Not only is the language shocking to a middle-class audience, but the writer's vision is far from the sentimental one generally associated with Jewish theatre. It was indeed gratifying that the production turned out to be an audience pleaser and that the most astute and admiring review came from the *Long Island Jewish World.* Critic J. Peter Brunswick wrote that "Rush brings us sharply face to face with the harsh realities of some discomfiting aspects of today's Jewish experience in the large urban jungles of the United States, in this case, Chicago . . . Rush's play asks painful questions and offers moral options it might be well for all of us to contemplate."

In 1984, the success of *Elephants* was repeated with a production at the Jewish Community Center of Baltimore.

Elephants was first produced by the Jewish Repertory Theatre in December 1981 with the following cast:

HENRY LEIDER	Lee Wallace
WOMAN	Marilyn Chris
BEN LEIDER	Richard Niles

Directed by Edward M. Cohen
Set by Geoffrey Hall
Costumes by Jessica Fasman
Lighting by Dan Kinsley

Time: During late afternoon and evening on a day in mid-December. The present.

Place: A small efficiency apartment, built into a large synagogue building located on the near north side of Chicago.

ACT I. 3 o'clock on a Sunday afternoon.
ACT II. Later that afternoon.

Act I

The apartment contains several living areas: a kitchenette, with table, two chairs, kitchen appliances and sink; a living area, an armchair, lamp and many, many places for books. The apartment is crowded with books and magazines. A window in the kitchen area, open at the start of the play, looks onto a residential street. There are three doors into the room: one leading to a bathroom; one leading to a short hallway which carries you to the outside door; and one leading to the rest of the building. On the wall near the exterior door is an inner-com buzzer system, which lets you speak to the rest of the building as well as buzz open the exterior entrance. On the wall near the kitchen is a keyrack.

The room is empty for a moment. Then the door to the outside is opened, and HENRY LEIDER *enters.* HENRY *is in his late sixties, wearing heavy winter clothes—coat, galoshes, hat, muffler, etc., which he removes and carefully puts in proper places during the scene.*

HENRY *(speaking to somebody following him):* I'll make a light. Who could believe it's so dark at three o'clock. We got a blizzard coming; it could be terrible. *(He flicks on a light)* How come it's so cold; I thought I left on the heat. *Oy,* the window, idiot. *(He goes to close the window, and finds a damp paperback book lying on the sill)* Idiot. Dumb-head. Look; look at this. Seven-ninety-five for Martin Buber, and all I got now is toilet paper. For such a thinker, a man should have more respect, right? Hello? You're there? Come in, come in already.

*(*WOMAN *appears in the doorway. She is a "bag lady," one of the elderly women who live in the streets of large cities. Her age is indeterminate—probably between forty and fifty. She is dressed in a large, shabby coat, woolen mittens, a ragged scarf and heavy shoes. She carries a large department store shopping bag.)*

WOMAN: Not so fast, Mister; not so fast. You didn't say you had stairs.

HENRY: Six steps from the street is not a trip to the lower depths. If you'd let a person help with the bag like he offers—

WOMAN: Touch the bag, Mister, you could lose your arm.

HENRY: Come, all the way in. I could close the door before we freeze. Look, I think my thumb turned into a popsicle. Never buy gloves from the army surplus. They use from World War II recycled cheesecloth. *(He pokes his finger through a hole in his glove.)* Bargains. Betrayals. Lady, what's the matter?

WOMAN: Where's the money? You said you had some money.

HENRY: No, no, no, no. I said you could *make* some money. There's a difference.

WOMAN: How much?

HENRY: Enough. Trust me.

WOMAN: Tell me.

HENRY: Two hundred dollars.

WOMAN: What do I have to do?

HENRY: First, you have to come inside.

WOMAN: I think it's bullshit, Mister. I think there's no deal or nothing here. You wanta rob me. It could be easy.

HENRY: I'm not going to—

WOMAN: I warn you, you gotta kill me first. You wanta do that? You wanta kill me? Let me tell you, all you'd get is $7.25. You're gonna commit murder for $7.25, you know that? You're crazy. You'll get the electric chair. It'll cost more than that just to turn on the switch.

HENRY: Please, will you trust me, you know who I—

WOMAN: Or maybe dip-the-stick? Is that it? A little fast fucky-fuck in the afternoon?

HENRY: What?

WOMAN: Ain't you ashamed of yourself, Mister?

HENRY: Lady!

WOMAN: You want that, better go down State Street. You could take your pick. They're all over the place down there. You can't miss 'em. Blue paint all over their faces, tits sticking out all the way to next Tuesday. You know what they use? They use grapefruits. They put grapefruits inside. A man thinks he's got a big thrill coming; he gets upstairs and finds out he's squeezing things that got SUN-KIST written on 'em. So what does he do? He runs out, stiff as a rod, and goes and rapes somebody. You tell me the city's a place to bring up kids? You gotta be crazy to live in the city. I don't know what you want from me, Mister!

HENRY: I want you to come in so we can talk.

WOMAN: Why couldn't we talk in the street?

HENRY: It's the North Pole out there! For the last time, look at me. I'm sixty-two years old. I retired from the drugstore because I had a stroke. I also got an asthma condition, a seven-year old grandson, high blood pressure and acid indigestion. My eyesight is so bad, in a car, I'm listed as a dangerous weapon. So enough already; this is very important here. You want to do business tonight, come inside and talk about it. If not, make up your mind and I could find somebody else.

WOMAN: Two hundred dollars?

HENRY: Yes.

WOMAN: First lemme see it.

HENRY: Inside.

WOMAN: It's something dirty.

HENRY: You're not gonna find out until you take five more steps. You won't be sorry, believe me. When you walk out from here, you'll be a happy person. *(She moves in the room. He goes to shut the door)*

WOMAN: Leave it open.

HENRY: What?

WOMAN: The door. Leave it open.

HENRY: What for?

WOMAN: So I could get out.

HENRY: What do you wanta get out; you just got in!

WOMAN: I don't like being closed up, you hear!

HENRY: I'm not paying Commonwealth Edison to warm up the street. *(He closes door)*

WOMAN: Help! Help! Fire!

HENRY: What are you doing; you want the whole neighborhood should know, for Chrissake!

WOMAN: Always holler *fire.* You holler *robbery,* nobody comes near a mile. You holler *rape,* little boys run over to watch. Always holler *fire.* You never learn good stuff like that in the public schools.

HENRY: We have to work out a compromise, lady. How about if I open up the bathroom door! Huh?

WOMAN: That window; what is that? Pine Grove Street?

HENRY: No. It's Wellington. Come here, lemme show you. *(He refers to bathroom offstage.)* See the window? You want to get out, drop down the toilet seat, climb up, and in fifteen seconds you're in the alley. *Nu?* Everything is hunky-dory, what do you say? It's wonderful. I'm warm. You're comfortable. Everybody's happy. I'll put on some tea.

WOMAN: I don't like it, Mister.

HENRY: Excuse me, but for two hundred dollars, you'll have to. I mean, it's nice we could be on the same bus, but, I'm sorry, I'm the driver.

WOMAN *(Points to the third door):* What's that?

HENRY: It goes into the rest of the building. You're better off with the toilet seat.

WOMAN: What kind of building?

HENRY: It's a *shul.*

WOMAN: A what?

HENRY: A Jewish church. I'm here the caretaker. This part belongs to me; that part belongs to God. Either way, I promise you'll be safe. Now please, you're dripping Niagara Falls over my books.

WOMAN: That's not Wellington Avenue.

HENRY: Trust me, huh? I lived here a year.

WOMAN: It ain't Wellington Avenue because I never *go* on Wellington Avenue. It's where the alligators live.

HENRY: What alligators?

WOMAN: It's true. They live in the sewers. You know the baby lizards they sell at Walgreen's? They call 'em sala—something? What they really are—they're baby alligators. People give 'em to their kids for Christmas. By February, the kids are sick and tired. Why not? You ever try to play with a baby alligator? It's not like a puppy. They don't roll over or fetch or nothing. So the kids, they flush 'em down the toilets. And where do they go then? They got some kind of instinct. They all go down there together in the sewers under Wellington Avenue. And then, every time there's a full moon, they come up, looking for old ladies to eat. They go for old ladies because old ladies, they can't run so fast. That's why I stay away. So don't tell me Wellington Avenue; I know the city inside out.

HENRY: You want to give me your coat, *nu?*

WOMAN: What, first the coat, then the pants, then the underwear, huh? What kind of dumb do you think I am?

HENRY: Then at least, sit down. We're not a couple of animals here, you know what I mean? God gives us manners; we don't have to stand and whisper in the street.

WOMAN: That means it's dirty. So long.

HENRY: It's not gonna hurt you to listen.

WOMAN: It will. It'll keep me here past Sesame Street.

(Phone starts ringing.)

HENRY: Just let me get the phone.

WOMAN: Down by the Polk Brothers, they got this big t.v. in the window.

HENRY: It's cocaine! *(She stops. The phone continues.)* All right? It's cocaine; will you wait. Don't make any noise, please. Nobody should know you're here. *(to phone)* Hello, what? *(to her)* It's my son, Ben. *(back to phone)* I'm out of breath because I ran. From outside, where else? . . . I went out because it was important; what is this, twenty questions here? . . . It's nice you should worry about my health, but do me a favor, don't. . . . I'll tell you what. I promise if I have another stroke, you'll be the first to know. I'll call you from the bathroom floor. . . . Yes, I called. You weren't in, I had to talk to that *mumzer* Kepler. Tell me, who decides down there on managers, why do they put such idiots in that position? . . . He IS an idiot, I had to tell him three times who I was. . . . Why do you defend him? What, is he listening? *(Louder)* Kepler, you *mumzer,* get off the phone, it's private business! . . . I don't care. YOU should be the manager, you got five years seniority there. . . . What I called, I want to see you. Tonight, on your way home, you could stop, *nu?* . . . You'll find out when you get here. . . . Maybe, it's about Sarah and maybe it's not; I'm not playing Sherlock Holmes on the phone, just come. . . . Of course, we'll fight. Just because it's *Hanukkah* doesn't mean a holiday from family. . . . *(hangs up, angry)* Where were we? You were on your way out or not?

WOMAN: You started talking about something, it sounded like Coca-cola. What was that?

HENRY: Now you're interested? Wonderful. Welcome to the human race. Only you'll have to wait a little bit. It's been a long day. I'm wet and I'm hungry; we'll have some tea; and start behaving in here like people.

WOMAN: You keep changing the rules, Mister.

HENRY: Trust me. We're gonna be partners. A partnership always begins with a meal. It's the eleventh commandment. Sit here, away from the carpeting if you don't mind.

WOMAN: How long is this gonna take?

HENRY: Why? You got some place to go? You got an appointment in the alley?

WOMAN: If I don't get to the Kroger before Marie, she grabs all the good boxes. I get left with the ones that still got lettuce stuck in 'em. Y' ever try to sleep in a box that got lettuce stuck all over? It gives you nightmares. Giant rabbits chasing you through the jungle!

HENRY: By the time we get through, you could get a room at the Hilton.

(A major decision: she moves over to chair and with a great sigh, sits. During the next beat, she changes her shoes, taking from some place in her possession a pair of tennis shoes. She takes off her large boots and puts these on.)

WOMAN: What about your kid coming over?

HENRY: Don't worry; there's plenty of time. And if not, you'll hide in the hall.

WOMAN: When I get to Heaven, I'm gonna say, "God, you know what you gotta do? You gotta give me a little blond boy, to sit here all day and all night and rub these suckers for me!"

(She rubs and stretches out her toes luxuriously.)

HENRY: What about your bag, you could put it down in the corner over here.

WOMAN: You got Jack Daniels here?

HENRY: No. We'll have tea.

WOMAN: I don't drink tea, Mister; you think I'm crazy?

HENRY: Tea is the perfect drink!

WOMAN: I don't drink anything, Mister, that you put in water and the water turns brown!

HENRY: I don't have any whiskey! I have a prostate condition!

(She lifts bag onto table.)

WOMAN: You're gonna make me use my own, goddamnit. You know how hard that stuff is to get hold of? It's like gold—

HENRY: Lady, don't put this on the table, please. I got— *(He reaches for the bag.)*

WOMAN *(She pulls from a pocket an aerosol spray can, aims it at him):* You ever read the labels on these things, Mister, the part that says keep outta your eyes?

HENRY: Lady—

WOMAN: I warn you; I'm old but I'm quick!

HENRY: All right! Just keep it off the table! *(She moves the bag; he cleans up the table)* Look. Look, see what you did? An expensive *Chekhov;* now a set of sponges!

WOMAN *(During following, she rummages through her bag and pulls out a very nearly empty bottle of Jack Daniels . . . and empties it.):* Come on, you got too many books anyhow. You're gonna get sick.

HENRY: I'm gonna get a heart attack that's what I'm gonna get.

WOMAN: It's true. Books make you sick. You keep books around, you know what happens? You get bugs. They crawl around, they bring worms. All kinds of little worms, with lots of legs. It's true. They live in the back parts; they eat off the glue. Then, when you read, you hold the book in your hands, the bugs and the worms and things, they get on your skin. They crawl under your fingernails. Then, when you eat, you got no idea what's going into your stomach. And when you piss, it's even worse. You touch yourself all over down there, and the first thing you know, you start itching, you start dripping. Take my advice. You don't want the clap; stop reading books.

HENRY: What do you have in that bag, anyhow? The crown jewels?

WOMAN: Look at this. *(She holds up whiskey bottle.)* They make the bottle with fake bottoms. You can't trust anybody.

HENRY: Every time I see you, it's never out of your hands. I thought for a while maybe it grew there, like a big tumor named Marshall Fields.

WOMAN: You been watching me a long time, Mister?

HENRY: Let me put these away to dry *(taking his wet outer clothes into the bathroom)*.

If the phone rings, don't answer.

(Speaking from offstage:)

You know something, I was surprised you let me get close to you. I mean, I used to see what happened on the street. A person gets inside ten feet, you start right away with the hollering and the dirty words. I said, "Henry, she'll never talk to you." It's a miracle you sat there, I couldn't understand why.

WOMAN: Because I know who you are Mister. You had the drugstore by the Pancake House.

HENRY: Thirty-five years! This is wonderful; like a reunion with an old friend!

WOMAN: You called the cops on me one time.

HENRY: Come on, never.

WOMAN: Wednesday night, November 13, 1979.

HENRY: No.

WOMAN: I made a place there in the alley, then Johnny Blue shows up. Citizens' complaint.

HENRY: You weren't in the alley. You were blocking up my front entrance. Customers had to step over you, it was disgusting.

WOMAN: They took me in the whole night, Mister. A room without even a window. I wasn't happy.

HENRY: So, *nu;* it's ancient history? Who's mad any more?

WOMAN: No. I ain't mad. Don't get me wrong. I don't get mad. I get even. There's a difference.

HENRY: Look, I had a business to run. What was I suppose to do? Put up a tent for you with plumbing?

WOMAN: After that, you know what I did? I always wanted to tell you. I used to come by every day. I used to stand across the street by the mailbox and look at you. I thought to myself, "There's that asshole that thinks he's so smart. Let's see how smart he is." I used to see your head sticking up from the prescription counter, but you couldn't see me. It got like a game, like a war. I kept on moving closer and closer, trying to see how close I could move without getting caught. One day—I always wanted to tell you—one day, I even got inside. I got inside and you never caught me. It was raining, see, goddamn pussies and puppies, and the place was filled up with people waiting for buses. And what did I do? I put on this big black raincoat and I snuck right in. You never saw. I stayed up in the front behind all the people and I moved around up there, and I kept pulling stuff off the shelves, too. Hershey Bars, Snickers, M & M's. That junk gave me the runs for two days straight, but it was worth every dump.

HENRY: Maybe instead you should have stolen Milk of Magnesia.

WOMAN: I did. Next time. I kept going back, you see. Every couple of months, when there was a crowd, or you were doing something in the back, I'd go in the front, and fill up. And not just junk, either. Sometimes real hard stuff. Contac. Super Tylenol. Vicks Extra Strength Cough Syrup!

HENRY: You got even. Wonderful. Can we change the subject?

WOMAN: I kept waiting for you to catch me, but you never did. Never. Ah, you stupid bastard. All the fun went out of the neighborhood when you sold off that place.

HENRY: I didn't sell it, Lady. I got sick, and while I was sick, it was stolen from me. Listen, you took a couple of chocolate bars and a box of pills and you think you hurt me? You were small time, Lady, believe me. Small time, compared to my son. *(He cuts up salami to serve during)* Kids. Nobody can betray you like kids. I had a wonderful business, that store, for thirty-five years. All right, so it wasn't Walgreen's, it's no sin to confess. But it was my life! So? One day, I was counting fifty nitroglycerin for Sol Shuster, when suddenly, like a snap in my head, there was a stroke. Just like that. The next thing, I was in a hospital bed, and I didn't get up for six weeks. And in the meantime, my son, Ben, what does he do? Like a traitor, he gets a power of attorney and right out from under me, he sells the store; and at such a loss. So what then? I found this. A janitor in a *shul.* I push a broom, wash a window, lock up a door, like a machine. It's no longer, let me tell you, such a wonderful life. *Oy,* I got diarrhea from the mouth. You'll have to put up with it. I mean, how often is there another person sitting here. So, tell me, you got a name? If we do business, I should know what to call you.

WOMAN: Business? What kind of business?

HENRY: Business like people do. I'm selling, you're buying.
WOMAN: What am I buying? I got $7.25.
HENRY: If not you, then Hector.
WOMAN: Who do I know named Hector?
HENRY: At the Pancake House, I remember, there used to be a Mexican who swept up at night. His name was Hector, and there were all kinds of stories up and down the street. I looked yesterday; he wasn't there any more.
WOMAN *(Looking down at the plate of sausage and bread he brought over):* What's this?
HENRY: Salami.
WOMAN: I never eat salami! You know what's in it?
HENRY: What difference does it make?
WOMAN: Parakeets! It's true. Pet stores, what they don't sell after a month, they slip in boxes to Gary, Indiana, by the Oscar Meyer plant there. They got a big factory: gas houses, stuffing machines, big bathtubs they use for coloring. And two weeks later, the birds, they turn up red like this in the Kroger. Why don't you gimme hamburger?
HENRY: Look, do you see any sign here that say *restaurant?* There is no sign here that says *restaurant!* All I got is tea, pumpernickel, and cooked canary.
WOMAN *(takes a sample):* You can even taste the feathers.
HENRY: Tell me already about Hector!
WOMAN: I ain't seen him in weeks. He got fired.
HENRY: How do I find him?
WOMAN: I don't know!
HENRY: All right! We're dribbling around and playing *dreidl* here, it's ridiculous. You have to do what you have to do, so here it is already. I'm holding, Lady—God help me—ten grams of pharmaceutical cocaine. I got it fresh, don't ask me how, but you should know it's very pure. For reasons I don't want to go into, it's very important that I have to make at least twenty-five hundred dollars cash out of it. Now I know Hector can do this.
WOMAN: I stay by myself, you know what I mean? I don't go around a lot.
HENRY: Help me get to him, and I'll pay you two hundred dollars.
WOMAN: Lemme see it.
HENRY: It's hidden away.

WOMAN: Unhide it.
HENRY: It's here. Trust me.
WOMAN: I don't trust anybody, Mister. That's how come I'm still alive.
HENRY: All right. All right. My God, what's happening in the world? I'm here, making a drug deal with a walking garbage can, who would believe!

(During the following, he goes to where he has hidden the dope.)

WOMAN: You deal with Hector a lot?
HENRY: Never. But he should know who I am; I had coffee there all the time.
WOMAN: Then who were you dealing with before?
HENRY: Before? What do you mean, before?
WOMAN: Before this?
HENRY: With nobody!
WOMAN: Come on Mister; you had a drugstore all them years.
HENRY: Which at all times was an honest business. I never, in my life did a single thing I couldn't talk about to another person.
WOMAN: Then what is this?
HENRY: This is an emergency.
WOMAN: Sure. The Water Tower is on fire. The lake is flooding over. Horseshit!
HENRY: I got a sister maybe dying, all right! You don't mind! Her name is Sarah. She lives now in Tel Aviv, and a few days ago, we got from there a telegram. She's in a coma. A tumor the size of an orange. You know what I *did* when I heard? I wept. I sat down, and like a baby, I wept. You should understand; I have for my sister, you see, a very great love. She was my best—my only true—friend in the world. Two things in my life gave me glory. The business that I built up, and the love I share with my sister. One of them is already gone. I have to go there. To fly all the way to Tel Aviv. To see her, to talk with her maybe one last time. But you know the cost? And what do I have here on my social security and petty cash? Not enough for a limousine to the airport. So then, what? First I went to my son. "Ben, send me to Israel." But, children only live so they can break your heart. Then I looked; what do I have to sell?

Nothing. A lifetime of books is only a couple hundred pounds of paper after all. So, I was in a terrible situation. Until, walking the day before yesterday on Clark Street, I saw you sitting there in the alley. And I thought—how is it that old lady stays alive? She eats, she has to get money someplace. And all of a sudden, I remembered about you and Hector and the stories all over the street, and I knew what I could do. *(Now, he holds up the vial of powder.)* So. What do you think?

WOMAN: Lemme see it.

HENRY: You don't mind. I'll hold it.

WOMAN: I can't pass it on, Mister, until I know what it is.

HENRY: It's fresh from the shelf.

WOMAN: A taste, Mister. Come on, one taste, or nothing happens. *(*HENRY *hesitates, then opens the vial.)* Come on, come on, come on. . . .

HENRY: Am I right?

(He shakes out a few grains. She licks her fingers, dabs up the grains, tastes them.)

WOMAN: I could tell better from a sneeze.

HENRY: No. *(Starts to close up the vial again.)*

WOMAN: Half a rail, you wouldn't even miss it.

HENRY: Get me in touch with Hector.

WOMAN: All right. I'll go looking tomorrow.

HENRY: No. It has to be tonight.

WOMAN: C'mon. He lives south of 95th Street. You go down there at night, you come home in six pieces.

HENRY: Then make a telephone call. Here. We got call-pak. *(He brings phone over.)*

WOMAN: What's the hurry! It's snowing out there.

HENRY: I don't want this garbage around me, lady; it makes me nervous.

WOMAN: Why? Is it running?

HENRY: Never mind.

WOMAN: It is. From where?

HENRY: I also have to be on an airplane at 9:30 in the morning. It's a twelve-hour flight—

WOMAN: From the hospital there on Fullerton? For the kids?

HENRY: No. I don't go stealing from hospitals. There are people who need this in hospitals.

WOMAN: Then where else? Come on, you been in this—

HENRY: Lady, I can call this off. It's not too late to call this off! Dial already!

WOMAN: All right! *(She digs around in her bag again.)* Keep it a secret. Who cares?

HENRY: What are you doing?

WOMAN: Lemme find the number! You gotta wait a minute, Mister, until I find the goddamned telephone number! I mean, your sister, she could hold out a little longer, so I don't wind up with some cop in Calumet City! "Hey, I got some snow here! Who's this? Office Kowalski? Sorry!"

HENRY: Lady, you're giving me such gas pains, I can't tell you!

WOMAN: Here it is. Save everything!

(She starts to dial; she stops and looks at him.)

HENRY: What, what?

WOMAN: You know, Mister I'm an old lady. Sometimes my mind gets fuzzy. It happens to old people. My cut out of this—how much were we talking?

HENRY: Two hundred dollars.

WOMAN: Two hundred dollars?

HENRY: Lady, finish dialing already, you'll get a disconnect.

WOMAN *(finishes dialing):* Ola, Hector? . . . Donde? . . . Aqui la vieja de Lincoln Park. ("Hello, Hector? Where? This is the old lady from Lincoln Park.") *(She turns to* HENRY.*)* You're in trouble. His sister says he ain't home.

HENRY: Where is he?

WOMAN: She says she don't know.

HENRY: When's he coming home?

WOMAN: Quando viene casa? . . . Veo. . . . Buen. ("When is he coming home? I see. Okay.") She says she don't know that either.

HENRY: Tell her she has to find him. Say it's life and death.

WOMAN: Es importante. Viv o muerto. ("It's important. Life or death.")

HENRY: What does she say?

WOMAN: Nothing. She's laughing. *(into phone again)* Digale es tan importante. Y es bien segura. Sabes le quiero decir. Azucar. Si. Yo le veo. Esta noche. Espera. ("Tell him it's very important. And very safe. You know what I mean. Sugar. Yes, I've seen it. Tonight. Wait.") He'll be home by midnight.

HENRY: He should call here.

WOMAN: Aqui. Tres, tres, dos, quatro, un, un tres. Digale tres y nueva tres, y pregunta—("Here. 332-4113. Tell him to ring three and then three again, and ask for—") *(To* HENRY*)* What's your name?

HENRY: Why do I have to give my name?

WOMAN: When he calls, he'll know it's clean. Come on, she'll think something's funny.

HENRY: Henry.

WOMAN *(into phone):* Henry. *(To him)* Henry what?

HENRY: What do you mean, Henry what?

WOMAN: Mister, everybody has to trust everybody!

HENRY: Henry O'Reilly.

WOMAN *(into phone):* Henry O'Reilly. Si. Adios. *(Hangs up.)* Okay. We have to wait.

HENRY: How long?

WOMAN: I don't know. She has to find him and give him the deal. Then he—

HENRY: How does she know the deal?

WOMAN: I told her.

HENRY: Over the telephone? Out loud like that?

WOMAN: I said *azucar,* don't worry.

HENRY: Azucar, shumcar. How could you do that?

WOMAN: It's *sugar,* Mister! You oughta learn Mexican, you know. Anybody who lives in this neighborhood thirty-five years and don't know Mexican is cutting his own throat. You should also learn a little Chinese—*(Spouts some Chinese:* ce-suo zai nar *means "Where's the bathroom?")*

HENRY: All right! After she tells him, what?

WOMAN: He decides he wants it and calls back.

HENRY: And how long could that take?

WOMAN: It could be half-an-hour, it could be Easter, how do I know?

HENRY: I need some Gelusil. *(Gets a bottle from kitchen.)* I don't like this. Maybe I should call it off. I have to talk to Ben. I have to talk hard to Ben.

WOMAN: We could sneeze on the snow, Mister.

HENRY: No!

WOMAN: Come on, Hector won't miss one little rail.

HENRY: Nobody takes any drugs in here! It's a holy place right next door!

WOMAN: You can't take 'em, but can sell 'em, what's the difference?

HENRY: I already told you, my sister—

WOMAN: Ah, your sister don't mind. She won't even know! What am I gonna do, write her a letter? "Hey, your brother's a junkie." No—

HENRY: Don't mock, Lady. An attachment is breaking apart here; it's not a subject for mockery.

WOMAN: What it is, Mister, is bullshit. You crimped that stuff, you're moving to sell it, there's no difference.

HENRY: I don't have to explain any more! I don't have to explain at all, Lady; especially to you.

WOMAN: Hey—

HENRY: You. You live in a gutter. What could you possibly know from an attachment! You know alligators and parakeets, that's all you know. For Chrissake, you don't even know your own name!

WOMAN: Frieda. How's that? They call me Frieda!

HENRY: Frieda! It comes from the Danish, *nu?* From Fredericka?

WOMAN: Or sometimes they call me Anna, the cops. Hector says Gertie. Marie on Sheffield hollers out shit-head, and when I talk to myself, I say Queen Elizabeth. And who are you? Saint Jesus?

HENRY: Look, you think I'm enjoying this, you're crazy. To steal cocaine, it's not like playing pinochle. But, my sister is in a coma and she's all alone, it must be a terrible thing. It's like the elephants. You should understand. When an old elephant dies—I saw it once on television, I never forgot—when an old elephant falls down and can't get up anymore, all the other elephants, do you know what they do? The big, strong ones, the females, the babies even? They all come around, they crowd in, they go to the elephant on the ground and—they try as hard as they can—to make the elephant stand up again. They push; they shove; and they make these sounds, like horns or something. It's like they're talking. And there they stay, as long as they have to. They stay there until it's no use any more. They don't let the elephant die all alone. They don't push him into some far away hospital room, or hide him away in some old people's home, or send him off to empty wastebaskets in a building. Do you know why? Because it's a living thing—with a life—and a life is not supposed to be lived alone. To leave my sister alone like that—would be a terrible act of betrayal. Elephants you see, they know that. And why should elephants be better than people? So I have to get to Tel Aviv, and if I have to break laws to do it, then that's what I'll do. So, at midnight, after I lock up from the teenager's social, if we haven't heard from Mr. Hector, we'll call a taxicab and go to the south side looking!

WOMAN: And we'll make it fifty-fifty.

HENRY: What?

WOMAN: The split. Fifty-fifty. Whatever Hector pays, I'll take half.

HENRY: We said two hundred dollars.

WOMAN: Now I'm talking fifty-fifty.

HENRY: That's over a thousand dollars!

WOMAN: Mister, I'm an old lady, have a heart. You see how I live. In August, I melt. In December, I freeze. And when they close down the public bathrooms in Lincoln Park, it's a terrible life.

HENRY: We made already a bargain!

WOMAN: I could get a new coat. You wanna know why I don't take this off? It's sewed on. Buttons are for shit keeping out the wind; I sew the sides up; it takes me half an hour to—

HENRY: What I said about Sarah, you didn't hear a word?

WOMAN: And shoes. I could get shoes. You wanna see my feet? I got sores all over 'em. I bleed every time I take a step. What do you—

HENRY: All right! I could go up to three.

WOMAN: I could also fix my teeth.

HENRY: Lady, don't push too hard.

WOMAN: I could eat salami like the pope!

HENRY: You won't get blood, understand. Three hundred fifty is all.

WOMAN: Six.

HENRY: Four.

WOMAN: Four seventy-five.

HENRY: Four fifty.

WOMAN: I'll take it.

HENRY: You got it.

WOMAN: Good.

HENRY: Drink the tea.

(They drink to seal their bargain.)

Confess, you don't have sores on your feet. They don't bleed.

WOMAN: Well, maybe not a whole lot.

HENRY: You did that good, I'm impressed.

WOMAN: Let me tell you, if I'd got to the ulcer, I could have taken you higher.

HENRY: So why stop?

WOMAN: You got too hot all of a sudden. I got nervous. Besides, four fifty is better than two.

HENRY: You should know, I would have gone all the way up to five!

(There is a moment, and they laugh with each other. A sudden sound—the front door buzzer—interrupts.)

WOMAN: What's that?

HENRY: The buzzer. Somebody wants to come in. Be quiet. *(Crosses to intercom, and works the speaker-response.)* Hello, what?

BEN *(The voice of* BEN LEIDER, *about mid-thirty):* Dad, it's Ben. Lemme in.

HENRY *(to* WOMAN*):* It's my son. Shhh. *(To box)* Ben, wait one second.

BEN: Come on, it's freezing out here.

HENRY: All right. *(To* WOMAN*):* You have to hide. Go sit in the *shul.*

(He begins to help her gather up whatever of her things are around.)

WOMAN: Where?

HENRY: In the *shul,* where the seats are! *(He opens the hallway door.)* It's down there. *(The buzzer again, impatient.)*

WOMAN: Somebody could see me.

HENRY: It's empty!

WOMAN: It better have a door, Mister.

HENRY: I'll call you on the speaker to come back.

WOMAN: A Jewish church. I been in some piss-ass places in my life.

(The buzzer continues to ring as he closes door behind her. He then goes to intercom and pushes buttons.)

HENRY: All right; it's open, come in.

(He opens apartment door for BEN. BEN *enters.* BEN *is in his mid-thirties, beginning to go a little bald, dressed as a hard working middle-class shoe salesman.)*

BEN: What's the matter?
HENRY: Nothing.
BEN: You're sure? You took so long, I almost went for my key.
HENRY: I was busy; it's not a major crisis.
BEN: What's the matter? Are you sick?
HENRY: No, I'm not sick. I was sitting on the toilet. From the toilet to the front door, it just takes a little time.
BEN: You answered the buzzer; how could you answer the buzzer if you were on the toilet?
HENRY: Ben, please; the inquisition ended five hundred years ago!
BEN: You called me at work; you pulled me away from a customer. It has to mean something!
HENRY: It means I wanted to visit. A father to visit with his son is not a capital offense.
BEN: It is at the store. I keep telling you that. Kepler gets on my case for a week.
HENRY: You let that snot-nosed kid walk all over you; it's a crime.
BEN: That snot-nosed kid happens to the manager.
HENRY: You should be the manager.
BEN: Okay, okay. Come on, get your coat. You can whip me in the car.
HENRY: Can you sit for a minute; don't be in such a hurry.
BEN: Andy's waiting. I called home; I told him Grandpa's coming for *Hanukkah.* You shoulda heard the kid scream. He's nuts over you.
HENRY: I got things to do here first. Sit.
BEN: What smells in here?
HENRY: Garbage by the *shul.* Before I leave, I'll take care.
BEN: I'll do it.
HENRY: No, I will. Please. It's my job, you don't mind.
BEN: I do mind; I don't like to see you doing it.
HENRY: It gives me pleasure.
BEN: Dumping garbage gives you pleasure?

HENRY: Why not? It's a useful occupation. God invented garbage; He also had to invent people to get rid of it. I consider burning the trash to be an act of holiness. It also gives me something to do with the rest of my life.

BEN: Look, if we're gonna talk about the drugstore, I'm walking out. You can hop the Howard L to my house.

HENRY: I'm not going to your house.

BEN: What? What do you mean? You called me at the store.

HENRY: I never go to your house. All I said was stop on your way.

BEN: I thought this time would be a world premiere. I told Nicolle to take out a Sara Lee.

HENRY: You had no business thinking.

BEN: Come on, it happens to be *Hanukkah.* People go by family on *Hanukkah.* So when a father calls his son, "Stop on the way," it seems a logical connection.

HENRY: I also got family in Israel.

BEN: Oh. That's what this is? What a surprise. I thought I was coming here for a handshake and a smile. I shoulda stayed to fight with Kepler.

HENRY: Don't be smart-mouthed, you hear me? I'm asking you a favor. Send me over there.

BEN: I can't. Wait; I'll write it in blood for you on my wrist!

HENRY: Ben, it's my sister. If she dies, Ben, you know what it would mean? I would be alone. I would become an old man alone.

BEN: Alone? What is this, a new strategy? What kind of alone all of a sudden!

HENRY: Who's to be left? Nobody!

BEN: Excuse me, what am I? I'm not a Martian, I happen to be your son. I got a house in Rogers Park with a back bedroom anytime you want it. Don't give me "nobody" here.

HENRY: It's not good enough.

BEN: Come on, you got there a son, a daughter-in-law, and a seven-year-old kid who thinks you're better than Bozo the clown.

HENRY: What I got there is a *shiksa* daughter-in-law, a grandson with a name like Anatole, and a French poodle with a rhinestone collar. Please, I'm in better company at the Lincoln Park Zoo.

BEN: Also, a table with potato pancakes and company. You could do a lot worse.

HENRY: I can't go live in your house. Please. It hurts me.

BEN: Why? Because my wife is Catholic?

HENRY: Your house is a coffin. Yes. I'm sorry, but it is. Why do you think I'd rather stay here, huh? It's so much fun washing out the garbage cans once a week? No. It's not fun. But at least it means something. I go to your house, and what do I become? An old man in the back room, you take into him an egg in the morning? A fixture around the house you place in front of a television set? Or better yet, a handy-dandy live-in baby-sitter for your *goyishe* kid. Thank you, I don't want it. All it is is wounds. You understand? Wounds?

BEN: We all got wounds, Dad. We all got failures. Look; you wanted to be a doctor, you became instead a druggist. So what. The world needs druggists. I wanted to be an architect; I became a shoe clerk. The world also needs shoe clerks. I mean, when doctors and designers want Hush Puppies, I become a very important person. You understand? Not everybody drives the bus; some of us ride in the back. But if you go with somebody else, at least the ride is comfortable.

HENRY: You could have been a doctor.

BEN: I never wanted to be a doctor.

HENRY: Because I wanted it. It was spite.

BEN: If it gives you pleasure to think so, go ahead.

HENRY: I want you to know what a disappointment you are. Benedict Arnold by comparison was a saint.

BEN: It's not gonna work, Dad; there's just no money.

HENRY: For the rhinestone collar there's money, for the *shiksa* with the big mouth—

BEN: Hey! Goddamnit, Dad, you're trying to make me feel guilty so I blow two grand, but for godsake, you're going too far. I don't deserve this. I mean, I treat you pretty damned decent and you know it. I got a wife and kid in Rogers Park waiting to give me hugs, but I break my butt slipping on the ice over Lake Shore Drive to come here. I send you cash once a month—

HENRY: Thank you!

BEN: I bring you salami from the Greek—

HENRY: Thank you!

BEN: I treat you pretty goddamned decent, and you keep giving me this Sarah crap; what for!

HENRY: Keep your mouth off Sarah, you hear me!

BEN: No, because I don't understand. Explain to me, okay? I mean, here I am, standing in the room; she's a million miles away.

You can't come to my house where people are waiting for you, but want to *schlepp* all the way over Arab territory to watch an old lady fall into the deep sleep. I mean—

HENRY: Maybe she's not, huh? Maybe she's just not dying after all. Did you ever think—

BEN: Oh, Dad, please!

HENRY: What did I read last week; this man they thought was already a corpse. They sent a psychiatrist in—Ben, these things are ninety percent in the mind anyhow. She's alone, she could be depressed. You understand? I could go there, I could—

BEN: You could do nothing! The telegram said loud and clear. There is nothing you could do for her!

HENRY: I could be there. It's enough that she's not alone.

BEN: Please don't start in with the elephants again.

HENRY: It's more than that! Understand something; I owe her this trip. For all the years she stood by me, gave me support I never got, let me tell you, from anybody else.

BEN: Wait a minute. Don't make me the villain here.

HENRY: Support I never got from anybody else.

BEN: All right. Would you like to know why? Would you like to know why you never got from anybody else? Would you like me to tell you? Because you were never around anybody else. It's true. I mean, Mom and me, we'd go looking for you. Where's Dad? He's at the store. Can you come watch Little League? No, I have to keep open the store. We'd look for you and all we saw was Prescriptions, Sundries and Open 7 Days a Week.

HENRY: The store was my livelihood; I should have stayed home and let it fail?

BEN: It failed anyhow, so what did you gain?

HENRY: Of course it failed; how could it not? I had people stabbing me in the back all the time.

BEN: Like who? Who stabbed? I sold the store because Walgreen's—

HENRY: I'm not talking Walgreen's. I'm talking years ago. I'm talking your mother and I'm talking you. Yes. Listen, why should I ever have stayed home; home was such a wonderful place? Your mother, every time I turned around, you know what she was doing? Taking. Mrs. Tessie Taker she was. A house in Skokie she had to have. A trip to Florida. A satin couch. Give me, give me, give me. Every time I got a little ahead, I turned around, and there was another gimme. I used to wonder, do you know; I used to ask myself, is she doing this on purpose? A wife is supposed to give; how is it that all mine does is take?

BEN: She had to have something, damnit. You don't have your husband, a satin couch is second best.

HENRY: And you, sonny boy; you were even worse. Another taker.

BEN: Me?

HENRY: Yes, from the very beginning. You opened your eyes, and you took away medical school. Zap. Just like that. You cocked up my life like a miracle. Did I ever thank you? Thank you for cocking up my life.

BEN: Hey, wait. Just wait. Nobody asked. Nobody asked a thing. You didn't want a wife, you shoulda said NO when the rabbi asked. You didn't want kids, you shoulda kept your zipper shut. Be a little fair, will you; you had a choice!

HENRY: Excuse me, would you like the truth? It wasn't a choice. It was no choice at all. You were a flaw in the merchandise. It was the depression, and the quality of rubber goods, you should pardon my dirty mouth, was not what it is today.

BEN: Wow. You go for the jugular.

HENRY: You forced me.

BEN: You know what I should do. I should write a letter to DuPont or Goodyear, which was it, and file a malpractice suit. What I get from the settlement, you can use to fly to see your goddamn sister!

HENRY: Ben, you're giving me such a migraine!

BEN: Believe me, I'm very sorry.

HENRY: Don't worry. I'll find the money someplace else. I gave you a last chance, now I don't need you. I'll get to Israel by myself.

BEN: Fine. Give my regards to the P.L.O. Don't get shot. Or, do get shot. Whatever you want. By the way, thank you very much for dragging me out here. I appreciate it. Not only do I appreciate the waste of my gas and my time, but I'm also very grateful for the heartbreak.

HENRY: What, are you gonna cry? A man your age, it's a shame.

BEN: Let me tell you something, not that you should be interested, but after you said, "Stop on the way home," I got very happy for half an hour. I phoned Nicolle. I said, "The old man's breaking down; it could be the start of something big." And you know what she said? "Don't hold your breath. You'll come home all tied up in knots." "Come on," I said, "He's an unhappy, lonely, old man. He needs a little sympathy." "You're wrong," she said, "He sits there in his dark room, reliving every failure and hurt and regret, picking away at his scabs and building up this incredible store of—" venom was the word she used. She says you're like a serpent, filled with venom, and you go looking for targets to spill it in to. That's crazy, I say, "Why would anybody do that?" And she said—"Because otherwise he would spill it all back into himself and he would die from it."

HENRY: Look at that; you married Sigmunda Freud. *Mazel Tov.*

BEN: Every time I come here, we fight. And I go home with a little more poison in my stomach.

HENRY: Then maybe you should stop coming here. You don't like what happens, stay away. I don't need this either.

BEN: Maybe I should. Maybe I have to protect myself.

HENRY: Likewise.

BEN *(Reaches into his pocket, takes out wrapped package):* By the way, Happy *Hanukkah.*

HENRY: What is it?

BEN: By Singer.

HENRY: I already read all of Singer.

BEN: So exchange it. The receipt's inside.

HENRY: Maybe. *(*BEN *exits.)*

*(*HENRY *puts the chain on the front door.* HENRY *goes to call on the intercom.)*

HENRY: Hello, Lady? Come back; it's all right now. *(She comes in.)* So what time will he call, Hector?

WOMAN: Sometime between now and later, what do I know?

HENRY: *Oy.* I should take a donnatal, I know it.

WOMAN: Why don't you give me a knife, Mister.

HENRY: What?

WOMAN: I might as well take off the coat, if I gotta sit here.

HENRY: God be praised.

WOMAN: But that's all I'm taking off, you hear?

HENRY: Please. I won't press my luck. *(Gets a kitchen knife for her.)*

WOMAN: You fight with him a lot? I could hear in the hallway.

HENRY: All the time. Hollering is the only way we know how to talk. Here. When you're through, keep it. It's easier than boiling.

WOMAN *(Cutting away at the strings of her coat):* You shouldn't do it. You should never fight with kids. They should grow up happy. They're the future of the world.

HENRY: Don't talk what you don't know.

WOMAN: You know, we could be stuck here all night, Mister. Why don't you break out some of that snow.

HENRY: No.

WOMAN: It would make life a whole lot easier.

HENRY: Change the subject!

WOMAN: Shit!

HENRY *(opens the gift):* It could have been worse. It could have been Sholem Aleichem.

WOMAN: Hey, who's the asshole that locked the door in here?

(She opens the front door, comes back in and resumes cutting. HENRY *leafs through the book, silently lights fade.)*

Act II

WOMAN *is at work in kitchen. Phone rings. She counts rings. She goes back to work. After a moment,* HENRY *enters, carrying wrapped bottle of wine.*

HENRY: I heard the phone.
WOMAN: It wasn't Hector.
HENRY: I told you not to answer.
WOMAN: I didn't answer.
HENRY: Then how do you know it wasn't Hector?
WOMAN: Because if it was Hector, I would have answered.
HENRY: What do you do, read phones?
WOMAN: Mister, settle down, will you? You been in and outa here all night like a yo-yo.
HENRY: Every time it rings I tremble.
WOMAN: Where'd you get the bottle?
HENRY: What bottle? From the teenagers, would you believe? I'm standing there, when that Becky Rose all of a sudden comes up and kisses me smack on the mouth. A real juicy kisser, that Becky Rose . . . and she says, "Happy *Hanukkah* to the sexiest man in Chicago." What do you think of that?
WOMAN: To a teenager on booze, a cucumber could be sexy. Lemme see.

(During following, she unwraps the bottle.)

HENRY: What happens to kids, huh? At seven, they're cute like puppies, but by thirty, they turn into vipers. Why?
WOMAN: How the hell do I know?
HENRY: Because you never had kids.
WOMAN: Because I don't know what the hell's a viper, do you mind?

HENRY: A viper is a snake. It bites, you get poison, you—I came here looking for something; what did I come in here looking for?

WOMAN: Look at this, Strawberry Ripple.

HENRY: I was talking to Danny, he was asking—*Oy,* idiot. It was the key. The supply room key, of course. You didn't see a red key hanging here, did you?

WOMAN: You wanna search me, Mister? I could lift up my dress.

HENRY: Lady, I'm only asking a question, you don't have to make a Nuremberg trial from every conversation!

(Goes to intercom buzzer.)

Hello? Hello?

DANNY *(from the box):* Hey, you guys, quiet down for a second.

HENRY: Danny?

DANNY: Yeah, Mr. Leider?

HENRY: The supply key? It's not on the hook here.

DANNY: I thought you took it back there with you.

HENRY: It's not here. And you wanted to use the record player.

DANNY: No hassle. We got Sammy Barlow; we'll chain him to the piano. Why don't you come back out; we're gonna sing for awhile.

HENRY: No . . . I need to do my candles. I didn't have time before.

DANNY: You're sure? You don't wanta be alone on *Hanukkah.*

HENRY: I'll feel bad if I don't get them up. Now, if I can remember where I put them.

DANNY: Okay, if you get lonely, call us. We'll send in Becky Rose.

HENRY: Please, I'm an old man, Danny. I could fall into my grave. I'll tell you what, though; you could leave the speaker on at your end. If I want later, I could listen from here.

DANNY: Okay. Talk to you later. Hope you like the wine.

HENRY: Bye. *(Clicks off. Takes a moment to think some more.)* I had it in my hand when I came back from setting up the table . . . You sure you didn't . . .

WOMAN *(holding up empty aluminum foil box):* Mister, you got any more of this?

HENRY: What? What is this? What are you doing here?

WOMAN: Putting into sandwiches, it's easier to carry around. Come on, you said help yourself.

HENRY: I didn't mean to move out the whole kitchen!

WOMAN: It's not the whole kitchen; it's some cheese, some lettuce, and a dozen eggs. I'm leaving you all the salami!

HENRY: You're gonna carry around a dozen eggs?

WOMAN: Don't worry; I'll hard-boil 'em first! Otherwise you know what happens? You put 'em in the bag, they break. All that yellow gunk goes spilling out, cats start following you for blocks. Come on, where's the tin paper?

HENRY: In the drawer.

(She goes rummaging in a drawer. He gets out his menorah, polishes, sets it up, etc.)

I know who the phone call was from; It was Ben. He called to apologize. He always does. And I always give in. But this time, no. Let him stew in his own . . . poison.

(HENRY finds candles in bookshelf.)

I don't need his house and I don't need his money.

WOMAN: You're right, Mister. You don't need kids at all.

HENRY: I'm a hundred percent right.

WOMAN: Especially when you got coke.

HENRY: Lady, you got a one-track mind.

WOMAN: Then what about the bottle? You don't have a rod up your ass about sauce, do you?

HENRY: I told you, there's no alcohol in my house!

WOMAN: You got Strawberry Ripple from the kids!

HENRY: I can't open that; it's holiday wine.

WOMAN: What the hell is this? Hey, in there, it's a party. Somebody gave you a present; there's music; and you got a kiss from a virgin. Why do you have to walk around in here like death?

HENRY: You know. You're absolutely right. We're sitting here like in prison; it's ridiculous.

WOMAN: It's murder.

HENRY: And the wine *is* here; it shouldn't go to waste.

WOMAN: It won't, believe me. Here, lemme—

HENRY: Only you have to wait for after the candles. It's part of the prayer.

WOMAN: Candles? What kind of candles? You're not lighting candles in here!

HENRY: It's my religion, do you mind? Ten minutes—and then we'll have the wine.

WOMAN: Hey, you don't believe in that bullshit, do you? It's all bullshit, every kind—

Marilyn Chris and Lee Wallace in the JRT production of *Elephants.*

HENRY: Please. It'll be the only thing that's pretty in the whole room. Also, on the bottom there, a couple of glasses. Very fine crystal from Rose's mother. Enjoy all the way, right?

WOMAN *(refers to candles):* You could cut 'em in half; they won't burn so long; they last you twice as long, you know what I mean . . .?

HENRY: All the way; it's a celebration, right? People get with people, light a candle, drink a glass, sing a bit—for a couple of hours, you forget the misery.

WOMAN: It's bullshit; it's a waste, believe me.

HENRY: Please. To you, everything is bullshit; it's disgusting.

(WOMAN falls silent, watching him prepare. Then he suddenly stops, listening to his own thoughts.)

On the other hand, maybe he meant good. After all, he drove out here; he bought me a present. Why did I get so angry? What do you think? Maybe I should call him?

WOMAN: Yeah. Call him now. Right now . . .

HENRY: Please; why am I asking advice from a person who never had kids?

WOMAN: But I did!

HENRY: You did?

WOMAN: Damn right I had kids. I might be ugly, but I work!

HENRY: What? Tell me?

WOMAN: I had a daughter.

HENRY: What happened to her?

WOMAN: She ain't around any more.

HENRY: Why not? What did you do, kick her out?

WOMAN: I sold her to the gypsies for a fix when she was three.

HENRY: Tell me?

WOMAN: She ran away from home. She was six months, she started walking early, and she just kept on going.

HENRY: Why don't you want to talk?

WOMAN: She got burned up in a fire when she was ten!

HENRY: She don't exist!

(The telephone rings. They stop to listen. It rings three times then stops. A pause. Then three times again. Pause. Then, while it begins to ring again . . .)

You answer.

WOMAN *(picks it up):* Ola, Hector. Aqui la vieja. Si. Tengo azucar. Muy pura. Si, estoy segura. Un viejo. ("Hello, Hector. This is the old woman. Yes, I have sugar. Very pure. Yes, I'm sure. An old man.") *(to* HENRY*)* You have to say where you got it.

HENRY: From the Children's Hospital on Fullerton.

WOMAN *(to phone):* Del hospital de los ninos on Fullerton. *(to* HENRY*):* How did you get in?

HENRY: Come on, they know me thirty-five years. I walk around there all the time.

WOMAN *(to phone):* Trabaja alla. Si. Es fiel. Diez grams. Si, lo he vista. Si. Tiene que esta noche solamenta. Si. Espera. ("He works there. Yes, I trust him. Five grams. Yes, I've seen it. Yes, it has to be tonight only. Very important. Wait.") One hour at the old bandshell.

HENRY: No. I can't get out of here before 12:30.

WOMAN: Diga que es muy temprano; que espellegrose. ("He says too late. It's dangerous.") *(to* HENRY*)* He says if we're not there by one, it's off.

HENRY: We'll be there.

WOMAN *(to phone):* Si. Oh, Hector. Quiero un favor. Digale que necessita una pequeno parte. Digale dime algo ahorita. No es posible qunque le diga. No me crees. Es culero. ("Yes. Oh, Hector, I want a favor. Tell him to give me some. Make him give me some now. He won't believe me. He's an asshole.") *(to* HENRY*)* He wants to talk to you. Come on, he'll get nervous.

HENRY: I don't know Spanish.

WOMAN: Don't worry; he'll make himself clear.

HENRY *(hesitates, then takes the phone):* So, buenos noches, what? Yes. Henry O'Reilly. . . . Because I used to be a pharmacist, I know from cocaine. . . . What? . . . She already tasted. . . . I see. All right. . . . Yeah, adios, why not?

(Hangs up, looks at WOMAN.*)*

All that Spanish babble, Lady? You made yourself a wonderful deal behind my back right here in front of my face, nu? This—sample—I'm supposed to give you all of a sudden; you didn't think I'd figure it out?

WOMAN: If he told you to give me a sample, Mister, maybe you better just do it, huh?

HENRY: I don't have to give in. I could say completely no.

WOMAN: You could say whatever you want. It's your sister.

HENRY: How much do you need?

WOMAN: Not much. You'll have plenty; don't worry.

HENRY *(As he gets out the vial of powder):* All of a sudden, Lady, you know something? You're making me afraid to turn my back. You'll stab me there all night if I let you.

(He shakes out a quantity of powder for her.)

WOMAN: You don't trust me, I don't trust Hector, Hector don't trust me, Hector don't trust you, I don't trust you. What assholes people are, huh? One more shake, come on.

HENRY: No. It makes me sick doing this.

WOMAN: Yeah, well, it can't make you all that sick. You lifted it.

HENRY: Not to see anybody using it!

WOMAN *(During the following, she takes from her bag a mirror, razor, straw.):* Of course people are gonna use it. And it's gonna make 'em mighty happy, too. Once this gets into the streets, Mister, there's gonna be people humming, maybe fucking each other with great big smiles on their faces—and they're gonna owe it all to you.

HENRY: Stop that. At least do that in the bathroom.

WOMAN: Sorry, I need the table.

(Proceeds to shake powder onto mirror. She takes a small vial of talcum powder and mixes it into the coke, then uses razor to clean it as she chants to herself.)

Little rails, little rails, what do I see?
Two little rails looking at me.
Little rails, coming, one at a time.
Coming to Momma, makes me feel fine.

By the way, let's get that wine poured. When I get these up, I'll be thirsty.

HENRY: For God's sake, don't ask me to help you.

WOMAN: You know, I gotta tell you something, Mister; I had a hunch this was gonna happen. It's true. All them months, I was crimping from you, I kept thinking: "He don't catch you. How come he don't catch you. How stupid can he be?" And then I said, "Sure. He knows what you're doing, but he's just waiting. Someday he's gonna get something outta you. And you're gonna get something outta him, and the two of you will be sitting one night together."

*(*HENRY *is now ready for his ritual. Moves to menorah. Pulls out yarmulke, stands with matches before unlit candles.)*

HENRY: *Boruch atah Adonoy, eloheynu melech ho-olohm; a-sher kidshonu, b'mitzvoso v'tzivohnu, l'hadlik ner shel Hanukkah.*

("Blessed art Thou, oh Lord, our God, King of the Universe, who has sanctified us by Thy commandments and enabled us to kindle the lights of Hanukkah.")

*(*HENRY *takes up lit candle, uses it to light the other.)*

Boruch attah Adonoy, eloheynu melech ho-olohm; she-o-so ni-sim la-a-bosaynu bayomim haw-lem bazman hazah.
("Blessed art Thou, oh Lord, our God, King of the Universe, who did wonderous things for our forefathers in days of old at this season.")
*(*HENRY *now lifts up a glass, fills it with wine, holds it over the menorah, and recites.)*
Boruch atah Adonoy, eloheynu melech ho-olohm, she-hekkiyonu, v'kimawnu, v'higiyonu lazman hazeh.
("Blessed art Thou, oh Lord, our God, King of the Universe, who has kept us in life and preserved us and permitted us to reach this joyous festival.")

(He then swallows from the glass, and reaches to pour another.)

WOMAN: That's all? It's over?
HENRY: What did you expect, a virgin sacrifice?

(He swigs down the second glass.)

WOMAN: Ready here.
(Now she is ready to sniff. She gets a small glass of water and brings it to her table. She dips a finger in the water and snorts a little bit of water up each nostril. Then she takes up the straw and leans over the rails, speaking to them.)
Little rails, I respect you, and I have been careful with you, and now I'm going to suck up the hell out of you!

(Then she sniffs up one rail through the straw, and then the other. She grimaces at the sting she feels in her sinuses. Then she repeats the use of the water, and then licks her fingers and, breathing a heavy sigh, leans back, to see HENRY *staring at her.)*

HENRY: That's all? It's over?
WOMAN *(Proceeds to pour herself a glass of wine):* What did you expect? A virgin sacrifice?
(She stops, suddenly, concentrating on her inner sensations.)
Rush it up, sweet Jesus; rush it up!

(She takes a deep breath, holds it, then lets it out with a loud "WHOOSH!" and gulps down the wine.)

God, what is this stuff; it's like piss?

HENRY: I think it's making me drunk.

WOMAN: Too bad you don't have any Jack Daniels. I really like Jack Daniels. When I can get it. You know what it sells for— but, wait. Hell, what am I talking about? After tonight, I can buy me a gallon. A case. I'll buy me a case. A carload. Because it's good. It's the best. Jack Daniels. I love it. I love it in a glass, or with that fuzzy stuff. Or with ginger ale. Or with Coca-cola. Or with water. Or with ice. Or with milk. Or with prune juice. Or by itself. Or, I could lick off the edge of the bottle or I could just smell the label. Tomorrow, I'll buy me a carload of labels.

HENRY: I used to have delicious wine on *Hanukkah.* From Sarah.

WOMAN: Not this stuff. This stuff is crap.

HENRY: It's from kids. What else can you expect.

WOMAN: You can't keep crap like this sitting around, Mister. You gotta get rid of it.

HENRY: To keep this, it's a sin.

WOMAN: There's only one thing to do. Empty it out.

HENRY: I agree.

WOMAN: Right now.

HENRY: As soon as possible.

WOMAN: Cheers!

HENRY: *Shalom!*

(They salute each other with full glasses, look at each other, grin, and get a case of giggles. They drink, and refill.)

WOMAN: You know what else? It's a party, right? Wait.

(She digs down into her bag again.)

HENRY: You got something else down there?

WOMAN *(She pulls out a large, broken but workable tambourine.):* Here we go!

(She begins to slap at it.)

HENRY: Music!
WOMAN: Fuckin' A Right!

(She starts loudly singing some gospel carol.)

HENRY: Shhh!
WOMAN: Oh.

(Conspiratorially, she lowers her voice, sings softer. She begins to move around the room, celebrating and banging the tambourine.)

HENRY: *Oy.* I got a Baptist here!
WOMAN: Come on . . .

(She continues to sing and slap and move around. He timidly claps with her. She comes to where the menorah is. Stops. Stares at it. WOMAN *bends over and suddenly blows the candles out.)*

HENRY: What are you doing? They're supposed to burn out!
WOMAN: Leave em!
HENRY: No. It means something!
(Goes for matches again.)
Oy, crazy. You're crazy, Lady, you know that? What kind of business, this is my house.
WOMAN: You leave things burning like that, how do you know what could happen? All this garbage in here, anything could—LEAVE 'EM!
HENRY: What? It's fire? You're afraid of fire?
*(*WOMAN *puts the tambourine back. The mood is again sullen, angry.)*
HENRY: Tell me.
WOMAN: None of your business.
HENRY: Lady, we're human beings. Talk to me.
WOMAN: Shit, I got eggs. What happened to my eggs.

(She goes to kitchen and continues preparing her hard-boiled eggs.)

HENRY: So sit here alone. There's nothing you could tell me anyhow. Maybe they could be finished; we could go already.

(He switches on intercom. Teenagers singing a happy Hanukkah song is heard. He switches sound off.)

No-goodnicks. Get through already!

WOMAN: You got some newspaper?

HENRY: Under the sink.

(She finds some, continues working. He pours another wine. Silence for a moment, then he goes back to intercom, switches it on to hear kids singing a sadder song.)

What a night. Sitting here, wine-drunk, passing out cocaine to a city dump wearing tennis shoes. A Baptist, too.

They sing that too fast. It should be pretty.

(He sings along for a moment.)

My sister could sing pretty. A wonderful voice. A beautiful person, a saint. We were the best of friends. When we were small, if I had candy, she'd get. If she had, then I would get. When I was in *cheyder,* we would sit up all night and I would teach her my lessons. She made me feel grown-up, like a regular rabbi. When we were older, Sarah could touch me on the shoulder and say, "A pharmacist is as good as a doctor" . . . and I believed her. I couldn't live with myself if I left her there alone.

WOMAN: She ain't alone. Stop driving yourself crazy, Mister; she's in a hospital: they got thousands of people hanging around.

HENRY: Machines they got. Idiots walking around in uniforms. But when she wants to talk, who listens? If she wakes up with some nightmare, who's around?

WOMAN: But how do you know she don't want it that way?

HENRY: Because I know how I would feel if it were me.

WOMAN: Ah. So then you're the one that got the nightmares . . .?

HENRY: Nothing gets past you, does it?

WOMAN: Look. I understand about nightmares, Mister.

HENRY: I wake up. Two to three times a night.

WOMAN: . . . Screaming . . .

HENRY: If there were only some way to stop them, huh?

WOMAN: There is, Mister. Fullerton Avenue. Figure it. You go out on Fullerton and, okay, maybe it's freezing, but then freezing is all there is. You crawl around in them garbage cans looking for junk to peddle off, and that's all you got time for. Or you spend hours wrapping yourself up in rags and piling cardboard boxes around your face so you don't freeze your eyelids . . . and maybe you luck into some number one shit . . . and, Mister, you sleep like a baby.

HENRY: You don't miss people?

WOMAN: You only go around people when you gotta get even with them.

HENRY: A vermin lives like that. A scavenger.

WOMAN: It's the only way, I'm telling you.

HENRY: What about an idea once in a while, a thought a little higher up than the gutter. Something you have respect for!

WOMAN: Hey, wait. Wait a minute. I'm giving you what I know here; what the hell are you climbing over my back for?

HENRY: Because what you're telling me, Lady, is disgusting; to spend a life getting even, you're talking killers in a jungle.

WOMAN: I'm warning you, Mister. Don't start pulling any holy crap on me. You're the same way.

HENRY: Me? I have a little respect, a little compassion.

WOMAN: You're a killer. You ripped off this coke from a children's hospital without even blinking.

HENRY: An emergency, I told you.

WOMAN: And what about what you did to your kid?

HENRY: To Ben? What does he have to do with . . .

WOMAN: I heard what you said to him. You grabbed him by the peaches and he died, Mister.

HENRY: Lady, nothing happened that didn't happen a hundred times yesterday and won't happen a hundred times tomorrow.

WOMAN: You think so, Mister? You think you didn't kill him and you think you didn't know you were doing it? He walked outta here like a corpse.

HENRY: And when I want him to, he'll walk back. A father fights with his son, it's not murder.

WOMAN: Show me I'm wrong. Show me how dumb I am. Call him!

HENRY: Why should I call him?

WOMAN: Because you been dancing around here pretending you're the pope and I'm crap. So call him. If you're so holy-holy, you'll have a terrific conversation and I'm garbage. But if you get nothing, Mister, you eat every one of them words outta your Saint Jesus mouth. Go ahead. Call.

HENRY: I don't have to prove anything, Lady.

WOMAN: Yes, you do. You goddamn know you do.

HENRY *(dials):* Hello? Nicolle, it's me, who else? I'm sorry too, but some other time. How's Andy? That's too bad. Keep him warm and give him orange juice. Listen, Sweetheart, let me talk to Ben a minute . . . What do you mean? I know he's home, he left my house hours ago. Put him on; it's important . . . Something I forgot to mention when he was here. All right . . .
(He waits.)
Hello . . . Nicolle, I said I wanted to talk to Ben. He's not sleeping. It's a lie . . . What? No, I don't believe you . . . a son doesn't say never again to a father. Put him on the phone . . . No, you're not sorry.

(Hangs up.)

WOMAN: If you ever came in the streets, Mister, me and Marie, we'd have to fight like hell for dry boxes.

HENRY: So. So, you're right. You showed me a wonderful thing. I hope you're proud of yourself.

WOMAN: I told you nobody comes at me, Mister.

HENRY: So. You got even. The sewer . . . pardon me, the fellow-sewer got even. All right, then it's my turn. You get even. I get even.

(He grabs her bag.)

WOMAN: Hey?

HENRY: Get away from me or I take it to the furnace!

WOMAN: Leave it alone.

HENRY: You been hiding God knows what in here. You been sitting on this like it was the Holy Ark. What are you hiding?

WOMAN: Go ahead. But I warn you, you hear me. I warn you. I don't get mad—

HENRY: You get even. Yes, wonderful. I'm frightened to death. You'll steal my frozen pizzas.
(He pulls out items from her bag. Ring of keys.)
Ah. Keys. You maybe got a key here to every door on the north side.
(Supply room key.)
And here. I should have figured right way.
(Tools.)

Tools?

(Spilling out contents of another package.)

Lipstick. Makeup. Powder. For the pump room?

(Rubber-banded package.)

Coupons . . . twenty cents off Grape Nuts. Ten cents off Ivory soap. That's one you'll never use.

(Manila envelope.)

WOMAN *(speaking through all of the above):* I get even. And I know how to do it too. Getting even. I'm an expert, you wait. I got ways and I got time. I can wait. One day you ain't gonna be ready. You ain't gonna be looking. People treat you like shit, they deserve what they get. Go ahead, Mister, keep going. See what happens.

(She continues to babble until she sees him holding an envelope.)

No!

HENRY: What? Here?

WOMAN: Leave it alone, gimme—

HENRY: Ah . . . it's in here, the heart of hearts . . .

(He tears open the envelope.)

WOMAN: Don't—

HENRY: So, what, what do I see, what do I learn?

(Picks up small photograph.)

What's this? Come on, tell me, or I'll tear it up.

WOMAN: Charlie.

HENRY: Who, your husband?

WOMAN: The number one asshole in the world. I kicked him out, I tell you. In the middle of the night, too. Served him right.

HENRY: Why?

WOMAN: Why? He was fucking every bitch in Humbolt Park, that's why. He'd roll in—3 or 4 o'clock in the morning. I wasn't gonna put up with it. You're married to me, I said. You do your bouncing in the sack here, or else you sleep in the zoo with the rest of the apes!

HENRY: You got even.

WOMAN: I kicked him out!

HENRY: Who's the kid?

WOMAN: Gimme some booze; you gotta have something left!

HENRY: You want it in two pieces, or three?

WOMAN: Yeah. It's the kid.

HENRY: What happened?

WOMAN: Charlie and me, we had a store one time, you see. It did lousy and it fell apart! They was all against us, every one of em. Right from the start. The landlord and his jewed-up rent. The supplier—no more credit, out of stock—the big guys first—they never, Mister, they never give you a chance.

HENRY: What happened? Tell me about the kid!

WOMAN: One day, Charlie says, we gotta do something. They're driving us into the ground; we gotta get out from under. What are we gonna do? We'll burn the place. Pick up the insurance money and get out. So, we spent a coupla weeks getting ready. Moving our stuff outa the flat—upstairs—and stuffing rags and papers in the stock room—and then, Friday night, Charlie lights a cigarette, and puts it in the ashtray, but not quite IN the ashtray, and we go out to see a movie. And when we get back, the whole place, burning like a son of a bitch. And then . . . and then . . .

HENRY: What?

WOMAN: I look at Charlie; Charlie looks at me . . . and where's Peggy? God, where is Peggy? The kid was always dumb. She never had sense. She was born with something wrong upstairs—doctors looked her over and said there wasn't a chance. They never give you a chance! We didn't even know what she went after. Idiot kid. Charlie shoulda held on to her; he was supposed to hold on to her. He told me to call the fire department, then he shoulda held on to the idiot kid. It was his fault. You bet it was, and I never let him forget it neither.

HENRY: Lady, tell me . . .

WOMAN: Gimme back the picture.

HENRY: Who was holding on?

WOMAN: Charlie.

HENRY: Who?

WOMAN: Charlie! Stop swinging at me!

HENRY: Why did you let go?

WOMAN: I didn't! She ran off before—no, wait, not me—Charlie, I keep telling you!

HENRY: You let go, and she ran back—

WOMAN: I hadda call the fire department! Charlie told me to make the phone call.
HENRY: You had the kid?
WOMAN: Stop swinging at me!
HENRY: And you let her go!
WOMAN: She was an idiot kid, goddamnit! She was goddamned better off! All of us—

(She stops . . . maybe having gone too far.)

HENRY: Lady, you're like a beast, I don't know—some terrible . . . I'm a monster, huh? While all the time you—you've been carrying around this filth? No wonder you live out in the street.
(Phone rings.)
It's Ben!
(Phone rings.)
It's Ben, you see. I know . . . Hello Ben! . . . What? . . . Yeah, Henry Leider, who's this? Cable . . . what cable? . . . From Tel Aviv?

(Hangs up.)

WOMAN: There. Mister, now you ain't got nothing. Get out in the goddamn street where you belong. Gimme the picture!

(Suddenly, HENRY *rips the picture apart.* WOMAN *cries out.* HENRY *stands there a moment.* WOMAN *is silent for a moment, then bends down to pick up pieces of photo. She is either crying or laughing or doing both at the same time.)*

HENRY: It fell apart. I should have known. Just like that. What was it so much that I wanted . . . to end up with nothing?
(Staggers to a chair.)
Lady, please . . . the room is spinning.
WOMAN: Put your head down. Low.
(Goes to him.)
You got any ice?
(Massages his neck.)
I been carrying that picture like some . . . concrete . . . block for centuries. I knew that, some day, some asshole's gonna come

and rip it outta me. You play your cards right, you hear? God . . .

(Intercom buzzer. HENRY *crosses to answer it.)*

HENRY: Yeah, what?
DANNY: Mr. Leider?
HENRY: What?
DANNY: We're all finished; we're leaving now.
HENRY: All right. I'll be out in a little bit.
DANNY: Everything's put away. You don't have to do anything.
HENRY: I have to put on the alarm, but it's all right. You go. Goodnight.
DANNY: Okay, goodnight. Happy *Hanukkah.*
HENRY: Yes. To you also. *(to* WOMAN) You got a strong hand there. Thank you.
WOMAN: I learned that from this Chinese sailor I met one night. We drank like fish for days. He taught me how to say "You want a blow job, $5.00" in Chinese. He said if I ever get to Shanghai, I could make a fortune. How soon can we go, Mister?
HENRY: Go? Go where?
WOMAN: Down to meet Hector.
HENRY: Oh. No, no, no . . .
WOMAN: I thought we had a deal!
HENRY: My sister's dead; there's no reason any more!
WOMAN: There's a thousand bucks in reasons! Come on, you still got the stuff; it's still worth a trip!
HENRY: No. I'm not sending this poison back into the street. Tomorrow I'm taking it back!
WOMAN: Gimme the bottle!
HENRY: No. Lady, I can't. Understand, I have to save myself something . . . some . . . respect.
*(*WOMAN *moves to get her stuff together.)*
What are you doing?
WOMAN: Gettin' outta here. I shoulda grabbed it when I had the chance, huh? Okay, next time I'll be faster.
HENRY: Huh? No, stay—
WOMAN: I been inside too much; I gotta get back out.
HENRY: What about your eggs here? You can't go until you pack up your eggs here!

WOMAN: No. I'll do without 'em.
HENRY: Don't. Please. Stay a little, please. I don't want to be alone. Not tonight.

(She continues her packing.)

WOMAN: Gimme the coke.
HENRY: You're not gonna leave me anything, are you?
WOMAN: I'll sit here with you all night.
HENRY: Okay. I have to lock up, I'll be ten minutes.
WOMAN: Lemme have it now. I don't want you dumping it someplace out there.
HENRY: All right. All right.
(He takes out vial and hands it to her.)
I'll be ten minutes.

(He goes into synagogue.)

WOMAN: Good.
(Alone, the WOMAN *moves quickly. She stuffs her belongings into her bag, carefully hiding the coke. She puts on her coat, scarf, etc. She picks up her bag, tests it for weight, and then goes to the door. She pauses, and turns back to see if there's anything else she wants. Then she chuckles to herself.)*
Elephants. What the fuck do they know.

(She exits. The stage is empty for a moment. Lights fade.)

Friends Too Numerous to Mention

a play in two acts by

NEIL COHEN AND JOEL COHEN

Dedicated to
Abe Cohen and Morton Cohen,
Our Fathers—Two Legit Guys

Neil Cohen,
Friends Too Numerous to Mention.

NEIL COHEN and **JOEL COHEN** are not related, but have been friends for twenty years. Their first play, *Rats Nest,* also a comedy, opened at an off-off Broadway theatre, was critically acclaimed and moved to an off-Broadway theatre for a successful run.

Friends Too Numerous to Mention, their second play, also found favor with the critics. Richard F. Shepard, in his *New York Times* review of the Jewish Repertory Theatre production, had this to say: "What could be tragedy, the death-of-a-theater-owner sort of thing, has been made into high comedy with sharp insights into human behavior abetted by good, snappy lines, a fast-moving production and a cast that throws itself joyously into the action."

The Cohens are currently involved in motion picture writing and production, and are working on a new play.

Joel Cohen, *Friends Too Numerous to Mention.*

Friends Too Numerous to Mention was first produced by the Jewish Repertory Theatre in December 1982 with the following cast:

PATTI OLIVER	Robin Karfo
ROSS BERNARD	William Wise
RONNIE NATHAN	Jack Kehler
KEVIN MORROW	Thomas Kopache
JOANNE BERNARD	Barbara Spiegel
VAL GUIDO	Grace Roberts
DR. WILLIAM BERK	Salem Ludwig

Directed by Allen Coulter
Sets by Geoffrey Hall
Costumes by Gayle Goldberg
Lighting by Naomi Berger

Time: The present.
Place: The executive offices of the Horace Music Stage, a suburban New Jersey theater.

Act I

Scene 1. Friday, mid-day.
Scene 2. Friday, 7:00 P.M.

Act II
Monday, late morning.

The characters and situations in this play are wholly fictional and do not portray, and are not intended to portray, any actual person or parties.

Act I

Scene I

There are two offices in the suite, a door between them. On the left is PATTI'S *office, efficiently laid out with desk, typewriter, coffee machine, and mountains of contracts, corporate records, sheet music, etc.*

On the right is ROSS BERNARD'S *office. A comfortable, plush contrast with thick carpet, deep leather chairs, panelled walls, mahogany desk and bookshelves with pictures of family, friends, and celebrities on the walls. There is a large photo of smiling buisnessmen cutting a ribbon in front of the suburban theater.*

To get to ROSS'S *office you have to walk through* PATTI'S *office.*

PATTI OLIVER, *slim, twenty-eight, and tough, wearing an expensive tailored suit, with the look of a successful businesswoman, sits in one of her office's expensive steel swivel chairs. She is finishing the complex and intricate construction of a tuna salad sandwich on black bread, which she has been carefully preparing.*

ROSS BERNARD *enters the office. He's in his forties, looks prosperous, but also overworked and emotionally drained. If he spent two weeks relaxing on a beach he'd be handsome. He's dressed expensively, but something is wrong; it's not the Gucci loafers, it's the epaulets on his sports jacket.*

ROSS *gives* PATTI *a quick smile, stops at her desk, looks at her sandwich, looks at her, she looks at him, he picks up her sandwich and drops in into the garbage can.*

PATTI *is too amazed to speak.*

ROSS: I saw that mayonnaise sitting here since this morning. You leave mayonnaise out in the heat it becomes poison.

PATTI: Mayonnaise? Not a new one, Ross.

ROSS: Why take chances? You're too valuable for ptomaine poisoning. If we're in the middle of a conference and all of a sudden they gotta come and pump your stomach, is it worth the aggravation?

(He glances into the garbage can.)

And where'd you get black bread? I haven't seen bread like that in thirty years. You know, Dr. Berk says this whole roughage thing is bullshit.

PATTI: Now I'm just going to have to go out for lunch.

ROSS: So you'll take an hour—you'll take half an hour. Just do me a favor, nothing with mayonnaise.

PATTI: How'd it go today?

ROSS: The CIA we know a little about—we'll never know everything. But the IRS is the most powerful organization the world has ever known. They have the power to destroy you. They can look at your records. They can take all your money. They're just as secret as the CIA, and I'll tell you something—they're even more dangerous.

PATTI: You've always said it's not a free country.

ROSS: You know I have, and it's true. You can't make a living anymore, they don't let you. I mean sometimes I think I'll go back to making $110 a week like everybody else. They all seem happy, they seem to get along all right. So why the hell do we knock ourselves out trying to make a living?

PATTI: Ross, what's bothering you? What's the matter?

ROSS: They call this a free country. A fucking garbage man is making eighteen thou, a garbage man. The guy drives a truck for four hours, goes home, and doesn't have a care in the world. But the businessman, the lawyer, the doctor—you work all day, your work goes home with you, you don't sleep at night, and then the government wants to take all your money. Well, it's my money.

(He starts for his office, turns, points at the garbage.)

Do me a favor. When I go into my office, don't pick it out of there.

PATTI: No, I thought I'd climb into the garbage can and eat it.

ROSS: You know, I was talking to Pete Roselle's secretary the other day. According to Pete this whole terrorism thing is gonna get worse.

(PATTI calls after him.)

PATTI: Ross, what happened today?

ROSS: I don't even know. All I know is that I'm getting a little sick of the lawyers, the IRS, the stock market, the FBI—I mean these people, they should be herded into a room, lined up against the wall, and . . . pissed on.

(He laughs at his own joke, she shoots him a look. ROSS *goes into his office,* PATTI *goes about straightening up her desk.*

ROSS *goes to his desk, sits in his plush chair, surveys the photos and awards on his wall. He seems very troubled. He presses a button on the side of his desk, the lights dim in his office, he puts his head on his desk.*

RONNIE NATHAN *walks into* PATTI'S *office. He's twenty-seven, wears black wraparound, outer space-like glasses, and a full baseball uniform from cap to cleats. He carries a bat, mitt, black motorcycle crash helmet. The back of his uniform is emblazoned with "THE HORACE STAGE." He wears a "Morrison Lives" button.*

RONNIE'S *hair trickles into a string down the back of his neck. One of the ends has a touch of red. He wears a tiny earring.)*

RONNIE: How ya doin'!?

(He dumps his equipment in one of the chairs.)

PATTI: Did we win?

RONNIE: Let's just say it couldn't have gone better—

*(*RONNIE *is not a dynamic public speaker. His eyes wander, he holds and waves his cigarette like Jerry Lewis, and sometimes his droll delivery can be misinterpreted as a slur. He also has a tendency to interrupt and finish people's sentences for them, usually incorrectly.)*

—I pitched an unbelievable game. Fourteen strike-outs. I got one double, one home run, and one sacrifice for a total of four RBI's, and made one play that, knowing you have no interest in softball I won't even try to describe, but it'll go down in the history of the Broadway Show League as the catch of the century.

PATTI: Did we win?

RONNIE: Remind me never to put a drummer in centerfield. We lost ten to four, all on errors.

(RONNIE *plops down into one of the swivel chairs, takes off his sunglasses, puts on round, black-rimmed prescription glasses. He puts his foot on her desk.*

PATTI *shoots him a dirty look, he puts his foot down, then gets up, leans over her desk, starts toying with her hair. She doesn't protest.)*

The haircut looks good. Couple of days, it'll look terrific. You shoulda let me cut it shorter on top.

PATTI: You did a good job. I like it.

(She moves his hand away.)

Come on, I'm trying to work.

(He sits back down. She seems a little annoyed with him, about something else.)

Listen, I want you to go in and talk to your brother-in-law. He had a meeting today with—

RONNIE: The Commissioner?

PATTI: No, the lawyers. We may be in trouble.

RONNIE: Yeah—? Was he acting bizarre?

PATTI: He threw out my sandwich cause it had mayonnaise on it.

RONNIE: He's got a thing about mayonnaise. When you walk out of restaurants you don't take the mints, do you?

PATTI: The mints!? I don't take the toothpicks. I thought it's toothpicks.

RONNIE: You don't take toothpicks, but you take mints? You put uncovered mints actually into your mouth? Patti, I'm surprised.

PATTI: Then he gave me the lecture about terrorism.

RONNIE: Well, now he's making sense.

(PATTI *just stares at him.)*

Hey, he spoke to Pete Roselle. It's an international thing. It's like a business. They have consultants now. You're a terrorist, you make an appointment and you go to Rome, or Caracas, or Switzerland, and you meet a guy in an office, and he teaches you how to blow up a bus, or you hire him, or he contracts it out. It's really not a joke.

PATTI: You're starting to sound just like Ross.

(RONNIE *leans toward her and smiles.)*

RONNIE: Look, the guy's good to me, and if he gets off talking about terrorism, or mayonnaise, what the hell, I'll listen to what he says and if it makes him happy, I'll agree.

*(*RONNIE *walks into* ROSS'S *office,* PATTI *goes back to work.* RONNIE *flicks on the lights in the dark office, sees* ROSS *with his head on the desk.* ROSS *opens his eyes, sees* RONNIE, *immediately perks up.)*

RONNIE: Did I wake you up?
ROSS: Just thinking. *(Sees uniform.)* Did we win?
RONNIE: Lost in the worst possible way. I personally strike-out fourteen guys and we lose the game. I'm serious, I'd do better without a team, just playing by myself.
ROSS: Or with yourself.
RONNIE: Yeah, right.
(He pats ROSS *on the back. These two like each other.)*
Rough day at the lawyers?

*(*ROSS *nods, then stares off into space.)*

ROSS: Ronnie, did I ever tell you about the time that me and Dr. Berk saved the Egyptian people from starvation?
RONNIE: Yeah.
ROSS: The entire five-year plan has collapsed. Agriculture? Forget it. Everyone's starving. You can't imagine the strife. No one wants to do anything. The Arabs? Forget it. They hate each other like you can't imagine. The U.N.? Yeah, right. They debate for twenty-six hours, and then they pass a resolution. Did this feed the people?—*(a look)*—So then Dr. Berk, who for my money is one of the world's greatest humanitarians, decided we had to step in, putting politics aside—Arabs, Israelis—and straighten out the situation. I mean, women and children, they're innocent, it's not their fault. And where was Jordan, and the Iranians, Arabs, Assyrians, Shittites—
RONNIE: I think that's shiites—
ROSS: Bear with me Ronnie, it was terrible. But if I ever live to be a hundred I don't think I'll ever be involved in something so noble and uplifting as this investment, this act of moral outputting, that Dr. Berk allowed me to be involved with. We said forget

about governments, forget about treaties, forget about exports and imports and law and all that bullshit—we got the ships, we loaded them with grains, we found the fertilizers, the machines, and we got those boats past all the bureaucrats and delivered it to the Egyptian people. You hear a lot of stories about the Third World—I don't even know what the goddamn first two worlds are, it's all one world to me and Dr. Berk—bribes, under the table payments, that crap—well let me tell you, Dr. Berk and I were treated like gods. They wanted to give *us* money. Ronnie, what can I say, I hope one day you can have a similar experience to the one I shared with Dr. Berk—it's an honor to be alive in the same century as this man. I mean, we were UNICEF, I still get letters from peasants, farmers, bureaucrats—

RONNIE: Ross, you're part of Egyptian history, and that's a long time, man.

ROSS: Ronnie, I'm in a lot of trouble.

RONNIE: Hey, whatever you need Ross, whatever I can do, I want you to ask me.

ROSS: I haven't even told Patti yet. I've got this new lawyer coming, a real heavyweight—

RONNIE: Well with you and me and Sonny Liston for a lawyer we'll beat anything.

ROSS: You know, when your sister asked me to bring you into the company I wasn't for it. You were a fuck-up. I'll admit it and you know it. But you've really been an asset to me, you've done just great. You're terrific, Ronnie, and I just want you to know it.

RONNIE: Ross, words can't express how I feel about you either.

ROSS: You know my offer still stands. We'll open you up a little haircutting place, right downstairs next to the restaurant. It'll be great.

RONNIE: I don't want to cut hair anymore for money. Ross, let me book Twisted Sister in here. Afrika Bambaataa. I want to open up a rock club. Ross. That's what I want to do.

ROSS: Well, I don't know. We'll have to talk about that. That's a whole different kind of money.

(They walk into PATTI'S *office.* PATTI *sees* ROSS' *long face.)*

PATTI: Who died?

ROSS: Maybe me. I've been subpoenaed to testify before the grand jury—on the set-up of the business here, the tax structure, tax evasion. It's communisim. It's fascism.

PATTI: I knew this was coming. Who's gonna handle it?

ROSS: Kevin Morrow. The lawyers want him to do it.

PATTI: I've heard of him. Good. He supposed to be strong, sharp, and—

RONNIE: Instinctively illegal.

PATTI: —the best. That's not what I was going to say, Ronnie.

ROSS: Well maybe that's what we need right now anyway.

*(*PATTI *glances at a note on her desk.)*

PATTI: Val Guido called.

ROSS: Shit.

RONNIE: What's the matter?

ROSS: Involved.

RONNIE: How's Val Guido involved?

ROSS: Investor. Another investor. In fact Val gotta go before the grand jury today.

RONNIE: I didn't know that Val Guido was involved. I thought it was for a job on the Salute to Israel Show.

ROSS: No. But the notion of Val Guido on the Salute to Israel Show is good. There's already seven Jews on the show, and for the live pick-up the network doesn't want it to be too Jewish.

PATTI: No, they said it could be Jewish. It just couldn't be too pro-Israel.

ROSS: I think they don't want it to be too Jewish. But anyway, I'll call Val later. *(He starts for his office.)* When the lawyer shows up, send him into my office.

*(*ROSS *goes back into his office,* PATTI *and* RONNIE *are quiet for a moment.)*

RONNIE: Is it bad?

PATTI: It's just a question of what we're getting busted for: the financing, the business, the accounting—we don't run this place like IBM.

RONNIE: I'm not worried. The money, the car, the apartment, the status, the money—I could walk away from it in a minute.

PATTI: You get used to a certain style of life.

RONNIE: That's *your* problem, not mine. You like driving that new BMW, the Eastside apartment, the expense account—you couldn't live without it. But I could get used to anything.

PATTI: Then you adapt too easily. That's part of your biggest problem.

RONNIE: This is a great one—"It's part of my biggest problem"—not my only problem, and only part of the biggest one. Who asked you anyway? And as for "style of life"—I know what you're talking about—money. Well, I like money, but money, honey, gives me sex and drugs and rock and roll.

PATTI: I just want you to get serious.

RONNIE: Patti, do you know what the key to getting through life is? Never have a serious discussion about anything. I don't. That's why everybody likes me. Now why are you getting on my case?

PATTI: Because I want you to see what's happening with Ross. Here's a guy who graduates with top honors from the Julliard School of Business or something and all of a sudden he thinks he's a wise guy, gets himself in over his head. Well, you gotta have some sense of where you're going. You can't just go off with a high cock and a bolero.

RONNIE: Ross is the guy in trouble, not me. And besides, I don't get the attitude. I though Ross was your hero.

PATTI: He's done plenty for me, but I know how we got here and I'm starting to lose my enthusiasm. A guy like Ross can't have a bunch of guys who look like juke boxes hanging around every night and not expect something to happen. He acts like he's a heavy guy and he's not. Look, I know you idolize Ross—

RONNIE: Idolize him? I don't idolize him. I just think he's a great guy. I mean, let's just say it's an honor to be alive in the same century as Ross Bernard.

PATTI: Ronnie, why don't you get a job?

RONNIE: What do you mean? I'm the music coordinator here.

PATTI: Ronnie, you don't do anything. Okay, you manage the softball team. But basically you don't do anything.

RONNIE: Don't give me sour grapes. I just happen to have a good job. Besides—I could say the same thing about you.

PATTI: What!!? I keep this place running. I supervise the contracts, deal with the unions, the musicians—

(He laughs, raises his hands, was only putting her on.)

RONNIE: Okay. Okay.

PATTI: You can't equate my work. I have a reputation in this business. I could go out and get a job tomorrow.

RONNIE: I could get a job tomorrow.

PATTI: I don't mean busing tables.

RONNIE: Hey, I could get a job cutting hair in some of the best places in the East Village.

PATTI: So why don't you let Ross open a haircutting place for you here?

RONNIE: In this place? Are you kidding? This ain't my crowd. And besides, I want to open a rock club. I got it all figured out. It'll cost $75,000 to start it, and I figure I'll make it back in six weeks. That's what Ross should give me the money to do. I've already got a storefront picked out on Avenue D, and I've got all the records—

PATTI: Dream on. You know, maybe if you'd take an interest in—

RONNIE: Don't start. Why don't you tell me how crazy you still are about me.

PATTI: Sometimes you really piss me off.

RONNIE: Well, that's cause you let your job get to you.

*(*KEVIN MORROW *walks into the office, smiles at both of them. He is in his thirties, thin but solid, intense, tough-looking, wearing an expensive three-piece suit. He speaks in an affirmative manner, his neck, head, and shoulders moving hypnotically liked an oiled ball bearing.)*

MORROW: Good afternoon. I'm Kevin Morrow.

PATTI: I'm Patti Oliver. Mr. Bernard's expecting you.

*(*RONNIE *shakes* MORROW'S *hand.)*

RONNIE: I'm Ronald Nathan. I'm known as Ronnie by people who talk to me.

MORROW *(eyes the baseball outfit):* I'm Kevin. You win, Ronnie?

RONNIE: Let's just say it couldn't have gone better.

PATTI: Please go in, Mr. Morrow.

RONNIE: What a guy.

*(*MORROW *goes into* ROSS'S *office.* RONNIE *exits, pops his head back in.)*

Hey, Patti, love ya live.

*(*ROSS *gets up to greet* MORROW *in his office. They shake hands.)*

MORROW: Kevin Morrow.

ROSS: How are you, Kevin?

MORROW: I'm doing just great, and I'm going to get you to feel the same way. Who was the young man in the baseball uniform?

ROSS: My brother-in-law. Works with us here booking talent. I literally pulled that guy up out of the gutter. He's a great kid.

MORROW: I like him. He's positive. And he likes you. That's important. And the girl?

ROSS: She's everything to me.

MORROW: What's she do?

ROSS: Everything. And she was nothing when we found her: a seventeen-year-old temp secretary from the Bronx whose parents had just died. She started working for me ten years ago. A genius, she's worked hereself up to the top. I mean I feely sorry for her sometimes, we're her entire life and family. But she's happy.

*(*MORROW *takes it all in,* ROSS *lifts the telephone.)*

Listen are you hungry? I can send Ronnie down to the kitchen for the Pupu Platter—you know, spare ribs, spring rolls—

MORROW: I've spoken with your lawyer and I have a good sense of what's happening.

(They are still awkwardly standing. ROSS *hastily pulls out a chair for* MORROW,*motions him to sit down while he goes around to his own chair.* MORROW *sits, then stands back up to unbutton his vest, exposing a revolver.)*

ROSS: Why the gun?

(MORROW *pulls his jacket back and looks down at himself, he acts surprised that* ROSS *noticed the .38 tucked into the front of his pants. He takes the gun out.)*

MORROW: Oh this? Well, I always carry huge sums of money.

(MORROW *reholsters the gun, sits back down.)*

ROSS: I've spoken to a few people. You come highly recommended.

MORROW: My legal reputation speaks for itself. Ross, let's start slowly. You have a theater here in New Jersey, sixty miles from New York. What sort of music do you have?

(ROSS, *eager and expansive, leans back in his plush chair.)*

ROSS: Well it's always been our policy to try to attract that middle-class audience that's moved out of the city that used to go to nightclubs and theater. We present the finest in music—a Liza, a Sammy— We try to give our audience a well-rounded evening of class entertainment. You see, we're looking for the sophisticated audience, or the family audience, or both. We provide convenient parking, competitive pricing, and the finest entertainment.

MORROW: Any rock and roll?

ROSS: We tend to shy away from that. We're not interested in the sort of audience that's looking to see some screaming *schmuck* set himself on fire.

(MORROW *has taken it all in, he leans forward and smiles.)*

MORROW: Okay now, let's get down to business. I've spent the last forty minutes, which I won't charge you for, looking around your theater. I've seen the setup. I've seen the bar, your dining room, and your snack bar. Mr. Bernard, do you operate the food concession here?

ROSS: No, I don't.

(MORROW *smiles seriously.)*

MORROW: I'm glad you told me that. You know, Ross, I receive $175 an hour for my time. I'm the best at what I do, so I deserve that much. But since you're paying me that much, obviously you're serious about trusting me and telling me the truth.

ROSS: Yeah—?

MORROW: Ross, let me attempt to lay out for you what I imagine is going on here at the Horace Music Stage in South Horace, New Jersey.

(MORROW *takes out a little pad on which he's made notes. His head and neck roll as he speaks.)*

You have 1900 seats in your theater. If the show is not sold out, and you are selling tickets at the door, close to showtime you will sell approximately two hundred tickets at half price, giving the customer a special pass to get in at the door and holding the real ticket at the box office. You will then report to the performer the official number of seats sold, not counting the special passes. At approximately $15 a ticket, you have the potential of making $3000 a night, multiplied by a ten-show run. This is a $30,000 loss to the performer in terms of his or her percentage, as well as a loss for the Internal Revenue Service. You split this pure cash profit with some of your select investors. You haven't stopped me yet. Am I correct?

ROSS: It's never $3000 a night.

MORROW: If the show is soldout, you erect portable folding seats, perhaps 250, around the perimeter of the theater. Usually 50 of these seats are not officially reported. So on top of your sold-out profit, you can earn an addition $500 or so each night for ten nights.

ROSS: I won't lie to you.

MORROW: I'm not making any judgments. I just want to know if I've anticipated the correct information. That's the only way that you can get your money's worth from my professional advice. Now your concessions, who operates them?

ROSS *(hates to have to say it):* Pinkey Hammond. Nephew of Solly Dubin of Las Vegas.

MORROW: Fine. I assume you know it's Mr. Solly Dubin of Las Vegas that people are probably interested in, or perhaps just Pinkey if the government doesn't want to work too hard. What else is Pinkey involved in here?

(ROSS *says nothing.* MORROW *continues, his shoulders moving.)*

Ross, I'm working for you. Everything you tell me is in the strictest confidence. Besides, I know the people you're talking about. Don't worry. I wouldn't think of putting you in jeopardy. But I have to know everything.

ROSS: Pinkey was involved in the construction of this place.

MORROW: Was the construction his investment?

ROSS: Basically.

MORROW: Let's get back to the concessions.

ROSS: Could we take a break?

MORROW: Let's try to get it all out. The concessions are ultimately operated by Pinkey and Sol Dubin of Las Vegas. Fill me in about the breakdown.

ROSS: The usual. At the bar there are three registers. Only the center one is reported to the IRS. You make 70 percent on booze to start with, 30 percent on food, and if you don't report it to the goverment the profits are ridiculous you make so much money.

MORROW: Do you have anything to do with these operations?

ROSS: No. We just get a percentage every week. We don't question the amount, and we don't ask questions.

MORROW: So, Sol Dubin's guys run the scams and you look the other way.

ROSS: Totally.

*(*MORROW *registers it all, seems satisfied.)*

MORROW: One more thing Ross—what's Dr. Berk's connection here?

ROSS: He's just an investor.

MORROW: Personally? Through his corporations? Through his foundations? Through the Eye Institute?

ROSS: His investment's through the Eye Corporation. They invested about $500,000.

(Even MORROW *is amazed at this.)*

MORROW: Wow—the Eye Research Corporation has a piece of the Horace Music Stage.

ROSS: Yeah, well, you see Berk's Eye Corporation has nothing to do with eyes—it's just his investment umbrella. It's the Eye Foundation that does the research and medical things, the Corporation just uses the name, but it doesn't have anything to do with eyes. Listen—I don't want Dr. Berk involved in this.

(MORROW *smiles, lets out a deep breath, nods knowingly.)*

MORROW: Okay, we've got a good start. Do you have some quarters? I want to make a few telephone calls.

ROSS: You can call from here.

MORROW: I only speak from pay phones.

(ROSS *has something on his mind.)*

ROSS: Kevin, what could happen to me?

MORROW: On the purest level, a number of things. You could go free and nothing would happen. You could go to jail, how long we'll see. Or—but if you listen to me, I think you'll go free.

ROSS: Why'd this all happen?

MORROW: Fate probably. No way to anticipate these kinds of things. When they happen, they happen—then you say, "This is day one. I look forward and not back." And you deal with the situation at hand. Let me make a few calls. Try not to worry. Look, what's the worst thing that could happen? You could be killed. So? You want to die like a weasel? If you gotta go, go out with class. Enjoy yourself. You have to understand that it's all a mental thing. So don't get hung up. Transcend the moment of what's happening now, and let me worry about getting you out of trouble. Ross, we'll speak later.

(MORROW *gets up, shakes his client's hand.)*

ROSS: My family, the people who work for me—I love those people. They're beautiful human beings. Keep them out of trouble.

MORROW: I don't want you to worry about that.

(RONNIE *walks back into* PATTI'S *office. He's changed out of his uniform into black pegged pants, irridescent jacket, green shirt, and pointy black shoes.* PATTI *acknowledges him, makes no comment on his outfit.*

MORROW *walks into* PATTI'S *office, smiles at* PATTI *and* RONNIE, *shakes* RONNIE'S *hand, then leaves.* PATTI *and* RONNIE *look at each other, share a laugh at the expense of the very intense* MORROW.

ROSS *has remained behind in his office, sitting back in his chair, feeling the tension race out of his body.*

The door to PATTI'S *office again opens and* JOANNE BERNARD *walks in.* JOANNE *is a very good-looking woman of forty, well-dressed with expensive jewelry. She's verbally and physically assertive. At the moment she's distraught. She kisses* PATTI, *hugs and kisses* RONNIE.*)*

RONNIE: How ya doin', Sis?

JOANNE: I spoke to Ross this morning. How do you think I'm feeling? *(to* PATTI*):* Our phone's probably tapped. I called my best friend to tell her and—

RONNIE: She hung up on you.

JOANNE: That's right.

PATTI: We're all in this together, Joanne.

JOANNE: You can't even go anyplace anymore. Europe? Terrorists. I don't see where these people's phones are tapped. Then all of a sudden it becomes civil rights. Well, what about my civil rights? I may be old fashioned, but I'm very frightened about what's going on in this country. It's appalling, it's nauseating, its—its—Ronnie, help me—

RONNIE: It's an American Tragedy.

JOANNE: Ronnie's always been a genius. And you know, maybe it's time for your hand grenades again.

PATTI: What's this one?

JOANNE: Yeah, he was the original hippie, throwing hand grenades all over the neighborhood when he came back from the Marines.

RONNIE: I was on downs all the time.

JOANNE: Ronnie was the original hippie.

RONNIE: I wasn't the original hippie. What kind of stupid expression is this? *(to* PATTI*)* You take the live powder out, and when you pull the pin it still fizzles but doesn't explode.

JOANNE: It wasn't so funny when you threw one at Mommy.

RONNIE: I told her to stop yelling at me.

PATTI: You threw a hand grenade at your mother?

RONNIE: I was on downs all the time!

JOANNE: This was a son-of-a-bitch kid. *(to* RONNIE*)* How's your sciatica?

RONNIE: It hurts, man.

*(*ROSS *steps out of his office, sees the small group.* JOANNE *breaks away and races to him, hugs him and smothers him with kisses, becoming very emotional.)*

ROSS: Try not to worry, Joanne.
JOANNE: You're so brave. Ross, tell me what's happening.

*(*ROSS *kisses her gently, pries her arms from around him.)*

ROSS: I have to testify about the business here. Come into my office, Joanne. I want to tell you about this guy Morrow. *(to all of them, impressed)* The guy wears a gun in his belt.

*(*ROSS *escorts his wife into his office, leaving* PATTI *with* RONNIE.*)*

RONNIE: What's going on?
PATTI: Just be thankful you don't know.
RONNIE: I have a general picture.
PATTI: But you don't know specifics. I know specifics. Oh, God, we could get in so much trouble.
RONNIE: I can be trusted. I'm not a child.
PATTI: Listen, if there's an investigation, everybody's being investigated. It might be a good idea to taper off the scams for a couple of months.
RONNIE: What are you talking about? Taking a few bets from Ross and his friends and laying them off on other friends? That's nothing. It's a goof.
PATTI: And selling coke. And selling grass. And selling—
RONNIE *(got to admit it):* Quaaludes.
PATTI: —boxes so people don't have to pay for long-distance calls. And selling cable t.v. hookups. And arranging for people to get electricity hooked into their apartments so they don't have to pay electric bills. Wise up. If your sister ever knew about all this—she thinks you're straight—she'd really go over the edge.

*(*KEVIN MORROW *walks into* PATTI'S *office, smiles at them, puts his hand on* RONNIE'S *shoulder.)*

MORROW: Tell Ross that Kevin's here.

*(*RONNIE *acts like he didn't hear the order, looks around the room. There is a long awkward pause, broken when* ROSS *and* JOANNE *re-enter* PATTI'S *office.)*

ROSS: Kevin, this is my wife Joanne.
MORROW: That's just great, glad to meet you.

(They shake hands firmly.)

JOANNE *(cold, to* MORROW*):* Do anything you have to.
ROSS: I think Kevin understands that. You don't have to—
MORROW: I'm not offended. I'm pleased to hear such a comment. I'm a strong believer in protective positive aggression. Joanne, I salute your strength. Ross, I've made some calls and I have some sensitive subjects to discuss with you.

*(*MORROW *raises his eyebrows,* ROSS *takes the cue.)*

ROSS: Uh Ronnie, if you could—
RONNIE: I'll talk to you later.

(He smiles to everyone and graciously leaves.)

ROSS: What a guy that kid is. He kills me.

*(*MORROW *glances at the two women, then back at Ross.)*

MORROW: Okay—?
ROSS: Sure. They can stay. There's chairs here. Let's sit in this office.

(The four pull up chairs and sit around PATTI'S *desk.)*

MORROW: I've spoken to some friends around the country, in Washington, New York, Nevada, and California. The government's building a case against Sol Dubin of Las Vegas, a tax case basically, and they're starting here and working their way up. Nobody's interested in your ticket scams, Ross, but they're willing to use it to pressure you. What they are interested in is where the money came from to build this place, and who takes a cut and doesn't tell the government about it.

ROSS: Yeah, well, I tell the government about Solly Dubin and I'm dead.

MORROW *(Sarcastic):*—Duh.

PATTI: So what happens if he doesn't talk? What kind of option is this?

MORROW: It's his only option.

PATTI: So what are we talking about?

MORROW: Maximum—thirty-six months in jail. That's maximum.

JOANNE: OH MY GOD!!! Thirty-six months. Thirty-six months. That's—

PATTI: Three years.

JOANNE: I know that's three years; that's not what I was going to say. All of a sudden she's Ronnie—

PATTI: I'm sorry.

JOANNE: That's absolutely unacceptable. There's been no crime. For what crime?

MORROW: Everyone just relax. Now we go to work so that this doesn't happen. We're all in agreement that you don't want to talk about anything, so what will probably happen is that you will be held in contempt and probably jailed for the life of that grand jury.

JOANNE: What about a trial?

MORROW: That's how they get you; a grand jury is not a trial. If you refuse to cooperate, if you refuse to answer questions, you're in contempt and you can be put in jail.

JOANNE: We'll leave the country. We'll go underground.

MORROW: I don't know if that'll be necessary.

JOANNE: Well I'm not letting them put my Ross in jail. It's as simple as that.

ROSS: We've been through this before. What would we do out of the country?

JOANNE: Ross—you're not going to jail. We'll escape to the Bahamas.

ROSS: The Bahamas—? *(maybe it's not so bad)* The Bahamas—

JOANNE: We'll go underground. We'll be the martyrs. If everyone else can do it, we can do it.

MORROW: Now everyone just relax.

JOANNE: This is my husband. I can't relax. Besides, we haven't done anything!

MORROW: Really, Mrs. Bernard . . . This place is run like the Belgian Congo.

(She is shocked.)

Mrs. Bernard. I'm not going to let your husband go to jail.

PATTI: Then tell us what you're going to do.

*(*MORROW *nods quietly, it's what he's about to do.* ROSS *is nervous, fidgety, trying to control his emotions. He says nothing, realizes he has surrendered control of his life.)*

MORROW: This is a man in trouble. Deep trouble. I'm glad I'm not in this much trouble. This is a man who is going to have to make serious decisions that will effect his life and the life of the people he loves.

PATTI: I think we understand that.

MORROW: No you don't. Because if you did, you wouldn't still be here.

(There is silence, PATTI *is offended,* JOANNE *doesn't know if she was included in the insult.* MORROW *continues to both women.)*

Right now we must be alone. It's the only way I can help.

*(*JOANNE *solemnly nods, gets up and kisses* ROSS, *takes* PATTI'S *hand and pulls her out of her seat.* PATTI *doesn't want to leave but* ROSS *nods for her to go and she doesn't want to fight. Obviously* ROSS *wants things done* MORROW'S *way.*

JOANNE *kisses her shell-shocked husband once again, then leaves with* PATTI.

There's a quiet moment after they've left.)

ROSS: Well?

*(*MORROW *smiles warmly.)*

MORROW: You have a wonderful wife, Ross. Happy marriage?

*(*ROSS *nods.* MORROW *tries to relax him.)*

Tell me about your children.

ROSS: Two girls. Twelve and nine. I love them more than anything. Felice and Nicole—Dr. Berk calls them Phyllis and Nickle. He'll never get it straight.

MORROW: You're decent. I like that Ross. I like you.

ROSS: I feel totally out of control of my life.

MORROW: Of course you do. And as your lawyer I hope that now, in your time of troubles, that you will be kind enough to let *me* take control of your life. Let me put things in order. I can do it. Ross, do you want to go to jail?

ROSS: No.

MORROW: Ross, it doesn't matter if I say blue and you say blue, if you think blue is purple. When I say blue, you have to know what I think is blue. And I have to know what you think is blue. But most of all—we both have to agree on what "No" means. When the newspapers print that you have been subpoenaed, your life will come close to ruin. Your children will be taunted at school. They will become nervous, paranoid, perfect candidates for drug abuse and cult religion. They may even come to hate you. The pressures on your wife will be terrific, at times even unmanageable. Even if your marriage stays intact, and most often they don't, the strains on both of you will take their toll. The strain will probably shorten her life.

(ROSS *nods.* MORROW *is just warming up.)*

Now what about you? Do you know what it's like to be personally humiliated in the *New York Times?* Should you go to prison, it'll cost you a fortune. You'll doubtlessly lose your house, and you'll go bankrupt. Your wife will have to go to work, and as a woman with no background in the labor market she will get a terrible job, perhaps a maid, quite menial, and very little money. So I ask you again, Ross—Do you want to go to jail?

ROSS: I told you no! What else do you want from me?

MORROW: A commitment to your innocence. You are paying me an unreasonably high sum of money to represent you, so I insist that you get your money's worth. If you go to jail it will destroy you, but it will also upset my ego. So before we proceed, I must insist that you cannot go to prison.

(ROSS *is exhausted, confused, he shrugs, nods.)*

ROSS: I don't want to go to jail.

MORROW: Very good. Now I want you to answer a few questions for me. When did your brother-in-law *(checks his notes)*—Ronald Nathan—come to work for you?

ROSS: Five years ago. When we started building this place.

MORROW: He had been arrested a few times?

ROSS: Bookmaking. Gambling. Selling grass. Disturbing the peace with his motorcycle—when he was a kid. Nothing. He never served any time—probation—suspended sentences. Maybe he was in the brig a month before he got kicked out of the Marines.

MORROW: So when Ronnie came to work for you five years ago he supervised the construction of the theater here, the building of the restaurant, the bidding on the concession leases, and when the theater was built, as music coordinator he supervised the bookings as well as the general year-round operation of the theater and restaurants.

ROSS: He didn't do any of that. I did it all. He barely knows about any of it.

MORROW: No. You barely know about it. He's run this place for five years. you've merely been the front. The operator of record. He's a young man with numerous brushes with the law. He's lived half his life on the underside of society, he knows his way around there. You're an educated businessman, his naive brother-in-law who he mesmerized and who he got to front for his shady operations.

ROSS: Wait a second. Nobody's gonna believe that.

MORROW: Of course they will. It's the truth. Ross, do you want to go to jail?

ROSS: Well of course not. But Ronnie—

(MORROW *comes down hard.)*

MORROW: You see Ross, we both don't agree on what "No" means. Ross, do you want to go to jail? Do you want to go to jail? Do you want to lose your house? Do you want to destroy your marriage? Do you want to destroy the lives of your children?

These are the questions you have to answer. They are all the things you have absolute control over. Ross Bernard, do you want to go to jail?

ROSS: No.

MORROW: Then Ronnie Nathan will go to jail for you.

(Lights fade.)

SCENE 2

As the lights slowly come up, JOANNE *and* ROSS *are marching around* ROSS'S *office, yelling at each other.* JOANNE *is particularly furious. It's 7 o'clock at night.* ROSS *wears a somber business suit.*

JOANNE: This is terrible. Just terrible.

ROSS: I know. I'm sorry.

JOANNE: "Sorry" doesn't solve anything.

ROSS: I know that. It's terrible.

JOANNE: Well, I know. It's terrible, Ross. It's wrong. But Ronnie's going to do it.

ROSS: I guess so.

JOANNE: I know so. He owes you, Ross. And he owes me. Where was he five years ago? We pulled him out of the gutter. Now let him do something for us.

ROSS: He's like my brother. I love the guy. That's why I've always tried to shield him.

JOANNE: Don't worry about him. He's been around plenty. And don't think he doesn't love you too, Ross. He'll jump at the opportunity to do something for you.

ROSS: I don't know if he's going to jump.

JOANNE: He'll fucking jump. I'll make him jump.

ROSS: I don't know if it's the right thing, Joanne.

JOANNE: What? For the children it's not the right thing? Ross, he idolizes you. He'll be happy to do it.

ROSS: Morrow says we'll set up a special fund for him, so that when he gets out of prison he'll have a tidy sum of money waiting for him.

JOANNE: A great idea. He'll love it. It's the perfect job for him. He gets to sit on his ass and tell stories all day. And at the end of the job, he's probably richer than we are.

*(*ROSS *isn't happy, wants to be convinced.)*

Ross, you have two Cadillacs. You have a $350,000 home. You have two kids in private school. Ronnie's got a one-room studio apartment in Manhattan. I mean, let's be serious—who should go to jail?

ROSS: But the guy's trusted us.

JOANNE: Listen here—that man is my brother. I raised that kid. I worried about him. I bailed him out of trouble—how many times? Times you don't even know about. I love him more than you can imagine. But Ross, I love you. You're my husband. And I'll do anything so you won't have to go to jail.

ROSS: Neither of us wanted this to happen. I'm sick. I just didn't want this to happen. But it seems like the only way.

JOANNE: Of course it's the only way, so I don't want you to worry about it. You just do whatever Mr. Morrow says, and if anybody want to get in your way, they're gonna have to get past me first.

*(*ROSS *hugs and kisses her.)*

ROSS: I love you Joanne.

JOANNE: Nobody's putting my Ross in jail.

ROSS: What do you think Patti's gonna say?

JOANNE: Fuck Patti. I'm getting a little sick of her opinions. She had her chance with Ronnie and she blew it, so now she says anything and I'll kick her right out of here on her ass.

*(*PATTI *enters her office, flicks on a switch; the sound of the audience entering the theater filters into the office. As* PATTI *adjusts the volume,* ROSS *and* JOANNE *walk into her office,* JOANNE *giving* PATTI *a big warm smile.)*

Hi, darling.

ROSS: How's the theater shaping up for tonight?

PATTI: Full house.

JOANNE: You seem upset about something, Patti.

ROSS: Is anything the matter, dear?

PATTI: I want to know who the hell is this Kevin Morrow, coming in here like this—

(She begins doing an impression of MORROW, *moving her shoulders, neck, and head while keeping her lower body stiff. The impression is fluid, funny, and accurate.)*

All of a sudden this guy comes in and I'm closed out. Listen, I don't mind lying for you guys. I've done it before, it wouldn't be the first time, and I do it well. But at least let me be around when the lies are being made up. It helps me to tell them.

ROSS: I know what you're saying. I understand, I'm sorry. But this guy Morrow, he operates differently, his own way. He's going to save me.

(She's still not happy. ROSS *wants to please her.)*

Patti, I don't want to keep secrets from you, but bear with me. Things'll clear up.

*(*RONNIE *strolls into the office. He wears a recycled pink suit, white shirt with polka dots, and a thin black tie.)*

JOANNE: He dresses this way just to annoy me.

*(*RONNIE *kisses her, smiles, she gives him a big kiss back, then grabs his tie.)*

What do you call this retarded thing around your neck?

RONNIE *(looks down at his tie):* This is what gets you?

JOANNE: I want you to come over tomorrow. The kids are starting to look live savages. Oh, Ronnie, you do such a good job cutting hair, you make other people look so nice, but when it comes to yourself—

RONNIE: I ran into Val Guido.

*(*ROSS *doesn't like this.)*

ROSS: Where?

RONNIE: On the way up.

ROSS: This I don't need now.

RONNIE *(to the others):* You guys know Val Guido?

*(*PATTI *nods,* JOANNE *doesn't.)*

Was once the funniest person in show business. You never saw the act?

(Neither woman has.)

Well, you'll have the honor in a few minutes. It's a funny bit, it always gets me. I used to see it in this club in Sheepshead Bay, but this is like eight years ago.

PATTI: I just know Val Guido, I don't know the routine. What's so funny about it?

RONNIE: It's hysterical. This is the person that everything happens to. I remember this one night at the club, Val Guido says—*(he gets into it, holds his head)*—"I just came from the doctor, I let a blister go and he's gonna have to amputate my arm. So I leave in a daze and I get arrested for jaywalking. They throw me in jail, there's a mix-up and I get a cell on death row. Suddenly this priest arrives with a lobster dinner, and I can't eat lobster—" You get the idea. Whatever happens, it's one thing after another.

PATTI *(dry)*: Sounds hysterical.

ROSS: I can't deal with that now.

*(*ROSS *goes into his office.* RONNIE *and* JOANNE *follow him. No sooner are they inside than the door to the suite opens and* VAL GUIDO *steps into* PATTI'S *office.* VAL GUIDO *is a woman in her seventies, frail, white hair and glasses, wearing a neat, well-tailored pants suit. She looks around tentatively.* JOANNE *peeks out at her from* ROSS'S *office.)*

JOANNE: Here's Val Guido.

ROSS *(to* PATTI*)*: Why don't you maybe discourage her from coming in here.

PATTI: I'll try.

*(*PATTI *goes out to speak to the old woman.)*

PATTI: I'm Patti Oliver. We met at—
*(*VAL *jumps up as if startled.)*
Are you okay?

*(*VAL *gives a sad smile.)*

VAL: Is Ross Bernard in?

PATTI: He's in a meeting right now—Is everything all right?

*(*VAL *holds back, looks up at* PATTI, *attempts a smile, settles on a frown.* PATTI'S *suspicious, doesn't want to be the brunt of a gag.* VAL *senses it.)*

VAL: I'm gonna be straight with you honey. I've had a bad day . . .

PATTI: So has Ross. I'm sure you have, but please, not today.

VAL: Please don't do this to me. I've been in the business for years. I have a reputation. But for once in my life I'm serious. It's like the worst of one of my routines. But today it's for real.

PATTI: You'd better let me go in there, I don't think they're ready for this.

*(*VAL *latches onto* PATTI, *won't let her go.)*

VAL: It's a bad bit. I can't believe it. My daughter passed away this afternoon. Twenty-five years younger than me, and I watch her die. It doesn't make sense. She was under an incredible amount of stress. Her fifteen-year-old-daughter had run away. She'd had a fire in her house a month ago, destroyed everything—a lifetime of memories. And then last Sunday she got into an automobile accident, went into a coma, and died this morning. She's dead. *(Pause.)* I want to go in and see my friend Ross.

*(*VAL *pushes past* PATTI, *maintains her composure as best she can, walks toward* ROSS'S *office.* PATTI *chases after her.* RONNIE *sees them approach.)*

RONNIE *(to* JOANNE*)*: Here she comes. Let's play her straight.

*(*RONNIE *takes one look at the old woman, a frown across her face, and breaks into a wide grin.* PATTI *gives* RONNIE *a hard stare.)*

ROSS: How you doing, Val?

*(*VAL *looks downward.)*

VAL: I've had—

RONNIE: A hard day. *(to the others)* Here we go.

VAL: My granddaughter ran away from home. Fifteen years old. She's probably on a street corner in East Harlem.

*(*RONNIE *grunts,* JOANNE *smiles politely.)*

Oh, then I guess you didn't hear. My daughter's been in a depression for the last few months. She started drinking again, it's not the first time she's had a problem—

RONNIE *(eggs her on):* She's having a few drinks, yeah—

VAL: So she started having a few accidents around the house. I don't know how, but her house caught fire and burnt to the ground. *(*RONNIE, ROSS, *and* JOANNE *start cracking up, but control themselves.)*
It's not funny.
(They love it. PATTI *turns away.)*
So she wasn't thinking. She took the car out. She got into an accident.
(They love it.)
She went into a coma—

RONNIE: She went into a coma—

VAL: And died.

ROSS *and* RONNIE: She died!!!

(They double over.)

VAL: My granddaughter ran away from home. My house burned down. My daughter got into an accident—

RONNIE: And she died!! She died!

(This is too much for them. Even JOANNE *is laughing it up.)*

VAL: I don't know what's supposed to be so funny.

*(*PATTI *can't take it, clutches* VAL *to her, yells at the others.)*

PATTI: Shut up, you bastards. Can't you see she's serious?

(They really go for this, then look at each other, then at VAL, *then they fall silent.* VAL *smiles warmly at* PATTI*)*

VAL: It's okay honey, I'm only kidding. *(to the others)* The old material still works. *(to* PATTI*)* Don't feel like a *schmuck,* Sinatra himself once fell for the routine.
*(*VAL *kisses the chagrined* PATTI, *then slaps the others to shut up.* PATTI *is embarrassed, then shrugs good-naturedly.)*
Listen all of you. I have to talk to my boyfriend Ross here for a minute. So just give us a little privacy.

ROSS: Yeah. Let us have a minute together.

*(*ROSS *walks over to get her a chair.)*
Walk this way, Val. Sit down.

VAL *(mimics* ROSS'S *walk):* If I could walk that way I wouldn't need the talcum powder.
(They all laugh.)
You're a great straightman, Ross. You should have gone into show business. Oh yeah, you are in show business.

*(*VAL *smiles again at* PATTI *as* ROSS *shrugs and shows* JOANNE, RONNIE, *and* PATTI *out of the office.* ROSS *is now alone with the old woman.)*

ROSS: Have a seat. Where have you been lately?

VAL *(sits down):* I've been playing Chicago. So what are you going to do, Ross?

ROSS: I got it all worked out. Tell your friends that they don't have to worry about anything.

VAL: Do I have to bother Dr. Berk?

ROSS: No.

VAL: So it's covered. You'll take the fall, but big deal. Behave or otherwise they'll take your life.

ROSS: Naturally I have to discuss some things with my people.

VAL: So Ross, you *schtupping* the secretary?

ROSS: You're a comedic genius, Val, but sometimes you go to far.

*(*VAL *grins, moves to get up.* ROSS *holds her down in the chair gently. He smiles slyly at her, puts her on the defensive.)*

ROSS: You've sunk twenty-six grand in this place. I'm a *schmuck* for getting involved, but Dr. Berk's an old friend of yours and Pinkey's your nephew. You knew how these guys played, how'd you get suckered?

VAL: I know Bill Berk from when we were both doing comedy together, so I think Bill Berk's gonna fuck me? What's he wanna fuck *me* for? The guy's richer than God. But with all his degrees, and hospitals, and his institutions, and the politics, he's still got this sleazy streak.

ROSS: But he's still a great man who does wonderful things for society. He was telling me once about the work his Eye Institute does with the medical schools in Korea—

VAL: You mention Korea, now there's a project I'm glad I invested in. Berk has a sweater factory there. They do beautiful cotton work, they have these cute little girls doing the sewing, they pay them something like ten cents a day. Berk got me to invest eight grand, and I've made back forty-five so far. So you see, you behave yourself, you pay your dues, and these are the kinds of projects he can get you involved in.

ROSS: I know that. That's why I don't make any waves.

(There is applause and a musical fanfare from the speakers.)

VAL: I hate that I had to come here to talk to you.

ROSS: I've got it all under control. I understand everyone's problems, and everyone knows I'm gonna keep my mouth shut.

VAL: Great. I'll see you during intermission.

(She shakes ROSS'S *hand then walks out to* PATTI'S *office with a smile.)*

See you all later. I gotta go see the competition.

*(*ROSS *leans out from his office as she leaves, motions to* RONNIE.*)*

ROSS: Could you come in here for a minute?

*(*RONNIE *walks across the room.* PATTI *starts to follow,* JOANNE *grabs her.)*

JOANNE: It's private. Between them.

PATTI: I'm sorry, but I want to know what's happening.

JOANNE: But why? It's just between them.

PATTI: Joanne, I spend more time here than anybody, so my head's the next one to fall. If I leave it up to these two "rocket scientists" to come up with a plan, we're gonna be in a lot of trouble. And besides, if you know what's going on, I want to know what's going on.

*(*PATTI *breaks away from* JOANNE *and walks into* ROSS'S *office.* JOANNE *races in behind, apologizes to* ROSS *with a look,* ROSS *isn't happy to see them.)*

ROSS: Hey, I want to talk to Ronnie alone.

PATTI: I'm not leaving, and Ronnie, don't say anything. It's time I knew what was in the works. I deserve to know.

ROSS: Fine. Okay. Sit down. But I want you to keep your mouth shut. You say one word, and you go right out of here.

PATTI: Why are you getting so tough with me?

JOANNE: I don't think she should be here at all.

PATTI: Well I'm staying.

JOANNE: This is a mistake. *(to* PATTI*)* Please, this is family.

*(*PATTI *glares at her.)*

RONNIE: Let me hear it already.

ROSS: Okay. Joanne, just sit down. Patti, you shut up. Ronnie, make yourself comfortable. Sit. Nice. Open your jacket. You'll all know eventually, so you might as well—

RONNIE: All know now. Ross, lay it out straight. I know what you're going through.

ROSS: Thanks Ronnie, but let me present this in my own way. I'll admit we got involved with, well, uh—

RONNIE: The wrong people.

ROSS: We were out of our league. We made a mistake, but we had no choice. When you think big, sometimes you have to deal with people of certain influence. If we didn't, somebody else would have, and then somebody else would be making the money that's established—

RONNIE: The quality of entertainment.

ROSS: No, the lifestyle we have today! Look, it's progress, we saw a swamp on the outskirts of suburbia and developed it into a strong business that provides employment, taxes, and beauty to a community that's accepted this theater with open arms. Now I didn't like to deal with the people we had to deal with. I didn't like their methods of doing business. But quite frankly, and I think we'll all agree, we really didn't have a choice—*(to* PATTI*)*—you disagree?

PATTI: Not yet, but I'm still listening.

ROSS: If you didn't like what we were doing here, you could have quit. You didn't, so shut up. Ronnie, I'm in trouble. And the lawyer says that you're the only person that can help me.

RONNIE: Me—!?? Well, I don't know. Me? I'm listening.

JOANNE: Well then listen.

ROSS: Joanne—.

(JOANNE leans over and kisses RONNIE to make sure his feelings aren't hurt. ROSS looks down, is trying to find the words.)

ROSS: Ronnie, would you be willing—this is very difficult for me—
RONNIE: Do I have to kill somebody?
ROSS: No, that's not it. It's—
RONNIE: You want to replace me. Somebody with a little more experience—?
(ROSS shakes his head.)
I leave the country. You say, I embezzled the money—?
PATTI: Well, is he getting warm?
ROSS: Ronnie, I want you to go to jail for me.
RONNIE: Sure Ross. I'll do it. What? I don't know. Jail? Okay, Ross, sure.
PATTI: What!? Oh God, we are going to get into so much trouble.
JOANNE: Shut up, Patti. We're in trouble already.
RONNIE: Whatever it is, Ross. Jail? You're gonna have to explain this whole thing to me.
PATTI: How's he gonna go to jail for you?
ROSS: We're gonna tell the grand jury that he runs the place.
PATTI: Oh, terrific. And what's Ross? The janitor?
JOANNE: Patti, be serious.
PATTI: Don't tell me to be serious. We're talking about Ronnie.
RONNIE: Will you let the man speak?
PATTI: You've just agreed to the stupidest thing I've ever heard in my life and now you want to hear more?
JOANNE: Now I'm starting to get annoyed.
PATTI: Who's gonna believe that Ronnie runs the place?
RONNIE: People believe anything. I was at this bar in Brooklyn and I saw these two great-looking girls. So we get into this great big discussion about puppies, so I tell them I'm a veterinarian—
PATTI: You're dealing with a grand jury, not two girls from Brooklyn.
ROSS: Look. Morrow's a genius and I've accepted him as my personal doctor to remove the tumor of crime that's troubling us.
PATTI: Please, Ross, don't fall in love with this Morrow like you fall in love with every jerk who comes in here. Even if you see him as your doctor, you're entitled to—
RONNIE: Two phone calls.

PATTI: Ronnie, shut up! *(to* ROSS*)* Get another opinion.
ROSS: I wouldn't insult the man.
RONNIE: I trust the guy too. But jail?
ROSS: Oh, it's not really jail. You're not going to Alcatraz or Devil's Island. Between Morrow, Dr. Berk, and the people we know, you'll go to one of those, you know, white-collar prisons, and it's only for a little while. They got tennis there, Ping-Pong—soft ball. And there's going to be people making sure nothing's going to happen.
PATTI: It's jail.
RONNIE: Yeah, I know. But I'm gonna do it.
ROSS: You're beautiful. I don't know what to say.
RONNIE: You don't have to say anything. You can depend on me. Look, I know I'm a fuck-up. I know I get in the way around here, that you've been carrying me, that half the time I don't know what the hell I'm doing with my life. That I'm a fuck-up—
JOANNE: Oh come on Ronnie, please, you don't have to say things like that.
ROSS: Wait a second, Joanne, let the man speak. I think he's making some good points here. Let's hear his opinion.

*(*PATTI *stands up and starts out; it's too much for her.* JOANNE *goes after her.)*

JOANNE: Try to understand.
PATTI: The guy is your brother.
JOANNE: But the other guy's my husband. One day, if you ever get married, maybe you'll understand what that means. You know, for a girl who's stolen my entire style, I can't believe how naive you are.
PATTI: You're selling him out.
JOANNE: You want Ross to take the rap? The man has a family.
ROSS: Uh, girls, would you try to transcend the moment for a minute?

*(*JOANNE *walks over to* RONNIE *and starts hugging and kissing him.)*

JOANNE: You're so brave, I love you so much.
RONNIE: I couldn't say no.

JOANNE: I never doubted you for a minute.

ROSS: Now don't worry, we'll pay for everything. And no matter how long this thing takes, when it's over, you'll have a pretty little stake set aside for yourself. We're setting up a fund, the Ronnie Fund, and the money'll be waiting for you when you get out.

RONNIE: Come on, that's the last thing I have on my mind. Um, like how much?

ROSS: There'll be plenty. The theater's doing great business, you'll be out of jail in a few months, and you'll never have to worry about money again.

RONNIE: I don't want to talk about the Ronnie Fund. I'm doing this because I love you, so I don't want you to feel guilty. *(to* PATTI*)* I'm not doing this because I'm stupid. *(to* ROSS*)* I'm not a fool. I wouldn't do this for anyone but you.

ROSS: I don't know what to say.

JOANNE: It's the best thing for everybody. You'll get out and you'll be rich. You'll open up an exclusive haircutting place on Madison Avenue.

PATTI: This thing'll never work.

JOANNE: Why don't you grow up?

ROSS: Patti, I want to talk to you. *(to* RONNIE *and* JOANNE*)* I wonder if you'd excuse us.

*(*JOANNE *is almost offended,* RONNIE *is eager to please. They leave.)*

Okay. Okay. I'm wrong. You think I'm wrong? Why am I wrong? Tell me I'm wrong.

PATTI: You're wrong.

ROSS: Listen, I know you love that guy.

PATTI: Twenty minutes two years ago is not love.

ROSS: Don't give me that. You're crazy about the guy.

PATTI: Everybody loves Ronnie, but this plan is not going to work.

ROSS: Sure it will. And after all this time I might have expected a little support. I mean we're gonna take care of the kid.

PATTI: By putting him in jail?

ROSS: We're setting up the Ronnie Fund! He gets to sit on his ass and he comes out rich. It's this guy's dream job. Hell, it's what he does anyway.

PATTI: You're ruining his life.

ROSS: Oh? I wish at his age that I had such an opportunity. I would have taken it in a minute. And besides, let's face it, the guy owes me.

PATTI: You gave him a job. He owes you jail?

ROSS: He wants to do it. He's gonna get rich. And besides, there's a thing called The Family, and what you're seeing here is The Code of The Family. Oh, it's not written down anywhere, etched on a tablet in a museum, but what it means is loyalty, trust, courage, will, and virtue—and it means that everyone helps each other out.

PATTI: Ross, look, it's me you're talking to. Not one of your birdbrained security men.

ROSS: If you can't handle helping me out, maybe you should go out of town for awhile.

PATTI: I'd like to help, Ross, but this plan—aside from the fact that Ronnie's not capable of sustaining a consistent thought for more than five minutes, it's just not right.

ROSS: That's my problem, not your's, and I think we should let Ronnie decide how he wants to solve it.

(He gives her a fatherly kiss, puts his arm around her and walks her out to the others.)

I'm proud to say we're all together on this.

(MORROW *enters.)*

MORROW: How'd it all work out?

RONNIE: Everything's fine.

MORROW: Then let us sit down and make plans immediately.

(ROSS *is stunned by how fast it's all moving.* MORROW *leans back in his chair.)*

MORROW: Now the first thing you have to do in a situation like this is to get a plot. Whether you're testifying in front of a grand jury, dealing with an employee, or trying to avoid paying a carpenter, or even—when you're dealing with family or friend, if you get a plot and stay with it—

RONNIE: Then you're always way ahead.

MORROW: I'm sorry, Ronnie, but no interruptions.

(MORROW *leans forward, as if to share a secret.)*

MORROW: Yesterday I came in here with a plot. I was brash, strong, successful, and busy. Am I really like that, or was it just an impression? Does it matter? You believed it, and that's why you're putting your trust in me. Now the best plots are surprises. A carpenter did some work on my house and hasn't been paid. Since getting paid is the first thing on his mind, he thinks paying him is the first thing on my mind. Well it is, cause I don't have the money to pay him. But if I act like that, I'm in trouble, I'm gonna have to pay. So my plot is that I'm on drugs because my knees were operated on, plus I'm spaced-out cause I found a burglar in my cellar and I smashed his skull in. He didn't die but now I'm all involved with police reports. So by the time we get talking about carpentry, this fool realizes that paying him is the last thing on my mind. I haven't been avoiding him, I haven't even thought about him. So when I tell him give me three weeks, he gives me three weeks. And in three weeks I'll give him a couple of bucks and he'll be happy to get it.

PATTI: But eventually you have to pay the guy.

MORROW: He'll be happy to get half. That's the way you have to deal with human garbage, and that's the way you deal with a grand jury. Boys, we're gonna totally surprise them. They'll be expecting one plot, but the story we give them is going to be so out to lunch that they'll definitely buy it.

ROSS: But I'm not the kind of guy who can—

MORROW: They're gonna think you don't want to talk because you're a hoodlum, a creep, a bona fide racketeer. So the D.A. starts to threaten you—

(MORROW *gets into it, loves building the story, his neck and shoulders working.)*

You don't want to talk, Ross, but they make you, only what you tell them isn't what they want to hear. The reason you haven't talked isn't because you're scared, or because you have information about the mob, and it isn't because you've done something illegal. The reason you're not talking is simple—you're trying to protect your brother-in-law. You're trying to keep your wife's little brother, the kid who never had a break, out of trouble. You don't know what's going on, honestly, because Ronnie handles everything. Ross Bernard just goes along with the program. You're a trusting guy, Ross, and maybe this kid's been using you. But you don't believe it. He's a good kid. And you've just been trying to protect him. It's the last thing anybody's gonna expect. It'll be beautiful. They'll be amazed. They'll call time-out. They'll look at each other and roll their eyes around their heads—and call Ronnie as a witness, because Ross, they're gonna believe it.

RONNIE: Hey, Morrow—were you ever abducted by a UFO and you know, given the intelligence booster?

MORROW: I take that as a compliment.

ROSS: I'm scared to death just listening to this. I can't put on a performance like that.

MORROW: There's no performance, you'll be perfect. You'll be pissing in your pants.

JOANNE: Now just a minute, Mr. Morrow.

ROSS: He's right, Joanne. I will be.

MORROW: And that's why they're going to believe you, because you're genuine. Ross, if you were the kind of guy who had ice water in his veins, we wouldn't be able to do this. But a guy like you, a worm, squirming, sweating, shaking—

JOANNE: Enough. enough.

ROSS: I just don't know.

MORROW: Ross, pull yourself together.

(ROSS *straightens up.* JOANNE *is shocked by* MORROW'S *attitude, but* MORROW *shoots her a look and she keeps quiet.)*

Ronnie, your job will be easier. You just say nothing. You'll be cited for contempt, and that's it.

RONNIE: Well, as long as I understand what's going to happen. You guys are gonna be there to take care of me and—

MORROW: What did you say?

RONNIE: All I said was I don't under—

MORROW: Ronnie, Ronnie, are you a chicken? Are you backing out on your obligations?

JOANNE: Is that what you're saying Ronnie?

RONNIE: Who's saying anything?

MORROW: I know you're scared. All that'll happen is that you'll be cited. We'll fight the citation, but at a certain time you'll probably be jailed for contempt.

RONNIE: Okay. That's all I wanted to know. I said I'd do it.

JOANNE: Any objections, Patti?

PATTI: None, if it's okay with Ronnie.

JOANNE: Now, Mr. Morrow. What about clothing? We're not going to let Ronnie dress like this, are we?

MORROW: Joanne, when this is all over, I want you to seriously consider a career in law. *(to* RONNIE*)* So you'll learn to feel comfortable in it, beginning tomorrow you'll wear a conservative dark suit.

(The door to the office suite opens and in walks VAL GUIDO. ROSS *instinctively gets up to greet her, as does* MORROW, RONNIE *waves to her,* JOANNE *is annoyed by the intrusion, and* PATTI *senses trouble.)*

VAL: Lousy comedian tonight. I just don't understand what this whole thing is with these "young comics." You never saw a young comedian in the old days. Even if they were twenty-three, a comedian had the decency to act like he was seventy.
*(*VAL *looks around.)*
Am I interrupting something?

MORROW: No, I think we're finished.

ROSS: Val, meet Kevin Morrow.

VAL: This is your lawyer?
*(*ROSS *nods.)*
You carry a gun? Very important.

MORROW: A pleasure to meet you, Mrs. Guido. You spoke to the grand jury if I'm not mistaken.

VAL: And I didn't say a thing. But then again, age has its benefits. Who's gonna push around an old lady. Ross, could we speak privately?

ROSS: Sure, But I'd like Kevin here—

VAL: He can stick around if you want him to, sure.

*(*ROSS *says goodbye to* PATTI, *kisses* JOANNE, *holds* RONNIE *by the shoulders, smiles, then hugs him warmly. He escorts them out of the office. He invites* VAL *to sit.)*

ROSS: Just get to it Val. I've had a long day and I want to get some sleep.

VAL: I just got a message from the consortium of investors. They've got a funny feeling about something . . .

(VAL *looks hard at* MORROW.)

They're very unhappy.

ROSS: Okay, so I've made some mistakes. So instead of just skimming off the concessions, why don't they send somebody out here to help me direct this damn thing.

VAL: Well, that's kind of the idea now. They've weighed the evidence, and I'm sorry to tell you that they're sorry, but in four months you're out of here. They're gonna pay you off, and they're gonna replace you. They'll make you an executive if you like somewhere down in sunny Florida. But as for this place, you're out.

ROSS: Val. This is my place. I built this place.

VAL: You're out Ross. Four months. It's over.

ROSS: Val, I have a family. My house. My kids. I have a life.

VAL: Sorry Ross. You've had enough.

ROSS: I'll be ruined. I won't let them do this. I built this place.

VAL: You gonna fight?

ROSS: Fight? No, of course not.

(VAL *smiles to* MORROW.)

VAL: It must be a pleasure to have such a smart client.

MORROW: It is, Mrs. Guido. There is one thing, though. We don't want Ross in jail. So we've made certain assurances to Mr. Ron Nathan, who will help us through Ross's present difficulties.

VAL: The jerk hairdresser?

MORROW: A certain fund has been promised to be set for him.

VAL: So?

MORROW: The man's going to jail for Ross. We want to cover his time. It's only fair.

ROSS: He's my brother-in-law. Val. I want to be able to set something up for him.

VAL: Money? Not our problem.

ROSS: But Val—

VAL: Oh, you mean set up a fund for the guy? Put aside some money?

ROSS: Yeah. Right.

VAL: No way! We're partners in profits, not in problems. Sorry, Ross. See you around.

(Curtain.)

Act II

As the lights come up, ROSS *and* PATTI *are sitting around the desk in* ROSS'S *office.*

ROSS: Patti, what do you know about Costa Rica?

(She drops her head into her hands.)

Just hear me out on this. It's amazing.

PATTI: When we sold the chemical company, we were all going to move to New Zealand. Now we're going to Costa Rica?

ROSS: It was Australia; we made some investments. We were never going to move there.

(She smiles at him, politely.)

You know Costa Rica's in Central America, which is actually part of North America. So it's not a South American country, it's a North American country.

PATTI: Ross—are we moving to Costa Rica?

ROSS: There's elections, democratic changes of government, a free press, no rioting—plus, it's a very beautiful land, many of its friendly people speak English, and for decades it's been a retirement haven for middle-class Americans who are respected and well loved.

PATTI: When are we leaving?

ROSS: Now we all know that America is moving in a direction that none of us are happy with. I'm terrified that we'll have a dictatorship here within the next ten years. Talk to Joanne, talk to Dr. Berk—they feel the same way. There'll have to be one. People will demand it as the only way to cope with terrorism.

PATTI: I get it—we make Dr. Berk the King of Costa Rica.

ROSS: No, no. Just listen. There's been a tremendous shift in the American population to the South—the Sunbelt—call it what you will. The great urban centers will soon be Atlanta, Houston,

Arizona, Florida. Now when these people want to go on a vacation, where are they gonna want to go?

PATTI: They don't want to go to New York, that's for sure.

ROSS: Exactly. So let's make a fortune. Even though Costa Rica's in Central America, it's hilly, lush, and temperate. Patti, we could go down there, and as the first ones with our expertise, literally make millions on the growing tourist trade catering to vacationers from the South. No one else is doing it. It's wide open. We would literally be rich.

PATTI: When are you leaving?

ROSS: I'll tell you Patti, I'm ready to go as soon as our present problems work themselves out. The kids and Joanne are learning Spanish from Lupe, and I've contacted the Costa Rican consulate. They're wonderful people these Costa Ricans, extremely polite, educated, very *European*—and I'll tell you the truth, as soon as everything's resolved, our bags are packed. Now I know you're young, Patti, but I know you think about your future. I know you think about something more exciting for yourself—well, this is it. I want you to come with us. I want you to be part of it.

PATTI: This is all very sudden.

ROSS: I know. It's just that circumstances have forced us to move up our plans and think a lot quicker. Remember that once our chemical company was in a closet. I was driving a cab at night to pay the phone bills for the calls during the day. That chemical company was a figment of my imagination. But you buy, you sell, you make believe you have money. First we made one deal, then another, and suddenly that company wasn't a closet, but it was a real office with a warehouse, and trucks, and when we sold it we made a lot of money. We've come a long way, through a lot of people and a lot of business. And even if we lost a lot of money on this place, we're going to go a lot further.

PATTI: Ross—we haven't lost all the money on this place, have we?

ROSS: Patti, I want to write this place off. I want to think big again. I want to think of new worlds to conquer.

PATTI: Ross, have you ever been to Costa Rica? Maybe you and Joanne should go down there for a week, or a month, before you plunge into something like this. Maybe you'll hate the place—maybe you'll love it—but I really think you should go down there before you make all these plans.

ROSS: The reason I am where I am today is because I act, I don't waste time thinking.

PATTI: But you'd be uprooting the entire—

ROSS: Listen, when these Jersey potato farmers didn't want me to put in the theater because of their farms, or ecology, or some shit, I decided to just put it in—and then we discussed whether we could do it or not, after it was done. That's the way you get things accomplished. I mean, I'm the guy who put New Jersey on the map, so I can move my family to Costa Rica if I want to.

PATTI: Ross, I know you a long time, and I believe in you, I'm just more cautious than you.

ROSS: Look, these are rough times. There are things I can't even discuss with Joanne, that I can only discuss with you. She's taking pills again, you know. These doctors are fucking amazing. They'll give you a prescription for anything, and she goes along with it.

PATTI: Ross, I'm sorry. I haven't noticed.

ROSS: There's nothing to notice. I mean, I shouldn't be complaining—we're getting along now better than ever. The fucking pills work, it just upsets me that she has to take them. But medicine's an amazing field. The thing's they're doing today would have been unheard of thirty years ago. You know, I was talking to Dr. Berk one day, and he told me that since 1910 there's been more progress in the field of science than in all of history before that. *(he thinks a moment)* It's just that some days Joanne'll repeat the same fucking story at breakfast, lunch, and dinner. You don't seem very excited about this new project. Why not?

PATTI: Well it just seems that—I thought this morning we were going to talk about what's happening with Ronnie, not Costa Rica. Ross, does Ronnie get to go to Costa Rica too?

ROSS: You know, you've been hurting me these last two days. I thought you knew me, had some confidence in me. Besides, the guy's Joanne's brother. You think we're going to desert him? We're gonna take care of the guy. That's what the Ronnie Fund's all about.

PATTI: But if the plan was to set up some kind of fund through the theater, and there is no theater, what's going to happen to Ronnie?

ROSS: We have not lost the theater, okay? Happy? And even if we did, it doesn't matter. We're selling our house when we move. That's $450,000 right there—it's all Ronnie's.

PATTI: Okay, Ross, what do you want from me this time?

ROSS: Ronnie's the kind of guy who wavers, so he's gotta be unsure about this whole thing.

PATTI: I don't blame him.

ROSS: Well, I just want you to tell him that he can trust us.

PATTI: That's my job? Great. And this whole thing is all right with Joanne?

ROSS: Of course, and with Felice and Nicole and Joanne's parents, everyone. That's why I wanted you here today, to share this with us. We love you, Patti, all of us, dearly. And no matter what happens I want to know that you'll stand with the family.

(He stares off, his mind elsewhere.)

PATTI: Ross, what's the matter?

ROSS: Oh nothing. I just hope Dr. Berk doesn't get wind of this. Don't get me wrong, the guy's my friend, but he's got a temper. *(*RONNIE *enters the offices, hears the voices from* ROSS'S *office, walks across and into* ROSS'S *office.* RONNIE *is wearing a conservative dark suit and tie, and a black motorcycle crash helmet with a black, mirrored visor pulled down over his face. Between the suit and the helmet he looks like a diplomat from outer space.)*

Ronnie! You look sensational.

RONNIE: How ya doin', Ross. *(pulls up the visor)* How ya doin', Patti.

PATTI: Look at this guy's tan. You look terrific.

RONNIE: I was at the beach. It was real polluted, man, like swimming in a dirty bathtub. It was great.

ROSS: Ronnie, you kill me. *(to* PATTI*)* I live vicariously through this kid. *(back to* RONNIE*)* I'll be back with Morrow. *(to* PATTI*)* I'll speak to you later.

*(*RONNIE'S *surprised that he's leaving;* ROSS *takes him aside, confides.)*

Talk to Patti, know what I mean?

*(*ROSS *smiles and exits.)*

PATTI: Okay, what's under the helmet?
RONNIE: What do you mean?
PATTI: Why are you still wearing the helmet? What's the surprise? Did you give yourself the Mohican Cut?

(RONNIE *smiles wryly, unbuttons the strap under his chin, removes the helmet. There's been no change in the haircut, though* PATTI *looks for one.* RONNIE *rubs his hair to unflatten it.)*

RONNIE: See? I'm taking this thing seriously.

(PATTI *gently tugs at the long hairs that trickle down the back of* RONNIE'S *neck.)*

PATTI: When are you going to cut this stuff?
RONNIE: When Morrow tells me to. Hey Patti, why don't you let me give you the rock and roll haircut?
PATTI: You're really going along with the program?
RONNIE: I'm getting off on it. It's heavy. Don't you think I'm doing the right thing?
PATTI: I'm so sucked in here I don't know anything anymore. Ross and Joanne, as crazy as they are, they're all I've got. But whether they're doing the right thing by you—
RONNIE: Come on, are you kidding? They care about me.
PATTI: I was thinking of leaving a couple of weeks ago, you remember, after my monthly screaming match with Joanne—but now, with all this trouble, it just wouldn't be right.
RONNIE: I've never seen you so confused. It's very attractive. It's the first time I've ever seen you act your age.
PATTI: If it wasn't you, Ronnie, I really wouldn't give a shit.
RONNIE: Well, the way *you've* been acting lately I'm just glad that I'm the one who has to stand up for Ross.
PATTI: Don't turn on me, you little creep. I've stood up for Ross plenty of times.
RONNIE: And got rich doing it. But now it's the big one, and I'm the one to handle it.
PATTI: Did you know he's got some deal cooking in Costa Rica?
RONNIE: So? He's always got something cooking somewhere.

*(*RONNIE *smiles sweetly, she looks at him, he stares at her hair, gently starts messing around with her haircut.)*

Remember when I first met you? You had that Norwegian haircut.

PATTI: What are you talking about?

RONNIE: You had that Norwegian haircut, like somebody put a bowl on your head. You looked like the Swiss Miss. That's it, it was a Swiss haircut—

(He gently keeps playing with her hair, examining, moving it around. She doesn't stop him. It is a warm moment.)

It was very uncool, but cute. That's it, you were cute.

PATTI: I like it the way it is now. Ronnie, is going to jail really okay with you?

RONNIE: You should let me cut it short on top. C'mon, Patti, why don't you let me give you the rock and roll haircut? I'll layer it. I'll cut it short on top and long at the back. You'll look great. How about it, Patti?

PATTI: Ronnie, I want to talk to you. Stop avoiding everything. You're just like Ross.

RONNIE: You gonna miss me?

PATTI: Of course.

RONNIE: So you'll come visit me. We'll talk through those goofy telephones.

(She looks at him, not amused.)

All I know is that I can take it and Ross can't.

PATTI: Yeah, he's going to take it all the way to Costa Rica. You know about this one?

RONNIE: Is that true? He's going there? Costa Rica?

PATTI: I don't know. He's talking about it.

RONNIE: So what else is new? Him and Joanne are always talking about moving somewhere.

PATTI: Well, if you're doing this because they're gonna set something up for you when you get out, you'd better make sure that they're still gonna be here when you get out.

RONNIE: Nobody's screwing me, Patti. Is somebody screwing you? You leave here after work, nobody knows where you go. You're probably uptown in Manhattan, dancing on a piano in a white tuxedo. Who knows? Or maybe there was something between you and Ross that didn't work out. Are you guys planning on doing some honeymooning in Costa Rica?

PATTI: You little shit. I never fucked Ross. Everyone thinks we have, but we haven't.

RONNIE: So what if you did. I don't care. I wouldn't have an opinion one way or the other.

PATTI: I mean, me and Ross? Don't you think that's a little sick.

RONNIE: No kidding. I'm sorry. You and Ross—look how confused I'm getting.

PATTI: I'm not trying to confuse you, it's just that you come to us, and—

RONNIE: I'm taken in—

PATTI: You're given a little love, and the next thing you know you've bought all of Ross' values and—

RONNIE: The whole family package. Yeah, well so have you.

PATTI: I'd be the first to admit it. But I'm not sure that these people have any idea what they're talking about anymore. I've seen them crazy before—you know all the delusions—but now they may be too far gone. I certainly don't know if they have the right to make you take their fall.

RONNIE: Nobody's making me do anything.

PATTI: You aren't doing this for the money, are you?

RONNIE: Patti, don't you see? It's the first time that people are taking me seriously, giving me some responsibility. I like it, and I'm sorry if you think I'm an idiot.

PATTI: I don't think you're an *idiot*—

RONNIE: That's why I'd do anything for Ross, 'cause he always makes me feel great. I don't have to do anything to show that I'm good enough for him. He just takes me in, gives me the big hello, slaps me on the back, confides in me—it's great. That he would think I'm worthy of that bullshit is great. So if I can do something in return, I'll do it. He's the only person that I mean anything to—and the guy would do the same for me. Besides, there's a time to think and a time to act, and this is a time to act. There are moments in your life when you just have to go with your impulses.

PATTI: You're even starting to sound like Ross, which means you're starting to sound like that *schmuck* Dr. Berk.

RONNIE: Dr. Berk's a great man. He's UNICEF.

PATTI: Oh, Ronnie, what do you know? I know Ross Bernard from when he was still Bernie Ross, and I know Dr. Berk from when him and Ross were selling shiploads of banned pesticides to the Egyptian government.

RONNIE: They fed Egypt.

PATTI: These two guys are running around afraid of mayonnaise and they made a fortune selling poison chemicals, so save the Great Man theory.

RONNIE: I don't want to hear it, cause I can't believe that Ross, or Joanne, or any of these people are taking advantage of me. I think I'm doing something good, on my own, for my sister and my brother-in-law and my nieces. And I'm gonna make some money. And my friends think I'm cool. And if I thought that I was being taken advantage of, I'd walk out the door.

(The door to the suite opens and in marches KEVIN MORROW. *He wears an expensive sports jacket, polo shirt, khaki slacks, brown shoes, no socks. He smiles at* PATTI *and* RONNIE. *There is an awkward moment as they all smile cagily at one another, then* ROSS *and* JOANNE *walk into the office.)*

ROSS: Well, it's great to see the gang's all here.

MORROW: Let's adjourn to the larger, plusher, and more comfortable office.

*(*ROSS *leads the way into his office.* JOANNE *pulls* PATTI'S *sleeve.)*

JOANNE: Who's side are you on?

PATTI: We're all on the same side, Joanne.

(They follow into ROSS'S *office. While* ROSS *is getting chairs for everyone,* MORROW *goes behind the desk and sits himself in* ROSS'S *chair.)*

MORROW: Everyone, please be seated.
*(*ROSS *makes no objection to the usurpation, just sits down.)*
I want to state for the record that Ronnie looks terrific in a dark suit. Now to reinvigorate our energies, I spent some time with my naturologist who has drawn up a plan of physical preparedness for all of us. The mind and the body are quite

closely linked. I can't force you to follow it, I'm a firm believer in the free will, but—

RONNIE: You recommend we follow it.

MORROW: Let's not get started, Ronnie. We'll start our program by cutting down on our intake of dairy products. Joanne, I want you to see that this family eats little or no mucus.

JOANNE: Mr. Morrow, what are you implying?

MORROW: Joanne, I don't know if you're prepared to become mucus-free, but I'd like to see you start to move in that direction. The next step will be morning calisthenics, followed by a program of high colonics and German foot baths—

*(*VAL GUIDO *enters the suite into* PATTI'S *office. She looks around, hears the voices, starts towards* ROSS'S *office.)*

This is not to suggest vegetarianism. Quite the contrary. I want you to increase your intake of organ meats, and red meats cooked extremely rare.

*(*VAL GUIDO *enters the office without knocking.)*

ROSS: Excuse me, Val. It's always wonderful to see you, but we're in the middle of a meeting here.

VAL: Sorry to disturb you.

*(*ROSS *tries to escort her out, she brushes past him, goes around the desk towards* MORROW, *smiling to everyone.* MORROW *stands.)*

ROSS: Is everything okay, Val? Is anything up?

VAL: Things are way up, Ross.

*(*VAL *is behind the desk, winks at* MORROW. MORROW *doesn't know what's up, doesn't know whether to smile at her or not. He sits down.* VAL *smiles, demurely opens her purse, fumbles around in it, looks at them apologetically for being a clumsy old woman, then suddenly whips out of her purse a small, pearl-handled automatic. She holds the pistol to the stunned* MORROW'S *head.)*

JOANNE: Oh my God.

VAL: Shut up, Joanne.

(VAL leans over the desk, pulls MORROW'S pistol out from the holster in his pants.)

MORROW: What do you think you're doing?

VAL: Young men with guns make me nervous. Get out of this seat. I'm sitting here.

(MORROW doesn't move.)

I'll blow your brains out.

(MORROW can hardly believe it, but does what the old lady says. He finds a seat on the couch. ROSS goes to close the door.)

Just sit down Ross.

MORROW: I expect to get my gun back.

VAL: Ross, people are upset with you. I had a conversation with Pinkey this morning. And I had a conversation with Solly Dubin last night.

ROSS: Solly doesn't think I'm going to do anything wrong, does he?

VAL: He thinks you've done something wrong already.

ROSS: But I haven't done anything.

MORROW: Let her speak, Ross.

VAL: Ronnie's a nice young man and I'm sure he's intelligent. But I don't know him. Pinkey doesn't know him. Solly Dubin certainly doesn't know him. Nobody knows him.

ROSS: Dr. Berk knows him. You've met Dr. Berk, right Ronnie?

VAL: We'll get to that in a minute. Look, Ross, don't make it difficult. You're being called to testify and people expect you to keep your mouth shut—not to concoct some hairbrained plot where we wind up worrying about whether this kid, who we don't know, is gonna break and say something stupid somewhere along the line. You're scared shitless of us, so you we can trust. Him we don't know.

RONNIE: You don't have to worry. I'm as big a chicken as Ross.

VAL: Kid, shut up.

RONNIE: I'm twenty-nine years old—I'm tired of being called a kid—

VAL: Kid, shut up. Now, Ross, you got to take your own knocks.

ROSS: I don't know if I accept this.

VAL: Oh Ross, I know you're confused and aggravated, that you don't know where to turn. That's why I'm here. You have a lot of problems.

ROSS: I'm glad to see that somebody appreciates that.

VAL: Everybody appreciates it. And they realize that because of all that's happening you can't really be worrying about the business. *(*ROSS *begins to comment, then falls silent, considers what's just actually been said. Everyone is looking at* VAL.*)*
We just can't trust you, Ross. You have an hour to clean out your desk, we'll take care of cleaning out the safe, thank you. And you'd better understand that this doesn't relieve you of any obligation to keep your mouth shut.

ROSS: I built this place, Val.

VAL: This'll all get straightened out when everybody's satisfied that you've behaved properly.

ROSS: I'm ruined. We're all ruined.

VAL: Not yet. I like you Ross.

ROSS: You keep saying that.

VAL: So I've contacted your old friend Dr. Berk and asked him to come here this morning and talk to you.

ROSS: YOU WHAT? How could you call Dr. Berk without discussing it with me?

VAL: I thought the guy was your friend.

ROSS: My God! Dr. Berk doesn't have to be involved in this.

VAL: Well, otherwise you don't have a prayer. You knew you were gonna be out, I'm just trying to help, to get you a reprieve. You know Berk is the only one who . . .

RONNIE *(to* ROSS*):* Whoa! What's she mean that you knew that . . . if you knew that you were going to be out of . . .

ROSS: Who said what?

RONNIE: I thought Val just said . . .

ROSS: She doesn't know what she's talking about. She'll say anything. She's senile.

VAL: Let's not get carried away, Ross.

RONNIE: So you don't know anything about—

ROSS: Little friend, if I said I was going to take care of you, I was going to take care of you. Now are you backing out on me and Joanne?

RONNIE: I just want to make sure I'm not getting ripped off.

ROSS: Number one, I take that as an insult. Number two, I want you to stop listening to Patti who's telling you God knows what.

PATTI: Hey Ross—

ROSS: Number three I want you to apologize to your sister for what you're inferring that we would do. Number 3A I want you to apologize to Val Guido for making me insult her. And number four—*(*ROSS *hugs* RONNIE*)* I want to thank you for staying. *(to* PATTI*)* Are *you* still on the team?

PATTI: Yeah. But I'm hoping to get traded.

ROSS: Ronnie, I happen to have a $550,000 house. Anything goes wrong, you get the deed.

JOANNE: Now just a second—!

ROSS: Relax Joanne.

*(*ROSS *summons all his energy.)*

Okay, I had a five-minute nervous breakdown, but now I'm okay. I'm going to take charge of this and we're going to work our way out of it.

*(*ROSS *just shoots* JOANNE *a look.* RONNIE *has calmed down, but now his face shows the signs of confused defensive suspicion.)*

I'm sorry I lost my head, Val. It's not that Dr. Berk scares me, he's just an important, busy man. But like plenty of people he owes me favors, and now I'm ready to call in the debts.

*(*RONNIE *whispers quietly to* JOANNE, *who is mesmerized by her husband's performance.)*

RONNIE: You guys weren't gonna screw me, were you?

JOANNE: How could you say that Ronnie?

RONNIE: I don't know.

JOANNE: Then just shut up!

(They all turn and look at JOANNE. *She smiles for* ROSS *to continue. He turns to* VAL.*)*

ROSS: Now, Val, I'm furious that people don't have confidence in me that if I work something out for my family—

VAL: People haven't been happy for a long time, and you know it. It goes all the way back to the tin roof.

ROSS: I had nothing to do with the tin roof.

VAL: Oh, Ross, you supervised the construction. How the hell could you build a tin roof on a theater in the suburbs? All you gotta do is call the weather bureau and you find out that they get sixty inches of rain out here. I'm backstage opening night, and with the rain hitting the tin roof it sounds like I'm back with Bob Hope in Vietnam.

ROSS: Val—it was Pinkey's contracting company that put on the roof.

VAL: So? That's part of the game. He was looking to make a couple of extra bucks. So you're supposed to have the brains to tell him to do it the right way.

ROSS: I'm supposed to know? The man is an investor in this place. I'm supposed to know he's ripping himself off, and I'm supposed to stop him? He's a dangerous man. If he wants to take a short-term profit, what am I supposed to do? He's a lunatic.

VAL: Well, you knew who you were getting into bed with. You loved the position, you loved all those gorillas hanging around this place as your assistants. You loved thinking you were a bad guy. But there's more to this scene than just lifestyle. You gotta be willing to put it on the line, and that's where you always backed off. If you hadn't, you might've gotten some respect.

ROSS: That kind of respect I don't need.

VAL: Then you shouldn't have played the game.

ROSS: And now Dr. Berk—.

VAL: Come on, I thought I was doing you a favor. If he buys what you're pitching, he can straighten everything out for you. *(to* RONNIE*)* Make an impression.

*(*VAL *walks out of* ROSS'S *office, makes herself comfortable in* PATTI'S *office.* JOANNE *runs up to* ROSS *and kisses him.* MORROW *butts in.)*

MORROW: I want my gun back.

JOANNE: Ross, ask Patti to leave. I don't want her here.

ROSS: Joanne—okay enough already. *(to everyone)* Ronnie, everybody—Dr. Berk is the one man who can pull us out of this. He's a brilliant and wonderful scientist . . . and a dangerous man. I expect everyone to show him the respect he deserves.

RONNIE: Let me just hear it again, so before you make any committments on my part—

ROSS: The committments have already been made. By you. And by us to you. So we all still love each other, right?

*(*RONNIE *nods.* ROSS *suddenly looks at him in horror.)*

RONNIE: What is it?

ROSS: Ronnie, take out the earring. You're meeting Dr. Berk.

RONNIE: I've met Dr. Berk.

ROSS: But maybe we're lucky. Maybe he doesn't remember. Come on, take out the earring.

*(*RONNIE *removes the earring.)*

And the hair—oh my God.

*(*RONNIE *glances at the mirror, doesn't get it.)*

Joanne, Patti, don't just stand there. Find me a pair of scissors. We gotta cut off that stuff trickling down the back of his neck.

RONNIE: It's gonna look worse, Ross.

ROSS: Not if you cut it.

RONNIE: I can't cut my own hair on the back of my head.

ROSS: Well then, what are we going to do? What are we going to tell Dr. Berk when he asks you about your haircut?

PATTI: Tell him it's a Duke Ellington haircut.

ROSS: That's great! Okay, everybody got that? It's a Duke Ellington haircut. Okay, Ronnie?

RONNIE: Yeah, sure.

*(*VAL *is sitting quietly in* PATTI'S *office when the door to the suite opens and in walks* DR. BERK. DR. BERK *is in his seventies, small, solid, very tan, with thin white hair, manicured hands. He wears a tuxedo, bowtie, and a doctor's reflector strapped cockeyed on his forehead.* VAL *gives him a big smile.)*

BERK: How are you?

VAL: Not good. Everything happens to me.

BERK: So? What else is new?

VAL: Thanks for coming.

BERK: I like Ross and his lovely wife Joanne. He's in over his head, but I like him. If I can do something, I'm happy to. Val, I must tell you, I've come from a very exciting conference. You know, the study of medicine, with all its setbacks and frustrations, is still man's highest pursuit. The work that some of these young physicians are doing would have been unthinkable even thirty years ago. Of course, if socialized medicine comes in, God knows what destruction it will wreak on the profession. God knows how many infants will never see the cures that are so near around the corner through properly funded experimentation. You know, when I left comedy to enter medical school—

VAL: Save it for a convention.

BERK: Get off my back, Val. Did you hear about the lox shortage?

VAL: You mean, Did you hear the one about the lox shortage?—

BERK: This is serious. Do you know why lox is so expensive today? It's because of the Russians. The Russians are hoarding lox. That's why it costs so much. It's a conspiracy, and the salmon are in the middle of it.

VAL: Do you want to see Ross?

BERK: Take me in to see the man.

*(*VAL *takes* DR. BERK *by the arm into* PATTI'S *office.)*

ROSS: It's such a thrill to see you, Dr. Berk. You know Felice and Nicole haven't stopped talking about the time you took them to the Institute.

BERK: Phyllis and Nickel, wonderful children. Both of them geniuses. And Joanne—this beautiful daughter of Zion, who, may I say, is responsible for numerous saplings in the Holy Land of Israel.

ROSS: Doctor, you know Patti, of course, and I think you've met Ronald Nathan, Joanne's brother.

BERK: There's a hole in your earlobe. Why?

RONNIE: Motorcycle accident.

BERK: He rides a motorcycle—?

JOANNE: Not anymore he doesn't.

BERK: Well, thank God for that.

ROSS: And this is Kevin Morrow. He's helping us out with our legal advice.

*(*MORROW *gets out of his seat, shakes* BERK'S *hand.* BERK *gives* MORROW *a hard look.)*

BERK: Never do that again.

MORROW: What did I do?

BERK: Never squeeze a person's hand when you shake it. You can cause irreparable damage. The hand has some of the most sensitive nerve structures in the body. I suppose you all know what happened to Jerry Sirola at the La Costa Spa? Like a fool, Al Martin comes up to him and shakes his hand. Jerry went down.

He had to be rushed to the university hospital in San Diego. The man was in a coma. He finally came out of it last week, but it was up in the air whether he was going to be paralyzed for life.

ROSS: Just from shaking somebody's hand?

BERK: It's an epidemic.

(They react. BERK *observes* MORROW'S *ankles.)*

What's the matter? Forget to put on your socks this morning? Ross, you got a lawyer who puts on his shoes and forgets to put on his socks.

MORROW: Dr. Berk, I didn't forget—

BERK: So what are you, a clam digger or something? There's an emergency clam to dig up, so you don't have time to take off your socks? But I gotta tell ya—I've spent an entire lifetime studying nerves and their symbiosis with the eyes. You look into a nuclear atomic microscope at a tiny sample of nerve, and what do you see? You see synapses meeting to give and receive information. For the imparting of information is the highest function that man can aspire to. The man who uses his mind—he's the man who works hard. Not the garbage man or sod carrier, no, it's the Doctor, the Scientist—

(He looks around, sees who he's got.)

—and the Entertainer, the Entrepreneur, and the Lawyer. *(right at* ROSS*)* But when you look into the microscope, you'll come to the Institute—it's just fascinating—and with these nuclear microscopes you can almost see the history of the development of man. But as hard as you look, into the double helix, into the microstructure itself, as hard as I have looked, I still can't understand why the fuck I have to be called up here to talk to you.

*(*ROSS *is speechless, tries to talk, just mumbles.)*

I don't like being involved in these things. I introduce people, I'm happy to give advice. But when things begin to heat up, I'm the last person you would want to get involved.

ROSS: I didn't mean to involve you. It was Val here who called—

BERK: It's already done. Now I have a young Korean doctor on my staff who's unlocked an almost invisible parasite that inhabits the fresh waters of Nicaragua and Costa Rica. If imbibed into the bloodstream, this parasite will travel into the brain and slowly consume the brain cells, until a year later the victim dies. With no brain.

ROSS: This is in Costa Rica?

BERK: We're close to solving this mystery at the Institute, and if we do I will have the opportunity of leaving an even greater legacy than the one that I've already carved out for myself. So you have to understand that the kind of shit you're into, if it got out and my name was attached, would make me more than a little annoyed.

ROSS: Dr. Berk, I wouldn't—

BERK: I was in business with you so I guess I can do you a favor. But you've pissed me off, so don't expect to ever hear from me again.

VAL: Go easy on the guy.

BERK: Val Guido, I salute you. You're a lovely daughter of Romulus and Remus and the delightful city they founded, home of His Holiness the Pope, whom I've had the pleasure of meeting, and for whose missions of peace I pray—but if you don't mind, keep your mouth shut for two minutes. *(to* RONNIE*)* Ronald, you'd like to do the right thing by your brother-in-law? To protect this man who's helped you, you're prepared to go to jail.

RONNIE: Dr. Berk, you're a heavyweight. It's great to have you on board.

BERK: You gotta listen to the young people, they have something to say. *(back to* RONNIE*)* And what would you like to do with your life?

RONNIE: Maybe open a rock club in the Bowery.

BERK: Ronnie, you may accuse me of archaic beliefs and values, but today's music is such a circus of queer performers and mongrels that it's an abomination to anyone who wears a wedding ring, *yarmulke,* or cross.

RONNIE: Yeah? Well then maybe I'll open a haircutting place.

BERK: I think that's more sensible. And if I may be so bold, how is your health?

RONNIE: I got sciatica, man. It hurts.

BERK: Well, there's a new miracle drug I've been prescribing for Joanne. And how about your mental condition?

RONNIE: Well, I've only been to a psychiatrist once. I had this tension headache for two weeks, right here—For two weeks I was in pain. I took every drug but it wouldn't go away, so finally Ross took me to a psychiatrist.

BERK: And what was his diagnosis?

RONNIE: He told me to relax.

BERK: Don't try to humiliate me, you little prick. I wrote that joke forty years ago.

RONNIE: But it's true.

BERK: Ronnie, I don't play the straight man for you, you play the straight man for me. You don't think I didn't know there was a joke there? If I wanted to hear a joke there I would have made a joke there.

JOANNE: Ronnie, apologize.

BERK: I wrote that joke. Val, what did they used to say about me? Put Berk and Shakespeare in a room, see who comes up with the jokes.

RONNIE: I'm sorry, Dr. Berk.

BERK: Ross, I can't believe this is the idiot you're hanging this all on. Where'd you come up with this idea?

MORROW: It's my idea. We discussed a series of options and agreed that—

BERK *(to* MORROW*):* Well, since it's your idea I'm holding you personally responsible—Wait a second, this is *my* idea!

(They all look at him. BERK *smiles warmly at* ROSS.*)*

Ross, I may be getting slow in my old age, but it's good to see my disciples have learned some of the lessons I've taught them—*(he smiles at* VAL*)*—It's one of my routines, the old Egyptian flimflam. Ross and me pulled this one off fifteen years ago. We found some joker in Cairo, what was his name—?

ROSS: It rhymed with "camel"—

BERK: Gamel! Right! We got this Gamel to set up a dummy importing company for us and we start running these drums of inert pesticides that we picked up in Jersey City for three cents a ton and we're selling if for eleven dollars a pound. If it wasn't for the Six Day War we'd be billionaires!

ROSS: Those were the days.

BERK: So this is the same thing?

ROSS: Of course.

BERK: Ross, I'm honored. This is better than a testimonial dinner. Makes me feel young again. Okay, let's take a flyer with this kid. I like a gamble.

Robin Karfo and Salem Ludwig in the JRT production of *Friends Too Numerous to Mention.*

RONNIE: What happened to Gamel?

BERK: Who cares?!

*(*PATTI *draws her finger across her throat.)*

BERK *(to* ROSS*):* You knew your time was limited here anyway, but you tried your best, and I'm actually quite intrigued to see if we can pull this off. I'm excited. I'll make some calls for you. Ronald can speak for you with the understanding that he says nothing, at all, about anything.

*(*BERK *puts his arm around* ROSS, *fatherly, takes him aside.* RONNIE *listens.)*

I'll see that you have a little breathing period, perhaps longer than the few months that Val originally discussed with you. As always, if things work out properly, when it cools down and you're resettled in Florida, we'll take care of you. Naturally I'm still holding you totally responsible for all this. It's not that I don't like you, it's not that I don't believe you, it's—

RONNIE: It's that you don't trust the guy.

(They all fall silent and look at him, too amazed to speak. RONNIE *also seems frozen, trying to control his anger.* BERK *doesn't get it, smiles to* VAL *that it's time to leave.)*

BERK: Well, Val, let's be going. God, I feel good about helping people, and I don't mind going out on a limb for Ross—

MORROW: Uh, she has my gun. I want my gun back.

VAL: I took it away from him. It made me nervous.

BERK: Do you want to give it back to him?

VAL: Actually, I'd rather keep it. It's a nice gun. I kind of like it.

MORROW: I don't believe this. I don't believe this. I want my .38 back.

*(*VAL *takes out* MORROW'S *.38, but holds it tightly.* BERK *looks at the .38, disapproves, looks at* MORROW, *shakes his head.)*

BERK: You don't want a gun like that. You want something more like a nine millimeter—nine shots in five seconds—it's the kind of gun a man like you should carry.

MORROW: I want my gun.

BERK *(to* VAL*):* I see his point. He knows what we could do with a gun with his prints on it.

*(*VAL *shrugs, gives the gun back to* MORROW. RONNIE, *who has been watching the whole scene, putting everything together, is getting angry.* BERK *and* VAL *turn to leave.)*

RONNIE: Uh, Ross—

ROSS: I appreciate it, Ronnie, but you don't have to say anything. This is what love is all about. Say goodbye to Dr. Berk.

RONNIE: Ross, I hate to disappoint you, but . . .

JOANNE: What?

RONNIE: You been putting one over me and I ain't gonna do it.

BERK: Oh boy, Ross.

ROSS *and* JOANNE: Ronnie, what are you talking about?

RONNIE: You knew you were gonna be out, so how were you gonna set up a fund for me? I know you guys don't have a dime in the bank—so just what the hell were you going to set up?

JOANNE: The little bastard's worrying about his money.

RONNIE: It's not the money. It was the setup. I was gonna take the fall and you weren't even gonna back me up. You wouldn't even let me know it was happening.

ROSS: Well, the more you know, the more liable you are. I was trying to protect you.

RONNIE: Even you tried to make a fool out of me. I feel so sick right now I wish I was dead.

*(*JOANNE *turns to* PATTI.*)*

JOANNE: You're behind all this, aren't you, you little bitch.

*(*JOANNE *goes for her,* ROSS *holds her back, embarrassed in front of* BERK *and* VAL.*)*

BERK: What's going on here, Ross? Can't you even control these infants?

ROSS: Everything's under control.

RONNIE: I'm not under control, not anymore. I saw your eyes when this jerkoff Berk started talking about Costa Rican parasite water. You were gonna take care of me? Set something up? Obviously the only thing getting set up was me.

BERK: Hey, punk, what did you call me?

RONNIE *(to* PATTI*)*: Their bags are packed, aren't they?

PATTI: Well, I don't know if they're packed yet.

JOANNE *(to* PATTI*)*: What did you tell him?

PATTI: Nothing. It's pretty obvious though what's happening.

RONNIE: Yeah. You guys have been rearranging the chairs on the deck of the Titanic.

MORROW: This isn't like you, we made a bargain. And when I know a guy, and I like a guy—

RONNIE: That's already two strikes against him.

MORROW: Now listen, Ronnie—

RONNIE: Just shut up. You're as big a jerkoff as Dr. Berk.

(At this BERK *lets out a yell and charges across the office, his hands out to grab and strangle* RONNIE. VAL *tries to restrain him, is slowly pulled across the office.* ROSS *turns quickly to* PATTI.*)*

ROSS: You gotta help me. Tell him I wasn't out to screw him. Tell him to apologize to Dr. Berk. Save me.

(She turns to RONNIE.*)*

PATTI: Don't wind up here like me.

MORROW: Oh, she's great. *(to* RONNIE*)* Kid, you've got to learn to transcend moments like these—

RONNIE: Enough of the Brave new World bullshit. Ross tried to screw me. I'm out.

*(*ROSS *turns mean, grabs* PATTI *by the shoulders.*RONNIE *picks up his helmet and baseball mitt to leave the office.)*

ROSS: You obviously have a lot of influence, and you've obviously forgotten all that you mean to us, to me, and to the kind of family we've been for the last ten years.
(He shakes her.)
So I'm going to ask you once. Tell him to do the right thing.

PATTI: What's the right thing?

ROSS: Tell him to do what we agreed to. Tell him to save me.

PATTI: He can't save you. It's too late.

*(*ROSS *angrily pushes her down.* JOANNE *rushes over to kick her, then* ROSS *readies to hit* PATTI *if she tries to get up.* RONNIE *turns from* BERK, *runs over to tackle* ROSS. MORROW *pulls back* RONNIE, *they struggle,* MORROW *pulls out his gun, holds it on* RONNIE.*)*

MORROW: Stay back. Those are my clients.

BERK: Okay. That's enough.

*(*VAL *whips her gun from her purse, waves it at* MORROW.*)*

VAL: Yeah. Knock it off.

*(*ROSS *turns, shocked to see* VAL *pointing a gun in his vicinity, points to* RONNIE.*)*

ROSS: He's the one you should shoot.

*(*BERK *glances at* ROSS, *shakes his head, disappointed. He then turns to* MORROW *who inadvertantly points his gun at* DR. BERK. BERK *frowns, carefully, removes the gun from* MORROW'S *hand, holding the gun like a fish, hands it to* VAL.*)*

BERK: You're not ready to carry a gun.
MORROW: I didn't mean to point a gun at you, Dr. Berk.

*(*VAL *helps* PATTI *to her feet.* PATTI'S *lip is cut.)*

BERK: Let me look at that wound. I'm a doctor.
PATTI: Just stay away from me.

*(*BERK *is stunned.* ROSS *sits down, hold his head.)*

ROSS: I'm going crazy. I can't handle it. I can't go to jail. I can't testify. Patti, I hit you. What am I doing? I'm going crazy.
VAL: Pipe down!
BERK: Morrow, I want you out of here now. *(to* RONNIE*)* Kid, stay of of New Jersey or you're in trouble.

*(*RONNIE *sneers at him, goes over to see if* PATTI'S *all right.* MORROW *speaks quickly to* ROSS.*)*

MORROW: Listen, maybe it's not so bad if Ronnie can't help us. I mean, this guy Berk is crazy—he's gonna hold me personally responsible. I mean he's a lunatic—don't get me wrong, he's brilliant, a great humanitarian—but this guy has killed people. He probably killed people on the operating table—
BERK: Are you going to leave under your own power or what?
MORROW: I'm leaving. I'm leaving.
(He starts to go, tries to be friends with BERK *at the expense of* ROSS.*)*

That guy's nuts. He beat up his secretary.

*(*MORROW *backs out quickly, waving goodbye.)*

ROSS: I *am* crazy. I'm sorry Patti, I'm crazy. That's it, I'll plead insanity.

BERK: Good luck, pal. You're a real disappointment. And I'll never forgive you for risking my Nobel Prize.

(He turns, grabs VAL, *drags her out of the office with him. The door closes behind them.* JOANNE *turns to* PATTI *and* RONNIE.*)*

JOANNE: How could you let us down?

ROSS: I'll become *Hasidic;* a born-again Jew . . .

JOANNE *(to* PATTI *and* RONNIE*):* This is what you've done. Are you proud?

RONNIE: Hey Ross, you got out of Egypt, you'll get out of Danbury.

PATTI: I'll come visit you, Ross. I've appreciated being part of the family.

JOANNE: Ha.

PATTI: Goodbye Ross.

*(*PATTI *leans in to kiss him,* JOANNE *holds her off.* PATTI *shrugs, turns and takes* RONNIE'S *arm.)*

RONNIE: Hey Joanne, think of me when you're trying to sell that $650,000 house.

*(*PATTI *drags him out the door,* RONNIE *yanks it closed behind them.)*

JOANNE: Well, it's nice to see the rats leaving the sinking ship. *(A beat—her hands on* ROSS'S *shoulders.)* Ross, darling, at least we have each other. At least *we're* still a family.

(He looks up at her, his eyes sad, inquiring.)

ROSS: Joanne, would *you* do if for me?

JOANNE: Oh Ross. Don't be a *schmuck.*

(Curtain.)

Taking Steam

a comedy in two acts by

KENNETH KLONSKY AND BRIAN SHEIN

Kenneth Klonsky, *Taking Steam.*

Brian Shein, *Taking Steam.* (Photo: Peter Higdon.)

KENNETH KLONSKY was born in New York City in 1946. He received his B.A. from the University of Vermont and his M.A. from the University of Toronto. He lives in Toronto, is a Special Education teacher in Scarborough, and an Education writer for *This Magazine.*

Born in Lindsay, Ontario in 1947, **BRIAN SHEIN** now lives and works in Toronto. *Theatrical Exhibitions,* a collection of his stage and radio plays and writings about theatre, was published in 1975. He also has produced a number of documentaries for CBC Radio and Vancouver Co-op Radio and a documentary film, *Potlatch: A Strict Law Bids Us Dance.* He won Canada's 1983 National Author's Award for Humour, and has worked as writer and editor for *National Lampoon.*

Taking Steam was a great success in its Jewish Repertory Theatre production, both with audiences and critics. Richard F. Shepard, in his *New York Times* review, wrote, "It is a good slice of life . . . one that unerringly rings true, down to its very feel, intonations and inflections."

It opened at the Leah Posluns Theatre in Toronto in October 1983. In an astute review, Mitchell Moldofsky of the *Globe and Mail* summed up the play and its characters as follows:

> They know each other too well to believe in the bold exteriors they wear with pride, as an armor against the creeping arm of death. When their time comes, these men will go out kicking and screaming, their very last breath an affirmation of life. Even when liquor is served in this "health" club, they cancel out the contradiction by offering the traditional Jewish toast, *"l'chaim."* To life.

TAKING STEAM was first produced by the Jewish Repertory Theatre in April 1983 with the following cast:

YANKELE	Felix Fibich
MAX GLASS	Herman O. Arbeit
BEN SAPERSTEIN	Jack Aaron
MOE PERL	Maurice Sterman
EDDIE FINE	Frank Nastasi
HENRY WALLACH	Harvey Pierce
JACK SHERMAN	Herb Duncan

Directed by Edward M. Cohen
Set by Adalberto Ortiz
Costumes by Melissa Binder
Lighting by Dan Kinsley

Time: The present. Winter
Place: The Men's Health Club of the old YMHA, Toronto.

Act I. Morning
Act II. Late afternoon

Act I

The stage is divided into two main areas. Dominating stage right and center is the larger area: the locker room. Characters entering locker room pick up their towels at an offstage check-in desk and enter the locker room through a door upstage left. There are several rows of lockers, all numbered, some with small strips of black tape on which the locker owner's name has been punched. An impression of many more rows of lockers stretching back upstage. Downstage are some benches and two bicycle machines.

Upstage right is an offstage steam room with a glass door.

On the downstage right wall of the locker room is a large mirror and basin, used for shaving. Stage left is the smaller area, perhaps at a lower level than the locker room: the TV room. It contains some chairs and a TV set that faces away from the audience and is perched high above the viewers.

Downstage right is an exit to the offstage whirlpool area. Throughout the club, many signs and notices—rules and warnings—are posted on walls. On one wall is a black button with the sign: "In case of emergency, push."

Downstage right there may be a room or closet from which YANKELE *brings such items as mops and bolt cutters.*

YANKELE, *about seventy years old, the locker room attendent, sits alone on a bench in the locker room sorting a pile of towels, placing the white towels into a bin. He looks up and addresses the audience.*

YANKELE: Welcome. Only you're not so welcome. Not unless you got one of these. *(holds up white towel)* You know what this is? No? Don't talk to me.

*(*YANKELE *returns to his sorting. He finds a blue towel in the pile, and holds it up with disdain.)*

You don't come in here with a blue towel. You got a blue towel—there's a door down the hall, goodbye.

(Discards the blue towel, and picks up another white one.) With one like this you're talking business.

*(*MAX GLASS, *seventy-three, hurries in through the check-in door. He is elaborately dressed for winter in headgear, galoshes, overcoat, and muffler. He carries two white towels. He goes behind the first row of lockers to his own locker to change.)*

YANKELE: You see? He's got his. Doesn't even have to show his card anymore. They give him the towels. *(holds up white towel)* Lifetime member, Men's Health Club, YMHA, Bloor and Spadina, Toronto, Canada.

*(*BEN SAPERSTEIN, *mid-forties, dressed in fashionable winter clothes, enters through the check-in door with his two towels. He goes behind the first row of lockers to change. Throughout this act,* YANKELE *collects shoes from various lockers.)*

That one, he still has to show his card. So now you know. With this . . . *(holds up white towel)* . . . you belong. One you should dry yourself, one you should step on. You want to wet your skin, you want to warm your skin, you want to burn it to a crisp, beat hell out of it? In short you wanna relax? This is the place. Somebody says it looks shabby. Old. Take a whiff. No, go ahead, don't be shy. Smells rotten, you bet. Stinks. But listen—a new branch up north they built, all new facilities, clean as your mother's kitchen floor. So Yankele, you're asking me, how come they still go here? What's the big deal? This is where it all began—south of Bloor. Spadina. Robert Street. Harbord. Palmerston Boulevard. Sure, the neighborhood's changed. But not when you come in here.

MOE *(from behind lockers):* He's dead. He's dead. He's dead. He's dead. He's dead. He's dead.

*(*MOE, *early seventies, lumbers into view. He carries an open school yearbook.)*

Howie Zuckerman, ten years ago in Me-ah-mee. Red Kaye—

YANKELE *(exiting, with bin):* There was a guy.

MOE: There was a guy! Me-ah-mee. Now Zavitz. Lenny Zavitz. Died in Pompano. Yesterday. I can't believe it. Lenny. Ziggy. Sammy. Al. Louie. Harry . . . Harry Vogel. Whatever happened to Harry Vogel?

EDDIE *(from behind lockers):* He's dead. You know he's dead. Forget it.

MOE *(closes book, holds it up):* You know what this is? Harbord Collegiate. Nineteen thirty-three. The class of Thirty-three.

*(*EDDIE*, early seventies, enters wearing a towel.)*

EDDIE: Enough already.

MOE: Vogel's our leader. Let me tell you the story.

EDDIE *(shouts, off):* Here comes the Harry Vogel story!

MAX *(from behind lockers):* Who died?

EDDIE: Zavitz.

BEN *(from behind lockers):* What?!

EDDIE: Lenny Zavitz!

BEN: No kidding!

MAX: Lenny!

MOE: No, let me tell you. This is at Harbord Collegiate. All these guys are in the class—Zavitz, Zuckerman, Kaye . . .

EDDIE *(shouts, off):* I was in the class. I sat right behind him.

MOE: And Harry Vogel. He sits right behind me. So let me tell you what happens.

MAX: Lenny!

EDDIE: Shaddup, Max!

MOE: No, no kidding, listen to me. We got this *goyishe* teacher. What's her name? I forget her name.

EDDIE *(mumbles):* Henderson.

MOE: Hands of Stone! That's it, that's what we call her. Hands of Stone. So she asks all of us to bring in a flag. She says, "Everybody bring in a flag from whatever country you come from. Or make one."

EDDIE: Why doesn't the guy shut up?

MOE: No listen . . . so who has the idea to bring in the Jewish flag?

EDDIE: Vogel.

MOE: Harry Vogel! He gets us all to bring one in—the Jewish flag. So the teacher, Hands of Stone—

EDDIE: We've heard it. *(shouts, off)* Haven't you heard it? The flag?

BEN *(from behind lockers):* Oh yeah. When old what's-his-name died. When Howie died.

MOE: No, stop kidding. I'm gonna tell you. Hands of Stone, she says, "The Jewish flag is not where you come from." So she takes Harry's flag to the front of the room—

EDDIE: Not Harry's. It was Zuckie's. He can't even get it right.

MOE: She takes the flag. She holds it up. She says, "See this flag. Here's what I think of this flag."

EDDIE: I know, they know, we all know.

MOE: No, she actually says it. "Here's what I think of this flag." Throws it on the floor. Steps on it. Rubs it into the ground. Our flag. Nobody says a thing. We're waiting—waiting for Harry. And you know what Harry does?

EDDIE: No, I don't know. I only sat behind you. Hey, will you shut up!

MOE: Harry Vogel stands up and says, "We're walking out. We're walking out until you're fired!" And we follow him out that door. All of us. They'll never forget.

EDDIE: Not with him around.

MOE: What a bunch of guys. *(opens yearbook again, looks at pictures)* Zuckie, Al, Red Kaye, Lenny.

EDDIE: Me.

*(*YANKELE *enters.)*

MOE *(shakes head sadly):* Lenny Zavitz. I'm the only one left.

*(*HENRY WALLACH, *eighty, in overcoat and hatless, cheerfully enters the locker room through the check-in door.)*

YANKELE: No hat!

HENRY: Uh-oh. Moshe's got the yearbook out. Who died?

EDDIE: Zavitz.

HENRY: Too bad. Am I in time for the Harry Vogel story?

EDDIE: You just missed it.

HENRY: Great!

*(*HENRY *opens his locker in the front row, and begins to change into a track suit.)*

YANKELE: Ten below outside.

(Oblivious to all, MOE *lovingly shuts the yearbook and exits past* YANKELE, *behind the lockers. He drops a towel on the floor on his way.)*

MOE: Nineteen thirty-three! What a class! They're still talking about us.

YANKELE: Celsius.

EDDIE: Yeah, talking. Look who's talking.

*(*YANKELE, *shaking his head, picks up* MOE'S *towel, and dumps it into the used towel bin.)*

YANKELE: Ignorant.

MOE *(from behind lockers):* Fiftieth reunion coming up. Wouldn't miss it for the world.

HENRY: He's gonna have a surprise. Nothing but Chinamen the last ten years.

EDDIE: You think that guy is gonna notice? He'll be talking Yiddish all over the school.

YANKELE *(points to sign on wall; reads):* "Members must place used towels in towel bins." They have to be told.

EDDIE: So we still playing tonight?

HENRY: The card game? Sure. It'll be in Lenny's honour. Did you call Monty?

EDDIE: Sure Monty. Get Silverstein.

HENRY *(chuckles):* Herb Silverstein. Only bets a winning hand. Marvin . . .

EDDIE: Tells too many jokes. Put him at Monty's table.

HENRY: Moe Perl?

EDDIE *(resigned):* Moe Perl.

HENRY: How about Sammy?

EDDIE: He's not around. He went over.

HENRY: No, he's back. He went down.

EDDIE: Okay, Sammy. Don't forget Saltzman, Murray, Irv—

MAX *(off):* Henry! Siddown!

HENRY: Max?

EDDIE *(shakes head, a definite no):* Please.

(MAX enters from behind the lockers. He carries rolled-up massage charts, massage oils, a racquet, a loofah sponge, and a tatami mat.)

MAX *(loudly):* I said siddown! You're not gonna believe it. The prime of life. Just like that—boom!

HENRY: You talking about Zavitz, Max?

MAX: Lenny Zavitz! What're you just standing around for?

EDDIE *(to HENRY, indicating MAX):* You gotta shut him up.

HENRY: Max, Max.

EDDIE: Jack'll be here any minute now.

MAX: For Christ sake already! Don't you remember Lenny's retirement party? Three years ago? The guy put out for us! Free case of whiskey . . .

EDDIE: If Jack hears it from The Mouth, he'll have a heart attack.

YANKELE: Listen, anything should happen, God forbid, push the button.

HENRY: Eddie, Eddie . . .

MAX: Who cared enough to get him a present?

EDDIE: Henry, do something.

MAX: Who? Me! Max Glass!

HENRY *(to MAX):* Shhh!

MAX: Ran all over town. Got it gift-wrapped. Got a card—a special card. Made a speech. "Lenny, you may be moving down there but you still got a special place in our hearts" . . . *(slaps LENNY'S locker)* . . . "just like you're keeping a special place in our club" . . .

HENRY: "Number four-one-six."

EDDIE: "Forever."

MAX: I gave him the present. Shook his hand. You saw!

EDDIE: We heard.

MAX: Told him! You're down there—go to Fletcher's. Order up the Crab Louie! The man was one-of-a-kind. There's nobody here anymore. I don't know what I'm gonna do.

HENRY: I never realized you two were that close.

MAX: Close?! *(intertwines fingers)* Like that! You needed a guy to play racquetball—Lenny Zavitz. A *schnapps*—Zavitz. Kept this club going. *(to EDDIE and HENRY)* You! You! He kept you alive with his jokes.

EDDIE: Lenny Zavitz never gave a damn about anybody.

MAX: Ask Jack! Jack Sherman. He'll tell you what Lenny did for him!

HENRY: Max. Let us break the news to him.

MAX: Jack phoned me, Friday midnight. He just got back. Couldn't sleep. Asked me, "Should I go to *shul* or should I come to the club?" Of course you come to the club! Sunday, ten-thirty.

HENRY: Max, shhh!

MAX: He's already a sick man! When I tell him about Lenny—

HENRY: Max, *I'm* going to tell him about Lenny. Not a word out of you. Promise.

MAX: I promise. Soon as you tell him, send him to the whirlpool. He's gonna need that treatment! *(flourishes charts)* Korean! *(exits to whirlpool)*

EDDIE: Max Glass is not coming to that card game tonight.

HENRY: Eddie, Eddie, you better calm down.

EDDIE: What're we carrying on for? Zavitz kicked off. If Jack were smart he'd celebrate. Live it up.

HENRY: Still, we gotta break it to him gently.

EDDIE: It's A-B-C. The boyfriend's dead.

HENRY: You think that's what Jack wanted?

EDDIE: Come on. Zavitz was camping out in Jack's condo for fifteen years. Every winter.

HENRY: You learn to live with it. You make adjustments.

EDDIE: Oh sure! Some fat slob is *schtupping* your wife, leaving his hair in your sink: sure, make adjustments!

HENRY: Jack never complained. Every winter Ceil's down at the condo. Lenny kept her happy.

EDDIE: Zavitz got the wife; Jack got the business.

HENRY: Well, Ceil gave Jack visiting privileges on the weekends. Now Lenny's left the both of them high and dry.

(JACK, *mid-sixties, in overcoat and hat, enters through the check-in door.)*

HENRY: Jack, you got a lovely tan.

JACK: Yeah, you think so? You don't notice I'm peeling?

HENRY: Not a bit. Here, Jack, let me help with your coat.

(MAX *enters.)*

MAX: Jack! . . .
HENRY: Not now, Max.
EDDIE *(to* MAX, *gesturing him off):* Shhhhh!
MAX: Jack Sherman!
EDDIE *(to* MAX*):* Get back in there!
HENRY *(to* JACK*):* Here, sit down.
JACK: Whatsa matter, fellas?
MAX: Lenny Zavitz—dead! Just like that! Dead!
EDDIE *(threateningly advances on* MAX*):* Max Glass . . .
MAX *(retreats into whirlpool):* You see what you made me do? *(exits)*
JACK: Lenny Zavitz? Naah. He's not dead. You guys are putting me on. He's not dead. No, tell me, Eddie, Zavitz isn't dead, is he?
EDDIE: Jack. It was bound to happen. The guy lived on chicken fat. *(exits behind lockers to change into track suit)*
YANKELE: Tch, tch, tch. *(exits)*
JACK: Come on, Henry, this isn't something you joke about. He's not really dead.
HENRY: Must've been great down there. How'd you do at the jai alai?
JACK: I saw him there. I saw him everywhere.
HENRY: Who, Lenny?
JACK: Yeah, the jai alai, the ponies, the dogs.
HENRY: Scotch in one hand, Yankee dollars flying out the other. Shooting off his mouth.
JACK: Even at the beach.
HENRY: That's how you're gonna remember him.
JACK: You're telling me he's dead.
HENRY: But you, Jack, you're the picture of health.

*(*JACK *starts to get undressed. He ends up wearing boxer shorts, shoes and socks, and a t-shirt emblazoned with the words "Rondela Fashions" in ugly block letters.* YANKELE *re-enters with a mop and pail, and starts mopping the floor in a desultory manner.)*

JACK: Me, I'm nauseous the whole week. I haven't been feeling well. I been eating wrong. The food down there repeats on me.
YANKELE: Excuse me. *(mops past* JACK*)*

HENRY: Really? Didn't you try that fish place Max always raves about?

JACK: *That* place! What's it called, Henry? The Lighthouse? The Swordfish? No, what's it called? The Fishouse?

HENRY: Fletcher's, Jack. It's called Fletcher's.

JACK: Don't remind me! You know the place I mean. By the water. Can you believe this? She insisted that we meet him there!

HENRY: Him?

JACK: Zavitz. What could I do, Henry?

HENRY: I don't know. Did you try the Crab Louie?

JACK: God! Don't even mention the stuff!

HENRY: Specialty of the House!

JACK: Too much mayonnaise—and they let it *sit!* I was up all night.

HENRY: You and Ceil and Lenny Zavitz—dining at Fletcher's!

JACK: I didn't feel good, let me tell you. I got on the phone to Toronto. The business was a mess. You think I wanted to get back to that table? What am I supposed to look at? Zavitz? The Crab Louie? Then she says, "We're going to a nightclub." No, whadya think?

HENRY: Hot spot?

JACK: It was in Lauderdale. Lenny drove. Had his foot on the floor the whole way. What could I do?

HENRY: Who'd you see there? Who was featured?

JACK: Ahhh, you know, what's-his-name. The guy.

HENRY: Don Rickles? Frankie Sinatra?

JACK: Ahhh, the Chinese Sinatra. No, no, what is he—Japanese? Hawaiian?

HENRY: You mean Don Ho. I know the place. The Luau. Lenny gets a piece of the action.

JACK: Yeah. It was dark.

HENRY: Thank God for that.

JACK: Fires in the floor. And down at one end they got a grotto and, would you believe it, they got the ocean coming out of there?

HENRY: Beautiful.

JACK: That's where Don Ho comes in on a boat with gorgeous girls, him singing.

HENRY: Aloha ho.

JACK: No, what do you think? Lenny was up on his feet throwing change at the girls. She was furious. Dragged him back to the table. Knocked over a lava lamp.

HENRY: Just like Lenny to kill a perfect evening.

JACK: I don't know. Two hundred plus tip. Don't you think that's too expensive, Henry? He only sang three songs! The boat went out, our bill came in.

HENRY: Don't tell me! That's when Lenny hadda go to the washroom.

JACK: Ahhh, what am I worried about? It's on the business. Thank God for that business. It costs you to sneeze down there. What do you think I gotta lay out to play golf? Take a guess. Green fees, caddie cart . . . No, come on, take a guess.

HENRY: Fifty, sixty dollars.

JACK: More. You know how much? A hundred and eight dollars. Ugh! It was hot. Lenny only played one hole.

HENRY: Did you say Lenny? Now you're playing golf with him? Jack.

(YANKELE *stops mopping, and stands with arms folded on top of mop, shamelessly listening.)*

JACK: He just showed up at the condo. She pushed the both of us out the door. She said, "You two boys go play. I'll be back here making pina coladas."

HENRY: So you only played one hole?

JACK: No, Lenny quit. He told me, "Get in your eighteen holes. Get the business off your mind. I'm gonna help Ceil mix those drinks." I hadda keep playing. What was I supposed to do?

HENRY: Jack.

JACK: I know. I know. It was bad. I couldn't find any shade. The doctor said I coulda died of sunstroke.

MAX *(yells from whirlpool, off):* JACK!! They finish telling?

(YANKELE *starts mopping again.)*

HENRY: I think Max Glass is calling you.

JACK: Max? What does he want?

(EDDIE *enters from behind the lockers, dressed in a track suit. He signals to* HENRY.*)*

HENRY *(cheerfully, to* JACK*)*: He wants to give you a massage. Go ahead. We're going jogging.
YANKELE: Jogging! On the ice they can't go jogging. They'll slip.
HENRY *(to* EDDIE*)*: So what'll we do? Go up to the gym?
EDDIE: Yeah, the gym.

*(*HENRY *and* EDDIE *exit through the check-in door.* BEN, *wearing a towel and carrying a shirt, enters from behind the lockers.* MOE *enters and walks right through* YANKELE'S *mopping toward the showers, dropping crumbs as he goes.* YANKELE *glares at him.)*

BEN: Haay, Jack, Jack baby. *(playfully slaps* JACK'S *face)* Lookin' good, lookin' good. Catchin' those rays. *(scornfully plucks at* JACK'S *t-shirt)* What's this? *(indicates his own shirt)* Hey, you know what they're lookin' for: the alligator. No little umbrellas, no penguins, no cheap ads. The real McCoy! That's what they go for. By the way, how's Ceil?

*(*MAX *enters.)*

MAX: Jack, I'm waiting for you.
BEN: Not now, Max.

*(*BEN *casually knots his shirt to the door of Lenny's locker.* MOE *stops to watch* BEN *and* MAX.*)*

MAX *(sees shirt)*: What's this?
*(*MAX *takes the shirt off the door and flings it at* BEN.*)*
Take it off.
BEN: Just staking out my territory. Four-one-six.
MAX: You want that? Lenny's locker? Don't you touch it! It's mine!

*(*MOE *exits to the showers.* YANKELE *shrugs, then exits carrying the mop and pail.)*

BEN: Yours? You couldn't get the time of day from Lenny Zavitz. Ben and Lenny. *(intertwines fingers)* Like brothers.
MAX *(dismissively, to* JACK*)*: You hear that?
BEN: Can't you see the man's busy?

MAX: What, with *you?!*

JACK: I'll be right there, Max. I just gotta talk to Ben. You know, business.

MAX: What kind of business! Your best friend just died!

BEN: Best friend!

MAX *(to* JACK*)*: You need a treatment. Hurry up. I'm in the whirlpool. *(exits)*

BEN: What are you doing with that old jerk?

JACK: I don't know. I did something stupid. Really stupid.

BEN: Stop right there. That's a put-down. It's coming from your wife.

JACK: He phones me Friday midnight. Says he can't sleep. Says he hasn't had a racquetball partner in three weeks. Asks me, "Should I go to *shul* or should I come to the club?"

BEN: Racquetball? In the whirlpool?

JACK: I didn't know how to get rid of him. Ahhh, what's the matter with me? I'm crazy.

BEN: Jack, that's Ceil talking again. I never took that crap from Fran. You're a beautiful guy.

JACK: Me? You think so?

BEN: Absolutely. Your friends know it. You gotta start believing it. Now what does Max want?

*(*MAX *enters, carrying charts.)*

JACK: He wants to give me a treatment.

MAX: Jack Sherman, come get your treatment.

BEN: A treatment. Max, we told you after Manny's son—no more treatments.

MAX: This is different.

*(*MAX *unfurls a chart which shows an outline of a foot.)*

JACK: He's got a chart.

MAX: I only do the foot now. I read the article. The foot's connected to everything—like a computer . . .

BEN *(to* JACK*)*: Not even you could fall for this.

MAX: You push here—the liver! Push here—the sinuses. Here—the sex.

BEN: Here—the quack.

(MOE *enters from the showers, drying himself. He stops in front of the towel sign, reads it, then lets his towel fall to the floor. He goes to TV room, turns on the TV, and seats himself with an elaborate ritual.)*

MAX: It's Korean.

BEN: Korean! Korean war torture, Jack.

MAX: I shoulda been a doctor! Doctors! I got stuff they never even heard about!

BEN: Jack, the guy may be seventy-three but he's strong as an ox. He'll break your bones.

MAX: Whadya put on a cut?

JACK *(to* BEN*):* Maybe he can help.

MAX: A *wound?* To stop the infection?

BEN: Stop his mouth.

MAX: Your own urine! Your own urine! On a cut you put your own urine! No doctor's gonna tell you that! You gotta come to Maxie! You guys need me. *(to* BEN, *indicating* JACK*)* Look at him, look how he looks. *(consults his chart; points)* The colon, I dig the thumb in.

JACK: I don't know.

MAX: Jack Sherman, get into that whirlpool!

BEN: He told you—later.

MAX *(grabs* JACK'S *arm):* Now! He's had a shock.

BEN: Let go! He's not interested.

JACK: It's no good. I'm dizzy.

MAX: He wants from me. Ask him.

(JACK *edges away into the TV room.)*

BEN: Jack, there you go again, getting pushed around. Don't let him manipulate you. Don't let anyone manipulate you. Quacks, wives, lawyers!

JACK: I gotta sit down. Really.

MAX: I know you! You got nothing to tell him. What, you're gonna take him for one of your singles weekends? I heard—you all lay in a pile and feel each other.

BEN: He's a very confused man, Max. You don't know what he's going through.

MAX: Ahhh!! Jack, where ya going?

(MAX *enters the TV room, sees* MOE, *dashes to the TV set, and turns it off.)*

You watching this? No? Turn it off. *(to* JACK*)* Look what you're doing, I'm losing my charts!

BEN *(from locker room):* Jack! Be strong! He's gonna try guilt!

MAX *(to* BEN*):* Shut up! *(mutters)* Little *pisher.*

BEN: It's what the wives do.

MAX *(to* JACK, *affectionately):* Come on, *schmucksie,* I don't have all day.

JACK: I don't know. You guys leave me alone. I'm not up for it. I don't feel well.

MOE: You gotta eat the right breakfast before you come in here. Anna brings me toast, you can put a little cream cheese and jelly. Black coffee. Boiled egg, three minutes. And a grapefruit.

(YANKELE *enters the locker room, pushing an empty towel bin with a squeaky wheel. He wears a black armband and carries a large bolt cutter.* HENRY *and* EDDIE *return from the gym through the check-in door.)*

BEN: Hey! They're gonna open the locker!

MAX *(rushing into locker room):* Who? What?

(YANKELE *slowly makes his way along the front row of lockers, stopping at each to read the name tape.)*

MAX: Here, this one, over here!

BEN: Four-one-six, open her up. She's waitin' for me. *(points to tape)* You see, Lenny Zavitz!

MAX: Yours?

BEN: Fifteen years I been listening to you guys bullshit. The least I'm getting out of it's a decent locker. Up front. Where the action is.

MAX: You're too soon now and you'll be too late then. Henry, you tell 'em.

(YANKELE *takes a piece of dark cloth from his bin, walks to the shaving mirror, ceremoniously covers the mirror with the cloth, and walks back to the locker. He points to the name tape.)*

YANKELE: Lenny Zavitz. Name's been here for twenty-five years.
MAX: Where's Jack? Jack Sherman, get in here!
YANKELE: Not such a long time.
MAX: Wait! *(runs into TV room)*
YANKELE: They like to see their names. It's an extra but they all want it.

*(*YANKELE *prepares to cut the lock with the bolt cutter.* MAX *drags* JACK *into the locker area.)*

MAX: They're opening his locker. Ya gotta see.
JACK: They can't do that, can they?
MAX: Shhhhhhh!! Show respect.
JACK: No—the body. Don't they have to have the body first? Isn't it a legal thing?
EDDIE: He's Perry Mason now. Watch out.
MAX: Silence!

*(*YANKELE *cuts the lock. All watch expectantly.)*

MAX: They're gonna open!
JACK: What's the matter with you guys? There's nothing to see.

*(*YANKELE *eases the door open a few inches. A bunch of stuff falls out: shorts, socks, running shoes, a jock strap.)*

MAX: Watch it! Watch what you're doing!
(As YANKELE *picks the stuff up,* MAX *speaks.)*
Pick it up! Whadya got there?

*(*MAX *pulls the shorts from* YANKELE *who dumps a few items into the bin.)*

BEN: Hey, that's quality! Where do they take it?
EDDIE: They re-sell it at the pro shop.
JACK: Hey, c'mon fellas, that's enough. You wouldn't want everyone staring at your stuff.

*(*YANKELE *holds up a brand-new jock strap. Like the rest of Lenny's stuff, it is huge.)*

EDDIE: Still got the price tag. Quite an athlete.
HENRY: A physical specimen.
BEN: Did Lenny ever tell you the one about the camel?
MAX: Hey, quit joking around.
JACK: I'm leaving. *(doesn't move)*

*(*YANKELE *opens the locker door wide. The locker is chock-full and a mess. On the inside of the door is an autographed photo of Peggy Lee. Hanging in the locker is a very long object wrapped in waxed paper.* YANKELE *removes it, and holds it out questioningly.)*

MAX: Take it out! *(grabs object, puts it on bench)* Put it here.

*(*MAX *unwraps the package and a salami is revealed.)*

YANKELE: Smelled for days . . . weeks . . . Funny . . .
EDDIE: Get rid of it.
MAX: It doesn't go bad.
BEN: Lenny! Front and centre! The man himself! Hey Jack, you get a load of that?
JACK: What's so funny?
EDDIE: Get rid of it. It stinks.
MAX: You don't throw out a perfectly good salami.
BEN: Hey, Jack. Did Lenny ever tell you the one about the camel? You know, the horny old guy in Miami Beach?

*(*HENRY *and* EDDIE *groan, recognizing the joke.)*

JACK: I want to know what's so funny.
MAX *(to* BEN*):* Silence! A man died! You think because you're young . . .
HENRY: For God sakes, Ben. Keep it down.

*(*BEN *quiets down.)*

MAX *(squints into locker):* What's the matter, you blind or something? There's tons of stuff in there.

(YANKELE *takes out a box of crackers, a jar of Cheez Whiz, a half-empty bottle of scotch, and some Dixie cups. He puts them beside the salami on the bench.)*

BEN: Good old Zavitz! He knew how to live!
MAX: Who're you? What do you know about him?!
YANKELE: Lot of get-togethers at four-one-six. Crumbs everywhere.

(YANKELE *finds a box of expensive cigars, and moves to throw them in the bin.* HENRY *steps forward and stops him.)*

HENRY: Yankele. Please.
MAX *(to* HENRY*):* Stop him. Don't let him do that.

(HENRY *hands out cigars to everyone.)*

JACK: You're not gonna do that, are you? Expensive cigars?
HENRY: Only the best.
BEN: You too, Jack. They're Lenny's.
JACK: No, really. I don't feel like it. *(takes cigar)*
BEN: Take it. You know how good they are.

(BEN *reaches into the bin, produces a gold-plated lighter, and moves to light* JACK'S *cigar.)*

MAX: Jack Sherman, no smoking! It's a health club.

(HENRY *collects the cigars.)*

HENRY: After supper.

(EDDIE *pours scotch into the Dixie cups, and hands them around.* MAX, *trying to help, only interferes.)*

MAX: Drink! Lenny Zavitz—a beautiful guy! A prince. A good word for everybody. Never too busy. Gave to the *shul.*
EDDIE: Sing us a song, Max. The guy thinks he's a rabbi.
MAX *(points to spot beside locker):* Right here! At the retirement party. He stood right here. He took my present. Gift-wrapped. Gorgeous! Special card.

BEN: Can you believe this guy—a complete egomaniac.
MAX: You got a lot to learn, young man! Nobody lives forever.

*(*MOE *lumbers in from the TV room, as if unaware of what is going on. He is given a cup and automatically toasts.)*

MOE: *L'chaim!*

(Pause. Everyone does a doubletake.)

HENRY *(shrugs): L'chaim.*

(They all drink. A party scene quickly forms around the locker. EDDIE *opens the crackers. A plastic knife is produced and someone slices the salami.* JACK *hovers nervously at a distance from the others.)*

JACK: It's good.
MAX: Hey, see if there's any mustard in there.
EDDIE: Max wants mustard.

*(*HENRY *rummages through the bin.)*

HENRY: What do you know. Here's my old stopwatch.
MAX: Look some more. I loaned the guy my goggles.

*(*YANKELE *finds mustard.)*

EDDIE: Mustard.

*(*MOE *has commandeered the Cheez Whiz and is seated apart.)*

BEN: So there's this old guy, he retires to Miami Beach. Hey listen! Lenny's favorite joke. Wants to set up a harem. So he figures, I gotta catch their eye. Buys a camel.
MAX: Hey! Tell Perl to pass that Cheez Whiz!
EDDIE: He wants the Cheez Whiz.
BEN: Shut up everyone! I got a joke here. Rides the camel up and down Collins Avenue, parks it at a restaurant. When he comes out it's gone.

Harvey Pierce, Herman O. Arbeit, Jack Aaron, Herb Duncan and Maurice Sterman in the JRT production of *Taking Steam.* (Photo: Adam Newman.)

MAX *(peers in locker):* Hey, is that my goggles! *(to* MOE*)* Moe! Moe Perl! The Cheez Whiz!

BEN: Give him the Cheez Whiz and shut him up. Okay, so he calls a cop. "Officer, mine camel's been stolen!" "What kinda camel?"

EDDIE: "It's a boy camel, officer."

HENRY: "How do you know it's a boy?"
EDDIE: "All day I been riding on Collins Avenue, I heard them shouting—
HENRY and EDDIE: "Lookit the *schmuck* on that camel."
MAX: What camel? Where?
EDDIE: Got any more jokes, Ben?

*(*MOE *slowly gets the last of the Cheez Whiz out of the jar with his finger. Meanwhile,* YANKELE *is taking items from the locker: a soap dish, deodorants, baby powder, baby oil, skin creams, shampoo, rinses. He dumps them into the bin.)*

MAX: What's that? What's in these? Shampoo! Throw it out!
JACK: Is that all? That the last of it?

*(*BEN *takes the empty Cheez Whiz jar from* MOE, *and shoves it at* MAX.*)*

BEN: Here. Now shut up.

*(*MAX *looks in the jar, and shoves it close to* BEN'S *face, pointing inside.)*

MAX: Lookit this! It's finished. *(shoves jar into* BEN'S *hands.)*
JACK: What? The locker's empty?
BEN: Haaay, we're just getting to the good stuff.
HENRY: Jack, come here. Look at this. You ever see one of these?
JACK: No, what is it?

*(*EDDIE *waves* JACK *over to the locker.)*

MAX: What? What? Hand it here!

*(*JACK *approaches. He is relieved when he sees what* HENRY *is holding.)*

JACK: Oh, a watch.
HENRY: See? World time. No matter where you are. New York. Miami. Tel Aviv.
JACK: Hey, no kidding. How do you do that? Do it again.

(EDDIE *finds a Polaroid camera in the locker, and holds it up.)*

EDDIE: Watch the birdie!
BEN: Lenny had a Polaroid.
MAX: Ben Saperstein, you keep your hands off that!
HENRY: Come on, we gotta have a picture. For the occasion.

(YANKELE *finds a blue religious bag in the top part of the locker, and holds it up questioningly.)*

YANKELE: Does he got family?

(No one hears YANKELE.*)*

MAX: Get outta here. I take a terrible picture.
HENRY: Over here.

(HENRY *leads* MAX *and* JACK *over to where* MOE *is sitting on the bench. They group around* MOE. BEN *tags along, and gets into the group.* EDDIE *aims the camera.)*

EDDIE: Move in a little Max. Yeah, that's right.
BEN: You're blocking me out, Max. Sit down.
YANKELE: Does he got family?
EDDIE: Ben, come here.
(BEN *comes over as if to help* EDDIE *adjust the camera.* EDDIE *hands him the camera.)*
It's all set. Just press this.

(EDDIE *goes to take his place in the group.)*

YANKELE: Does he got family? *(shrugs, puts bag on bench)*
EDDIE: Cheese, everyone.

(BEN *snaps the picture.* MAX *leaps to his feet, rushes to* BEN *and grabs the camera.)*

MAX: Don't touch it! Here, pull the tab! *(pulls picture out)* Open it!

EDDIE: Max, not yet!

(MAX rips the cover off the picture. Everyone gathers around MAX.)

JACK *(looking at picture):* It's dark.
BEN *(to MAX):* You idiot! There's no more film. You ruined the last shot.
MAX: Whadya talkin' about? It's fine! Look, there's Henry.
HENRY: That's Eddie. I think.

(YANKELE finds a blonde, woman's wig in the locker. He holds it out and waits, puzzled.)

MAX *(to BEN):* You didn't do it right! You clicked too fast.
BEN *(seeing YANKELE):* Haay, all right!
EDDIE: Big joker, Lenny.

(BEN takes the wig from YANKELE, goes behind the lockers and puts it on.)

BEN: Remember his Belle Barth routine? In the steam room?
(BEN enters, singing and dancing.)
"I lined a hundred men up against the wall. I bet a hundred dollars I could bang 'em all . . ."
(BEN gets a pair of rhinestone-encrusted harlequin sunglasses from YANKELE, who has pulled them from the top of the locker.)
Oooohh, look what we found!
MAX: My goggles!
BEN *(puts on glasses; imitates woman's voice):* Hey, Maxie, wanna cool off in the pool?
MAX: What, those ain't my goggles!
JACK: Gimme those!
BEN: Finders keepers.
JACK: Goddammit, gimme those! You see what you guys done?
BEN *(in woman's voice):* Why Jack, you're so forceful.
JACK: I told you to leave that locker alone!
HENRY: Jack?
JACK: They're hers! He knows they're hers! What's she trying to do to me?

EDDIE: Ceil?

BEN: Jack, these your wife's sunglasses?

JACK: She said she lost them. Made me buy her a new pair.

BEN *(as Ceil):* Oh Jack, I must have left them on the beach.

HENRY: Ben, enough.

BEN: *(removes wig; dumps glasses into bin):* Who are you protecting? Her? They're all the same. *(exits behind lockers)*

MAX: Little *pisher.*

HENRY *(to* JACK*):* Don't worry about it. It'll all be forgotten by tomorrow.

JACK: Ahhh . . .

HENRY: Jack, Lenny's out of the picture. Everything's changed. You've got a nice place down there. You can enjoy it now.

EDDIE: Sure, let him go down tomorrow.

*(*BEN *enters, goes to the shaving basin, lifts the cloth off the mirror and tucks it back. He starts shaving.)*

BEN: Sorry, Lenny.

*(*MOE *examines and appropriates the blue religious bag. He disappears momentarily behind the lockers.)*

JACK: What are you talking about—tomorrow?

HENRY: Why not tomorrow?

MAX: Hey, whatsa matter with you guys? They haven't finished yet.

JACK: I got business here! What does he mean?

EDDIE: Tell him to retire.

JACK: Retire?!

HENRY: Retire.

JACK: Line up at Publix Market for sales on tomato juice?

HENRY: Sure. Pick up your Golden Age card. See a few movies.

EDDIE: A dollar-fifty.

JACK: That's children's prices! I'm an executive.

EDDIE: Oh. Rondela Fashions.

JACK: Thirty-two years! You've seen the place. They're coming down every day from Forest Hill. Asking for Jack.

MAX *(to* YANKELE, *pointing to top part of locker):* Back there! In the top! There's something!

*(*YANKELE *finds and removes a gift-wrapped package.* BEN, *shaving, tweaks his own cheek.)*

BEN: Haay boychik! How ya doin'?

*(*MOE *reappears with the yearbook and sits by himself.)*

HENRY: Let them ask for someone else. Jack, you don't have to pretend anymore.

JACK: But the house. The garden. What if the kids visit?

EDDIE: The garden! He's crazy.

YANKELE *(reads card on package):* "To Lenny. On your retirement . . ."

MAX *(grabs present):* My present. From the party. Three years ago!

EDDIE: The present. The present!

MOE: "Everybody bring in a flag from whatever country you come from. Or make one . . ."

EDDIE: Harbord Collegiate! He's crazy.

MAX: Sitting here for three years. At the back of a locker. I buy the guy a present and he doesn't open it. He's crazy!

JACK: My business, my house, my kids—my life!

HENRY: Stop pretending, Jack. That's not your life. Your life is down there.

JACK: What? With her?

EDDIE: Yes, with her!

MAX: Put myself out. Ran all over town. Got it gift-wrapped. A special card.

MOE: She says, "Here's what I think of this flag!"

MAX: Not cheap either. Goddamn right not cheap!

EDDIE: This place is a nuthouse! Tell him to leave while he can.

JACK: I know what she'll do. Run me around shopping malls. Dress me up in white pants. Make a fool out of me.

MAX: Throws it in the locker. Slams the door. What does he care?

MOE: "We're walking out. We're walking out until you're fired . . ."

JACK: What the hell's down there? Golf?

HENRY: Ceil.

EDDIE: Ceil Sherman.

JACK: I don't wanna play golf for the rest of my life.

MAX: You know what I think of Lenny Zavitz?

EDDIE: Lenny Zavitz—a beautiful guy! A prince!

MAX: He never gave a damn. He never gave a damn. Lenny Zavitz never gave a damn about anybody! *(dumps present into bin; exits. Lights out.)*

Act II

HENRY, EDDIE, MAX, JACK *and* MOE *are in the TV room. A lull.* YANKELE *is slicing bagels and smearing cream cheese on them. A coffee urn and styrofoam cups sit on a table.* JACK *is in undershorts, t-shirt, shoes and socks. A pair of pants is draped over the chair next to him.* MOE *is dozing.* MAX *is reading the paper.*

YANKELE: They wear themselves out. They complain. They need a snack. Some people can get for themselves. These ones. . . . A smear of cream cheese, a little grape jelly for taste. . . . Every day it's the same. More or less.

JACK *(to* MOE*)*: Another thing about Raisin Bran—You know those little boxes. I betcha never knew what the dotted line was for.

*(*MOE *snores.)*

JACK: You know what I mean, Moe—the dotted line they got going down the middle of the package.

*(*MOE *makes a noise as if awakening, but remains asleep.* EDDIE *takes a bagel, and starts to eat it.)*

YANKELE: For shame, they eat a bagel with only the towel on.

JACK: No, come on, take a guess. I heard Saltzman talking about it. All these years I been eating the stuff.

EDDIE *(pours himself coffee)*: Leave him alone.

YANKELE: And hot coffee from the urn!

JACK: All right, Eddie, I'll give you a hint. You cut along the dotted line and pull the flaps open. Okay, now what's it for?

EDDIE: To take a crap in.

JACK: No really, it's fantastic! You actually eat from it!

EDDIE: Jesus.

HENRY: Jack, I told you you've been working too hard.

JACK: I know what you're thinking. Why doesn't the milk leak out? Right, Henry?

(MAX slowly lowers his newspaper, and stares incredulously at JACK, then raises the paper again. MOE slowly awakens.)

JACK: Well, I'm gonna tell you. When you cut the box, you're cutting through wax paper at the same time. The wax paper holds the milk in. See, Henry, just like a bowl. Now all's I got's a cup, kettle, knife, a spoon, toaster. That's one less thing to wash.

EDDIE: For God's sake, why doesn't he use the dishwasher?

JACK: *The dishwasher?* She never taught me.

MOE *(half-asleep, gets to his feet)*: Is it lunch time?

(MOE goes to the table, and loads up with bagels and coffee.)

YANKELE *(to MOE)*: Eat.

JACK: Every winter she goes down. I got it all worked out.

HENRY: You're not fooling anybody, Jack. You need your wife.

MOE: No, we had lunch.

JACK: You know what Normie told me? When Shirl goes down he buys himself extra underwear, extra socks. So whadya think I did? December twenty-fifth she left, April first she's coming back. That's ninety-seven days. So I got myself ninety-seven pair of underwear, ninety-seven pair of socks. Wholesale.

(MAX lowers his paper, looks at JACK, then raises it again.)

HENRY: Jack.

JACK: And the shirts I send to the cleaners.

MOE: Soon it's my supper.

JACK: You know something else?

HENRY: I'm not sure I'm ready for it.

JACK: I sealed off the master bedroom, the boys' room, the dining room. Put plastic over everything. I'm using Ronnie's bedroom, the kitchen, the downstairs washroom. Three rooms, that's all I need.

EDDIE: Disgusting! You live like an animal—like an I-don't-know-what, a subterranean.

JACK: What, I should open up the master bedroom?
MOE: Anna. She makes a gorgeous pot roast.
EDDIE: We told you, sell the house.
MAX: Move out!
JACK: What if the boys come back?
EDDIE: They're too old.
YANKELE *(shakes head sadly):* Tch tch tch. *(exits out check-in door)*
HENRY: You got the condo. You got Ceil, a good-looking wife.
JACK: You never know. Daniel—he's brilliant.
EDDIE: An intellectual.
MOE: On a cold day there's nothing like it. You open the front door. A gush of warm air. Smell it—*pot roast.*
EDDIE: Mothballs.
JACK: Eddie, you remember my Daniel. Talking in the Harbord Bakery to his fiancée about MacDuff. I told him, he's a natural businessman. He shoulda stuck it out.
EDDIE: Forget Daniel. Forget the business.
MOE: Got buttered carrots.
MAX: Now he's going to start on the *kugel.*
MOE: It's a good *kugel.* A *lukshon.* With cinnamon and raisins. Melts in your mouth.
HENRY: Ceil makes a *kugel* like that.
JACK: Okay, forget Daniel. The youngest—he's out west. Says he's a choreographer. What the hell is that?
EDDIE: Dancing.
HENRY: So what's for dessert, Moe?
MOE: Honeycake. Maybe a fruitcake.
JACK: You think he's a fairy?
MOE: And a grapefruit.
MAX *(to* JACK*):* What'd you say?
MOE: Doctor Krantz says, "Eat whatever you want. Only don't forget the grapefruit."
JACK: I can't leave! I gotta be there for when the customers come in.
EDDIE: He's too important. They'll dig him up to run the place.
MOE: You want a snack any time of day—cheese, a smear of chicken liver, a drink—go ahead.

*(*YANKELE *re-enters the TV room, shivering.)*

YANKELE: Gentlemen. What it's like out there I wouldn't tell you. A deep freeze. Outside you shouldn't poke your nose out. Stay here. *(starts to clean up table)*

MOE: It's the enzymes. The grapefruit cuts through all the other stuff, breaks it down to practically nothing.

*(*BEN *enters from behind the lockers.)*

BEN: Hey Moe, how they hanging?

MAX *(to* BEN*):* You! I see you! You get away from that locker!

BEN: What locker, Max? Oh, you mean Lenny's? *(slaps Lenny's locker)* Four-one-six?

*(*BEN, *teasing* MAX, *sits in front of the locker.* MAX *exits behind the lockers.* MOE *exits to the steam room.)*

JACK: It's not so bad. I'm happy here.

EDDIE: He's happy.

JACK: You don't go down there to stay. It sets in.

EDDIE: Whadya got here? Room and kitchen, houseful of dirty laundry, box of Raisin Bran. You call that living?

JACK: April first'll be here before you know it.

EDDIE: So?

JACK: April first she's coming back. April first she's cleaning up.

EDDIE: That's great, Jack. You got it made.

*(*EDDIE *and* HENRY *exit to the locker room.)*

JACK: Hey, wait you guys!

HENRY: Take it easy, Eddie.

JACK: We're talking.

EDDIE: We told him. I can't stand he doesn't listen.

*(*MAX *enters, and crosses to the showers.)*

MAX *(to* BEN*):* Don't you try nothing.

HENRY *(to* EDDIE*):* Listen, about tonight. I've been thinking about Max.

EDDIE: No! Never! Absolutely not!

HENRY: We can't do that. He's got to be at the game.

(A terrible silence.)

BEN: Card game tonight?

*(*HENRY *and* EDDIE *ignore* BEN.*)*

HENRY: Just an idea. Put him at the back and forget about him.
EDDIE: You're soft in the head.
HENRY: Maybe for later. For cake.
EDDIE: Sooner. Later. Never!
BEN: Whose house?
HENRY: They'll wonder.
EDDIE: Forget it. Under no circumstances! No Max Glass! He's not invited.
BEN: It's time we got tough with Max.
EDDIE *(notices* BEN*):* Hey, playboy. Mind your own business.

*(*BEN *goes to the TV room.)*

JACK: Henry, you really think I should use the master bedroom?
HENRY: What?
JACK: Like we were talking about. The master bedroom.
EDDIE *(to* HENRY*):* Don't answer him. He's crazy.
HENRY *(to* EDDIE*):* Look, it's Sunday. You're all worked up. Relax, have a good time.

*(*EDDIE *stops behind the lockers.)*

EDDIE: You call this a good time? It's the health club, that's all.

*(*HENRY *gets on a bicycle, and starts pedalling.)*

BEN: Haaay, Jack. The master bedroom! You're hitting the scene! Don't tell me, I don't wanna know her name.
*(*JACK *is at a loss.)*
No, two of them. Sisters! I gotta hand it to you, Jack. That's getting back at Ceil—hey, in her own bedroom.
*(*EDDIE *comes out from behind the lockers wearing a track suit. He climbs on a bike and pedals.* YANKELE *has finished cleaning*

up the TV room. He walks past HENRY *and* EDDIE *carrying the bagel box, then exits.)*

So what's her name?

JACK: Who?

BEN: The girlfriend.

JACK: No, what do you mean?

BEN: Who's this woman you been taking into your bedroom?

JACK: Are you implying sex? *(laughs)* I'm a married man.

BEN: To Ceil.

JACK: I get nauseous thinking about it. I got pains up here—in my shoulder. No kidding, I get indigestion in my shoulder.

BEN: Avoidance, Jack, avoidance. What were we talking about? Your marriage, Jack. *Empty*—like the house.

JACK: I got terrible gas.

*(*MAX *enters the locker room, then goes into the steam room. While the steam room door is open,* MOE'S *voice is heard.)*

MOE: I can have anything I want . . . even a *bobka* . . .

(The door closes.)

BEN: Get rid of her. I dumped Fran. It's not the end of the world. Jack, how old are you?

JACK: Old. You know, sixty-five.

BEN: Old? You wanna see old?

*(*BEN *drags* JACK *into the locker room, and points to* HENRY *who is still pedalling.)*

Look at this guy. Seventy-nine years old.

HENRY: Eighty.

BEN: All right, eighty. His mind's acute, his body's great, runs five miles every morning. Early to bed . . .

EDDIE: Eats his Wheaties.

BEN: He gets it up anytime he wants.

HENRY: No, that I got some trouble with.

BEN: You mean it gets you into trouble.

HENRY: It can be troublesome, let me tell you.

BEN: It doesn't go away. It's waiting. Latent.

HENRY: It's asleep.

BEN: Aw, he's modest. Look who we got here. A legend. Eddie the *Trenner*. Two, three times a day. Rat-tat-tat.

EDDIE: No, I don't.

BEN: Well, maybe he's wound down a little.

EDDIE: I can't. Not anymore.

HENRY: But Eddie—the memories. It's like the supermarket. There's the memories stocked along the shelves. You pull them down, you re-taste them. It's better than the real thing.

EDDIE: No it's not.

BEN: Sure. I told you. He still gets the real thing.

EDDIE: What's it to him? If I lie he's gonna believe me. If I tell the truth he thinks I'm lying. I told him—I can't do it.

(MAX *enters from the steam room.* MOE'S *voice is heard again.)*

MOE: . . . just don't forget the grapefruit . . .

MAX *(slams door):* The guy's bugs! He's talking to the walls! *(indicates bicycle machines)* You staying on those all day? Give somebody else a turn! *(turns to shower room)* Ya hear that? The showers. Drippin' away. I gotta run in there twenty times a day to turn them off. *(rushes off to showers)*

JACK: Henry, I gotta talk to you.

BEN: Okay Jack. Take some time. Breaking free from that bitch—I never said it was gonna be easy.

HENRY *(to* BEN*):* Are you talking about this man's wife?

BEN: Wife? Chapter Last. The End. They're rolling the credits.

JACK: Henry, please. It's serious. I gotta talk to you alone. *(re-enters TV room)*

BEN: I tried to build the guy up! Whadya giving him this can't-do-it stuff. That's not what he needs to hear. Ya gotta think young. *(pats his face)* Time for my steam.

HENRY: Ben, how old are you?

BEN: How old do I look? Forty-three.

HENRY: You got one or two good years left.

BEN: Buncha wise guys.

(BEN *exits to the steam room, and shuts the door.)*

EDDIE: He never had them.

HENRY: Eddie the *Trenner*. A real pair of balls.

EDDIE: You better believe it.
HENRY: The girls are still talking about you.
EDDIE: Never missed a day.

*(*YANKELE *enters carrying a "NO SHOUTING" sign. He sees* EDDIE *and* HENRY *still on the bicycles.)*

YANKELE: Slow down, slow down. It can happen sometime. A little knot here. But listen, anything should happen—God forbid—push the button.
*(*YANKELE *shuffles along with the sign, and starts to position it on the wall.)*
Yankele's gonna come running.

*(*HENRY *gets down from his bicycle.* MOE *emerges from the steam room, begins to shut the door, then deliberately leaves it open.)*

BEN *(inside steam room)*: Hey! Shut the door! *(shuts door)* That stuff is precious!

*(*MAX *charges into the locker room.)*

MAX: The whirlpool! Ya hear it goin'? Who's in there? Nobody!

*(*EDDIE *gets off his bicycle, and escapes to the whirlpool.)*

EDDIE: I am.

*(*MOE, *carrying shaving gear, enters the TV room, turns on the TV set, settles himself in a chair and lathers up, making a mess of his surroundings.* HENRY *enters the TV room.* MAX *smacks his side where a pocket would be if he were wearing clothes.)*

MAX: It's coming out of our pockets! The bastards'll raise the dues again.
*(*MAX *enters the TV room, and heads straight for the TV set.)*
You guys watching this? *(switches TV off)* Turn it off!
HENRY: Max, keep your voice down. We're trying to talk.

MAX: Talk!

(MAX *tries to show attentive concern.* MOE *lumbers up to the TV, turns it on, returns to his seat, and starts shaving. He shakes out his razor on the floor, making a bigger mess.)*

JACK: Henry, how can I even talk to her after what she's done to me?

HENRY: Jack, I know. We all know. Now it's finally over, you gotta bury the past.

JACK: She lied to me!

HENRY: Jack, you knew what was going on.

JACK: Her sunglasses. Right out there, in front of everybody.

HENRY: What?

(MAX *notices the TV, and angrily turns it off.)*

MAX *(to* MOE*)*: Shhh! They're talking!

HENRY: She still loves you. She wants you back.

JACK: No, she doesn't. She didn't make my breakfast the morning I flew back here. I waited hours for her to get up. I hadda call a cab to the airport.

HENRY: You could have woken her up.

JACK: Not that one. She's got earplugs. She's got eyeshades.

MOE: Krantz tells me I got too much stress. "Watch your heart, Moe." Valium. *(continues shaving)*

JACK: She leaves the cereal box on the table in a bowl. A little note: "The milk is in the fridge."

HENRY: Weren't you just telling us how you look after yourself?

JACK: Henry, I don't want no Raisin Bran when I'm down there.

HENRY: So she missed a breakfast after forty years.

JACK: You think she ever missed a breakfast for Lenny? White fish, lox, Brother's coffee cake. I saw the scraps.

HENRY: You go looking for trouble you're gonna find it.

JACK: I know you're all laughing at me. You got no idea how it feels. Lenny's gone. Who's she gonna find down there next? Some guy I don't even know.

HENRY: You think that's what she's doing now? You know her, Jack. You know how she's feeling. She loved the guy. She needed him.

JACK: Don't you think I know that?

HENRY: You needed him too, Jack. Now it's just you and Ceil.

JACK: Ahhh, Henry, I wish to hell I was your age. Does the worrying stop?

HENRY: It stops. Either that or you stop.

JACK: That's what I'm worried about.

HENRY: That's what I mean.

MAX *(notices* MOE *shaving)*: No shaving in the TV room. We got a rule. Whatsa matter, you deaf or something? Moe Perl, I'm talking to you!

HENRY: Max, your voice. We're trying to have a serious conversation.

MAX: This is serious!

MOE: Krantz. He's a master. Puts me on Epsom Salts.

JACK: Henry, for God's sake! What do I do?

HENRY: Phone her.

JACK: What do I say to her?

HENRY: I love you.

MOE: Then prune juice. Anna brings me a little glass before bed. *(shakes razor out on floor)*

MAX: You see that? You see what he's doing?

JACK *(referring to* MAX*)*: Henry, tell him to stop it!

MAX: You better warn him, Henry. I'm gonna punch his face in. Like I did at Harbord Collegiate! In the yard! With everyone watching!

*(*MOE *finishes his shave, and tosses the disposable razor onto the floor.)*

MOE: Sometimes an enema.

MAX *(approaches* MOE *threateningly)*: We got rules. We got rules in here.

HENRY: Max, Max, he's stopped. Calm down. He's stopped shaving.

MAX: I don't care he's stopped. It's no good he's stopped. He shoulda stopped when I told him to stop!

*(*MOE *turns on the TV again and exits to the whirlpool.* YANKELE *enters the locker room, and looks for a new position for the "NO SHOUTING" sign.)*

JACK: I can't tell her I love her!

HENRY: You'll tell her. You know you will, Jack. You'll move down with her.

JACK: Like hell I will!

MAX: Get back here, Moe Perl! Get back here and turn off that TV set!

(In his rage, MAX *switches off the TV.)*

HENRY: Jack, you're wasting your time. You've got someone. That's more than the rest of us. Max, it's off. *(exits)*

YANKELE: Here maybe. No. He still won't see it. This is the place.

*(*YANKELE *posts the sign, then exits out the check-in door, muttering.)*

JACK: I won't do it!

MAX *(sees the sign)*: Who's shouting?! Talk to Moe Perl!!

*(*MAX *enters through the locker room and goes behind the lockers.* EDDIE *enters the locker area from the whirlpool, gets a bristle brush, shaving mug, and straight razor from behind the lockers. He goes to the basin and prepares to shave.)*

JACK: I'm talking to Moe Perl! From him I'll get advice. *(exits to whirlpool)*

EDDIE: Sure. Rub his head a little. It's a crystal ball.
*(*BEN *enters from the steam room, towelling himself.)*
Henry, make it fifty.

HENRY: What? Fifty, blue? Too high.

EDDIE: No, no, no! Red! I said red.

HENRY: I thought you said blue.

EDDIE: Blue? I told you blue. Blue's twenty-five.

HENRY: So what's white?

BEN: Hey, you got it hot? *(feels water in sink)*

EDDIE: White? Low boy.

BEN: It's cold! *(runs hot water into basin)*

HENRY: Five? Ten?

EDDIE: Ten.

BEN: Here, treat yourself good. You need the hot to lift the whiskers.

HENRY: Ten's high.

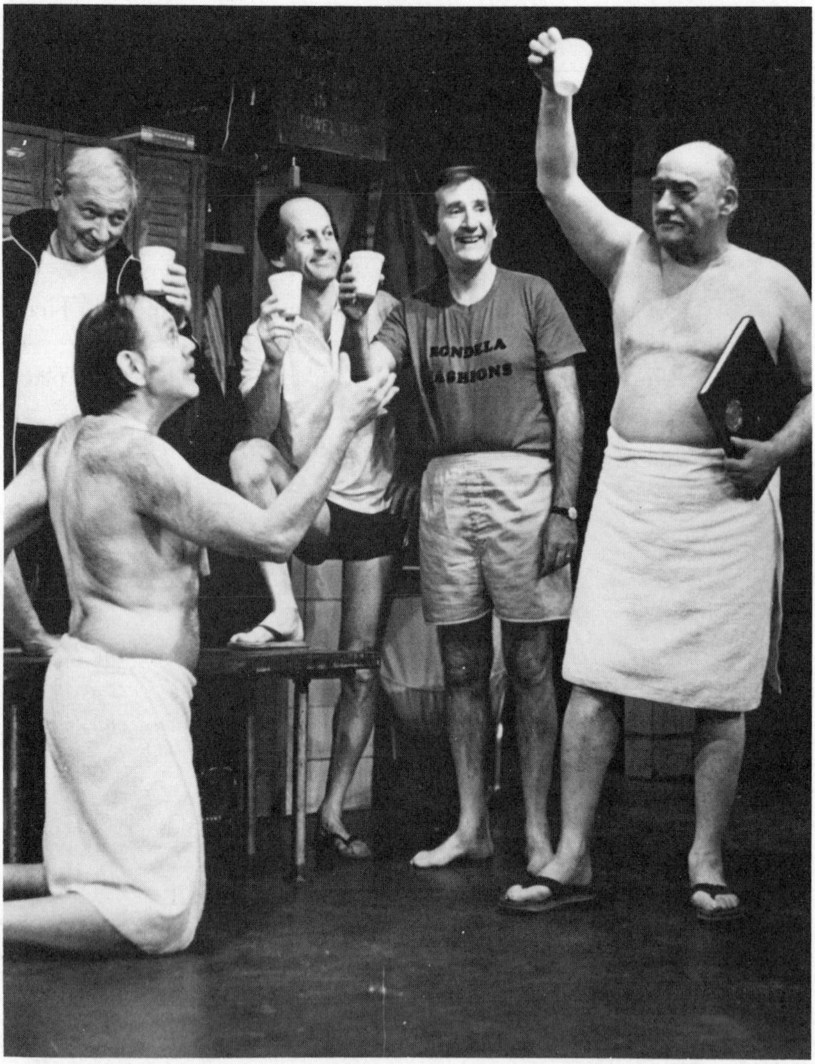

Jack Aaron and Harvey Pierce in the JRT production of *Taking Steam.* (Photo: Adam Newman.)

(EDDIE *finishes lathering, puts the brush down, and picks up the straight razor.)*

EDDIE: High for who?
BEN: Haay, now that's a razor! Machismo!

(EDDIE *starts shaving quickly.)*

HENRY: It's high for some of them.
BEN: Eddie! Against the grain. Like this. *(mimes shaving)*
EDDIE: He's gonna teach me how to shave.
HENRY: Make blue twenty-five.
BEN: Twenty-five cent ante? That what you mean?
EDDIE *(to* HENRY*)*: That's what I said. Blue twenty-five.
BEN: Now that's the kinda game I can get into. Whose house?
HENRY: I meant red. Red twenty-five.

(EDDIE *takes bits of toilet paper from a wad on the edge of the basin and applies them to his cuts.)*

EDDIE: What is this? Old maid? Red's fifty.
BEN: C'mon Henry. Where's your nerve?
HENRY: Blue ten.
BEN: Ten? Let's get serious.
EDDIE: I'm the bank.
HENRY: You'll break us.
EDDIE *(to* HENRY*)*: We'll talk later.

(EDDIE *pushes* HENRY *towards the TV room.* BEN *calls after them.)*

BEN: Call me when you get it back to fifty.
EDDIE: So who asked him?

(HENRY *and* EDDIE *enter the TV room, pick up newspapers and shuffle the sections of the newspaper.* BEN *is momentarily stranded in the locker room, alone and at a loss. After a moment, he exits behind the lockers.)*

HENRY: I still say blue ten.
EDDIE: No, no, no, no . . .
HENRY *(offers* EDDIE *section of paper)*: Business?
EDDIE: I got no business.
HENRY: You should read about Saltzman here. He's busy with no business.
EDDIE: I got no business and I'm not busy.

HENRY: Sports?
EDDIE: I'm tired. Gimme Homes and Gardens.

(They settle down to their reading. JACK *follows* MOE *onstage.* MOE *climbs on a bicycle machine, and pedals sluggishly.)*

JACK: Moe, that's brilliant! Am I ever glad we put our heads together. Moe Perl—who would have thought. So yeah, Moe, that's exactly what I'm gonna do. Bring Daniel in. Put him at the helm right away. President of Rondela Fashions. Vice-president.
MOE: Twenty-three . . . twenty-four . . . twenty-five . . .
JACK: He can stay at the house as long as he wants. His room's waiting for him.
MOE: Who's this, Jack?
JACK: Daniel. My oldest.
MOE: Danny! Anna loves that boy. *(pedals a few times, more slowly)*
JACK: Nothing has to change! Nothing!
MOE *(gets down from bicycle)*: I'm not doing no more.

*(*BEN *enters.)*

BEN *(to* JACK*)*: So what's your decision? You're gonna drop her. Sure, that was no marriage. So when does the bitch get the word?
JACK: Ben, you got it all wrong. Moe and I worked the whole thing out. Nothing has to change.

*(*MOE *starts doing knee bends, barely bending his knees.)*

MOE: Do ten of these.
BEN: Look, I'll walk you to the phone. I'll put in the coins. Hit her before she hits you. Then get out fast before she takes you to the cleaners.
MOE: You could damage the tendons.
JACK: Winters, she's got the condo. April first . . .
BEN: Oh no you don't. Jack Sherman, you're gonna confront.
JACK: What do I gotta confront? Haven't you heard? Daniel's coming in.
MOE: You gotta help me with this one, Jack.
JACK: What?

*(*MOE *demonstrates another exercise. He places one hand behind his lower back, the other hand back over his shoulder.)*

MOE: The hands are supposed to touch. Pull 'em together.
*(*JACK *tries to help* MOE *with the exercise.)*
You gotta be careful with this. Krantz says you could get a hernia.

BEN: You hear that, Jack? You could get a hernia.
*(*BEN *speaks to himself, as he exits behind the lockers.)*
Coupla basket cases. *(turns back)* Jack, do it! It took me forever with Fran. All she left me was the guilt. *(exits behind lockers)*

MOE: Boy, that feels great.

*(*JACK *and* MOE *separate.* MOE *lies on the bench.)*

JACK: Did you hear that guy? That's the kind of stuff they've been telling me all day. Leave my wife. Sell the business. Do this. Do that. You're the only one here with any sense.

(Behind the lockers, BEN *slams his fist against a locker again and again.)*

BEN: Whore! Bitch! Take it—take it all! It's yours! Hey, what about my balls? You want 'em? Sure you want em. Beg!

JACK: Moe, you're the only one with any sense.
*(*MOE, *doing leg raises, barely lifts his legs. He counts a set of raises.)*
You know what Daniel's like. Sure, I made a mistake with him. Maybe I shouldn't have made him carry my samples. One month only. He quit. He tells me, "I never want to see the inside of that place again." I even offered to put him on salary.

MOE: Eight . . . nine . . . That's it.

JACK: Whadya think, Moe? Ahhh, he's gone. I never hear from him. He's not coming back.

*(*MOE *stares at* JACK *as if seeing him for the first time.)*

MOE: Jack, you look terrible. You got something on your mind. Listen, I bet you never thought of this. Whyn't you get rid of that business of yours? Hasn't amounted to much the last few years. Well, it's just a suggestion. *(exits behind lockers)*

*(*JACK *turns to Lenny's empty locker, opens it, shuts it. He wanders toward the TV room, stops, and turns back. He moves to go behind the lockers, shakes his head, turns back. He slumps down on the bench, head on hands.)*

JACK: It's not so bad. Ahhh, what the hell.
*(*JACK *tries to get up, cannot, and slumps back down again.)* It's not so bad. It's not so bad. *(slumps further down)* I'm gonna have to call her. Oh God, I'm gonna have to call her.

(In the TV room, HENRY *and* EDDIE *speak from behind their newspapers.)*

EDDIE: So what do you figure? Fifty pounds of meat?
HENRY: Fifty pounds? How many guys are we having?
EDDIE: Twenty. Twenty-five. Four tables.
HENRY *(lowers paper)*: *Fifty pounds?*
EDDIE: Okay, have it your way. Thirty-five.
HENRY: Couple of *kugel?*
EDDIE: It's oily. It'll get on the cards.
HENRY: Oh. Here comes the Earl of Sandwich.
EDDIE: Naah, nobody eats that shit anymore. Sticks in your gut.
HENRY: Dave's a caterer. He'll know.
EDDIE: No *kugel.* Potato salad. *Knish.* No *kugel.*
HENRY: Cole slaw?
EDDIE: Sure, cole slaw. Chopped liver. Three cases of beer. Light beer.
HENRY: Some guys eat *kugel,* you know.
EDDIE: Ice cream cake.
HENRY: That gets on the cards.
EDDIE: Okay, have your *kugel.* *(exits to locker room)* Figure fifty pounds of meat.

*(*JACK *is still sunk in deep depression.* EDDIE *walks behind the lockers, retrieves his clothing, and comes out front to change.* HENRY *exits to the showers.* YANKELE *enters through the check-in door, and shows* JACK *a badly-polished pair of shoes.)*

YANKELE: Yours?

(No response from JACK. YANKELE *shows the shoes to* EDDIE. EDDIE *shakes his head, and points to his own shoes.* YANKELE *shrugs.)*

EDDIE: Time?
YANKELE: Late. *(exits, carrying shoes)*
EDDIE: Another day, another day. You going home, Jack, or you wanna grab a bite with us before the game? Tide you over.

(No answer. EDDIE *half-turns to look at* JACK, *gives a low whistle, and continues dressing.* BEN *enters from behind the lockers. He carries a neatly folded pile of clothes plus an athletic bag. He stacks it all on the bench beside* JACK.*)*

BEN: All right, Eddie, what time's the game tonight?
EDDIE: Very late. Past your bedtime.

*(*EDDIE *exits behind the lockers.* BEN, *wandering about, notices* JACK'S *pants draped over the bench.)*

BEN: What's this stuff you're wearing? *(picks pants up, looks at label)* Simpsons. Ceil pick these for you? See how she cramps your style? Jack, it's a jungle out there. They're waiting for us and they're hungry. Give 'em something they can sink their teeth into. Jeans!

*(*MAX *enters from the other side of the lockers carrying a pile of his stuff. He stacks it on the other side of* JACK, *goes behind the lockers.* BEN *doesn't notice* MAX.*)*

EDDIE *(from behind lockers)*: The Canadian gigolo.
BEN: Hey Eddie, you see what he's got on here? Boxer shorts. What's the matter with this guy? *(to* JACK*)* Give 'em the real stuff! Bikini briefs. Ebony.

*(*EDDIE *enters, dressed.)*

EDDIE: He's got bad circulation.

(JACK *moves to the TV room.)*

BEN: And wear some gold. Chains of gold. Jewish letters. *(sees* MAX'S *pile of stuff)* Hey, what's that?

*(*MAX *enters with the last of his stuff, gathers as much as he can from the bench in his arms, strides to Lenny's locker, and starts jamming the locker full. It has the look of a well-planned maneuver.)*

What the hell!

*(*BEN *strides over threateningly to* MAX *who ignores him and continues to fill the locker.)*

Clear it out! Get your junk outta there! That's Lenny's locker. It's mine.

*(*MAX *has an open lock in his hand, and is ready to put it on the locker.* BEN *grabs* MAX'S *wrist.)*

EDDIE: Come on, you two. Break it up.

*(*MAX *and* BEN *ignore* EDDIE. BEN *keeps his grip on* MAX *and deliberately scoops* MAX'S *things onto the floor.* MAX *breaks free, and tries to retrieve his belongings.* BEN *restrains him, and tries to throw some of his own stuff into the locker. The two struggle furiously. The locker is once again empty. As they fight, they exchange insults.)*

MAX: Who're you? Mr. Nobody.
BEN: Old quack!
MAX: You don't belong!
BEN: Loudmouth!
MAX: Mr. Fancy Pants. We're all laughing at you.

(The fight ends. MAX *and* BEN *glare at each other.)*

BEN: Oh, they're laughing at me. So how come I know about the poker game tonight and you don't?

*(*MOE, *fully dressed and with Lenny's religious bag in his hand, has entered from behind the lockers with a pile of his own things. He dumps them into Lenny's locker, shuts the door and*

locks it. The sound of the door shutting alerts MAX *and* BEN *who hadn't noticed* MOE'S *entrance.* MOE *walks insouciantly past them to the check-in door. He pauses at the door.)*

MOE: I'm going to *daven. (exits)*

MAX: Moe Perl! *(to* BEN*)* Now look what ya done, ya Polack! Moe Perl, get back here and take that lock off! *(to* EDDIE*)* Whose house?

*(*BEN *exits through the check-in door.)*

EDDIE: What's it to you, Max? It's another locker, that's all. Smells the same as the rest of them.

MAX: It's better! I miss too much back there. Poker game! I'm getting Henry. *(exits to showers)*

*(*BEN *re-enters with a bolt cutter.* YANKELE *follows him, futilely trying to restrain him.)*

YANKELE: Gentlemen, gentlemen.

*(*BEN *grimly positions the bolt cutter over* MOE'S *lock. He tries to cut the lock, fails, and throws the bolt cutter to the floor in disgust.)*

So. Not so easy as it looks.

BEN *(to* YANKELE, *indignantly)*: Fifteen years and they still wanna keep me in the back. Look, this locker belonged to Lenny . . . Mr. Zavitz. He wanted me to have it. There's no argument—it's for me. Period.

YANKELE: And what is your name?

BEN: Nobody is ever screwing me out of anything again! Nobody! *(picks up his stuff)* You'll hear about this. And clean up back here! It's a pigsty! *(exits behind lockers)*

YANKELE: Shah, shah! They'll wake the dead. *(sees* JACK*)* That's better. *(exits)*

*(*EDDIE *picks up his athletic bag as if to leave.)*

EDDIE *(to* JACK*)*: Hungry yet?

JACK: No.

EDDIE: C'mon. Ya gotta eat. We got a card game.

JACK: No.

EDDIE: We'll go in my car. Put your pants on.

(Silence.)

Okay, don't eat. Don't play cards. Go home at least. Put your feet up.

(No response.)

What's the matter, you don't wanna go home?

JACK: No.

EDDIE: Cut it out. That's enough.

*(*JACK *gets to his feet and begins to dress.)*

Atta boy. Stop feeling sorry for yourself. Put the pants on. Where you wanna go? Jack! You coming?

JACK: No. *(continues to sit)*

EDDIE *(with controlled fury)*: Goodbye! *(shouts in direction of showers)* Henry, ya ready to go?

HENRY *(from showers)*: I'll be right there.

MAX *(from showers, to* HENRY*)*: Talk to me. Whose house? I wanna know whose house!

EDDIE: *Oy.*

HENRY: Not now, Max.

*(*HENRY *enters the locker room, followed by* MAX, *who is in a huff.* HENRY *starts getting dressed at his locker.)*

MAX: Henry, you're in. Whose house you goin' to? Normie? Marvin?

HENRY: Max, Max. Sit down. Let me pour you a drink.

*(*HENRY *reaches into his locker, and pours a drink into a Dixie cup.* MAX *swallows the drink in one gulp, then wipes his lips.)*

MAX: Cocksuckers!

HENRY: Is this how a mature man behaves?

MAX: I'm seventy-three years old and he's calling me mature.

HENRY: I'm not talking to a crazy man. *(turns away from* MAX; *continues dressing)*

MAX *(sits; waits)*: Well?

EDDIE: It's at Eddie's.

MAX: Eddie Fine?

EDDIE: Sure. So?

MAX: Don't give me that. You know what I'm talking about!

EDDIE: Max, it's just a little poker game. What're you getting so hot about? Yankele! My shoes!

MAX: Is Normie coming?

EDDIE: Why not.

MAX: Joe?

HENRY: Mmm.

(YANKELE enters with the shoes he carried earlier.)

MAX: Monty? Herb? Murray? Syd?

YANKELE: Yours?

HENRY: Yeah. *(takes shoes)*

(YANKELE exits, muttering.)

MAX: What about Moe?
(HENRY grunts noncommittally as he puts on his shoes.)
Moe? Moe Perl? That *schmuck?*
(No one pays attention to MAX. HENRY continues dressing.)
Don't play around, Henry. What about me? What about Max Glass? Didn't I drive Normie and Shirl to Malton to catch the plane? Didn't I pick them up?
(HENRY starts to pack his athletic bag.)
Murray! He wouldn't be married again without me! Five hundred miles off the Buick, running back and forth to the caterers. Broke my balls for you guys. So what's wrong? What's the matter with Max Glass? Don't just stand there!!

EDDIE: Tell him, Henry.

HENRY: Maxie, sit down.
(MAX hesitates, then sits.)
It's your voice, Max.

MAX: My voice. What about my voice?

HENRY: It's too loud.

MAX *(quietly):* My voice is quiet.

EDDIE: It's not too quiet.

MAX *(slightly louder):* I think I'm fucking quiet.

HENRY: Max, you're always talking to the whole world. Everybody takes offense.

MAX: Who? Who takes offense? Name one person.

EDDIE: The rabbi.

MAX: That guy takes offense? Henry, you were there. You heard what he said! In a crowded *shul!*

HENRY: Well, he probably should have waited.

MAX: You're goddamn right he should have waited. Hollering at me. Pointing his finger. "Max Glass—silence!"

HENRY: On the other hand, you were yelling so loud you disrupted the whole service.

MAX: I wasn't yelling!

EDDIE: When he *whispers* everyone can hear.

MAX *(leaps to his feet, shouts):* Are you crazy?! You outta your mind?

HENRY: Max, look at yourself. What'd you just do?

MAX *(sits, chastened):* I yelled. I always yell. How do you control it?

EDDIE: See a throat doctor.

MAX: Yeah? So?

EDDIE: Have him cut your throat.

MAX *(jumps up):* That does it! I'm finished with you guys! *(pause)* You're right. I'm too loud. I can't help it. You gotta tell me what to do.

HENRY: Well, you can start right now by keeping your mouth shut.

MAX: You're right. You're right.

HENRY: Promise, Max. Not a word.

MAX *(whispers):* I promise. Can I come? *(mimes playing cards)*

*(*EDDIE *gestures a frantic "No" to* HENRY.*)*

HENRY: Not a word, Max. All evening.

*(*MAX *puts a finger to his lips, and elaborately promises silence.)*

HENRY: Okay.

EDDIE: Great, Henry! Just great.

*(*EDDIE *glares at* MAX *who basks in silent triumph.)*

EDDIE: Come on, let's get outta this place. *(shouts loudly over lockers)* We're leaving!

*(*MAX, HENRY *and* EDDIE *start to put on hats and overcoats.)*

HENRY: Sai Woo? Kwongchow?

(MAX gestures that he might be interested.)

EDDIE: Forget it. No Chinese please. The Bagel.

(MAX gestures his disgust.)

HENRY: Eddie, we've ordered in a whole load of food for the game. We just want a snack. Some sweet and sour. Moo goo gai pan.

EDDIE: We had that last time. United. You can eat light.

(JACK rises from his seat. He speaks in a small, hesitant voice.)

JACK: I'm gonna do it.

(No one hears.)

HENRY: United? What'll I order?

(BEN, dressed in street clothes and carrying an athletic bag, strides from behind the lockers and past JACK, heading for the check-in door.)

JACK: I'm gonna do it.

BEN: What?

JACK: Phone. *(exits)*

(The three older men move toward the check-in door.)

HENRY: Where's Moe?

BEN: Hold it right there! Don't move! Jack Sherman . . . is about . . . to phone . . . his wife! Sit down. You don't wanna miss this.

(The three sit, loosening their overcoats.)

The guy's got balls after all. *(calls to JACK)* No chit-chat. Straight to the point. Outta my house! I'm cutting you off! Not a cent! But, hey Jack, be compassionate. She's been through a lot. If she starts to cry, hang up. He's doing it. He's actually doing it.

(YANKELE *shuffles through the check-in door, pushing a mop and pail.)*

YANKELE: They're here all day. They never leave. *(exits)*
BEN: He's talking. Put it to her!

(JACK *re-enters locker room.)*

JACK: I did it. I did it.
BEN: Sure you did. Sure you did. Tell us how it feels. A free man.
JACK: I told her. I've had enough. I'm selling the house. I'm selling the business. I'm moving down.

(HENRY, EDDIE, *and* MAX *get up and move toward* JACK.*)*

BEN: You're doing what?!
JACK: I'm moving down with my wife. Now!
BEN: Jack Sherman, after all I've done for you.
JACK *(to* HENRY*):* I told her. What you wanted me to say. I used to think I had all the time. She's scared. She needs me. Me! I gotta get outta here.
EDDIE: Goodbye Rondela Fashions.
JACK: Rondela Fashions! That goddamn *shlockhouse.* Hey, you guys come down tomorrow—I'm gonna push the racks right into Lake Ontario.
EDDIE: Have a flood sale.
HENRY: Jack. You and Ceil are gonna have a lot of good years.
JACK: Yeah, you think so? I guess I gotta get going. *(puts on coat)*
BEN: Would somebody please tell me why I'm wasting my time with you people? I try to breathe some life into this place and look at the thanks I get. I don't have to stay here. There's another club up north. With young people. YMHA, not OMHA. That's the trouble. You think old. What should I expect? You are old!
MAX: You should live so long.

(BEN *speaks as he exits through the check-in door.)*

BEN: Finished! I got no time to waste on old men!
MAX: Wash behind your ears!
HENRY: See you tomorrow, Ben.

MAX: See what you made me do! I yelled!

JACK: You guys have been great. Just great. So whadya think? I sell. I invest the whole bundle. Just like Saltzman says. Gold.

HENRY: Wonderful, Jack.

JACK *(goes to check-in door):* I'll try to drop in here before I leave. Be seeing you.

MAX: Jack Sherman! I owe you a treatment.

JACK: Uh, later Max. *(exits)*

MAX: I got no friends. It's true. I offend people. My mother, may she rest in peace, had a saying: "The empty barrel makes the most noise." Why didn't I listen to her? I was too busy talking.

JACK *(sticks his head back inside door):* So gold's no good? You're not buying? What about real estate? Jojoba beans? *(steps back inside)* Listen, I gotta get some advice from you guys.

*(*EDDIE *pushes* JACK *out the door.)*

EDDIE: Your wife's waiting for you. Now get the hell out of here, Jack!

JACK: Okay, okay . . .

MAX: Even in business. I coulda made a fortune if I kept my mouth shut.

HENRY: Max.

MAX: If I want friends, I gotta keep my mouth shut.

HENRY: Max!

MAX: I know. I know. I swear to God I won't say a word!

*(*MOE *enters through the check-in door.)*

MOE: I said a *bruche.* For Lenny.
*(*MOE *goes to his locker, and prepares to leave.)*
For Zuckie . . . Al . . . Red Kaye . . .

HENRY: Time for supper, Moe.

MOE: I also said *Kaddish* for Anna.

HENRY: We're going to United.

MOE: Dairy.

EDDIE: Sure. Good for you.

MOE: Not like Anna. She made better.

HENRY: She did. She did.

(YANKELE *enters.)*

YANKELE: Gentlemen, before you leave you should know. Twenty-six degrees below freezing. Celsius.

*(*YANKELE *goes up to* MOE*, and fusses over him.)*

YANKELE: Put on the hat. That's right. Cover the throat. There. That's better.

*(*HENRY, EDDIE, MOE, *and* MAX *exit out the check-in door. A flurry of voices is heard from outside.)*

MAX: I said you won't hear a peep outta me. YOU WON'T HEAR A GODDAMN PEEP!

EDDIE: Shaddup, Max!

HENRY: Eddie, Eddie.

YANKELE: They have to be told. Every day.

*(*YANKELE *begins to clean the locker room.)*

Appendix One

Plays Produced by the Jewish Repertory Theatre—1974–1984

1974–75

God of Vengeance by Sholom Asch
Lady of the Castle by Leah Goldberg

1975–76

A Night in May by A.B. Yehoshua
The Closing of Mendel's Cafe and Relatives by Eve Able
Andorra by Max Frisch
East Side Justice by Isaac Metzker

1976–77

Middle of the Night by Paddy Chayefsky
Jonah by Guenter Rutenborn
Cafe Crown by Hy Kraft
The Condemned of Altona by Jean Paul Sartre
Cakes with the Wine by Edward M. Cohen
Ivanov by Anton Chekhov

1977–78

The Cold Wind and the Warm by S.N. Behrman
Dancing in New York by Julius Landau
The Merchant of Venice by William Shakespeare

Anna Kleiber by Alfonso Sastre
I am a Camera by John Van Druten, based on Christopher Isherwood's *Berlin Stories*
I am a Zoo by Bonnie Zindel

1978–79

Triptych and Sammi by Ernest A. Joselovitz
The Halloween Bandit by Mark Medoff
Unlikely Heroes by Philip Roth, adapted by Larry Arrick
Loyalties by John Galsworthy
The Gentle People by Irwin Shaw
Rocket to the Moon by Clifford Odets

1979–80

Liliom by Ferenc Molnar
Benya the King by Richard Schotter, inspired by *Tales of Odessa* by Isaac Babel
The Matchmaker by Thornton Wilder
Green Fields by Peretz Hirshbein, translated by Joseph C. Landis
Come Blow Your Horn by Neil Simon
36 by Norman Lessing

1980–81

Me and Molly by Gertrude Berg
Success Story by John Howard Lawson
The Birthday Party by Harold Pinter
Marya by Isaac Babel, adapted by Christopher Hampton from a translation by Michael Glenny and Harold Shukman
Incident at Vichy by Arthur Miller

1981–82

Awake and Sing! by Clifford Odets
Elephants by David Rush
Delmore: Shenandoah by Delmore Schwartz and *Luna Park* by Donald Margulies, based on *In Dreams Begin Responsibilities* by Delmore Schwartz.

Pantagleize by Michel de Ghelderode, translated by George Hauger
Vagabond Stars by Nahma Sandrow (book), Raphael Crystal (music), and Alan Poul (lyrics), based on material from the Yiddish theatre

1982–83

After the Fall by Arthur Miller
Friends Too Numerous to Mention by Neil Cohen and Joel Cohen
Ivanov by Anton Chekhov
Taking Steam by Kenneth Klonsky and Brian Shein
My Heart is in the East by Linda Kline (book), Raphael Crystal (music), and Richard Engquist (lyrics)

1983–84

Up from Paradise by Arthur Miller (book and lyrics) and Stanley Silverman (music)
Gifted Children by Donald Margulies
The Homecoming by Harold Pinter
Escape from Riverdale by Donald Wollner
Kuni-Leml by Nahma Sandrow (book), Raphael Crystal (music), and Richard Engquist (lyrics), based on *The Two Kuni-Lemls* by Avrom Goldfadn

Appendix Two

Scripts Developed at JRT Writers' Lab 1978–1984

Writer	Play	Subsequent History
1978–79		
Richard Ploetz	*The Dead-end Gang*	
Brooke Breslow	*Corners*	Counterpoint Theatre, NYC
Israel Horovitz & David Boorstin	*Cappella*	American Jewish Theatre, NYC
Richard Schotter	*Benya the King*	JRT, JCC of Cleveland, New City Theatre, Pittsburgh, New York State CAPS grant, 1983 Berman Award
Nathan Teitel	*The Keymaker*	American Jewish Theatre, NYC
Shimon Wincelberg	*Resort 76*	Whole Theatre Company, N.J., University of Pittsburgh
1979–80		
M. Z. Ribalow	*Honey*	American Theatre of Actors, NYC
Elissa Ely	*Three Theatre Pieces*	
Susan Merson	*Exile of Sarah K*	Ensemble Studio Theatre, NYC
Lionel Abel	*Play Golem*	

Norman Lessing	*36*	JRT, JCC of Cleveland
Donald Margulies	*Luna Park*	JRT
Edward M. Cohen	*The Complaint Department Closes at Five*	
Dan Ellentuck	*Fat Fell Down*	

1980–81

Elliot Tiber & Andre Ernotte	*The Music Keeper*	South St. Playhouse, NYC
Michellene Wandor	*Scissors*	Almost Free Theatre, London
David Rush	*Elephants*	JRT, JCC of Baltimore
Donald Wollner	*Badgers*	Manhattan Punch Line, NYC, Published by Samuel French, 1984 New York State CAPS grant
Rae Edelson	*The Enamel Pot*	Playwrights Platform, Boston
David Rush	*Estelle Laughing*	Northwestern University
Nahma Sandrow, Raphael Crystal, Alan Poul	*Vagabond Stars*	JRT, Hunter College, NYC

1981–82

Gene Ruffini	*The Choice*	
Jay Neugeboren	*The Edict*	
Donald Wollner	*Rookies*	JRT, Ensemble Studio Theatre, NYC
Michael Taav	*Movie Love*	
Neil and Joel Cohen	*Friends Too Numerous to Mention*	JRT
Susan J. Kander	*When the Days Grow Short*	New Vic Theatre, NYC

Kenneth Klonsky and Brian Shein	*Taking Steam*	JRT, Leah Posluns Theatre, Toronto, Published by Playwrights Canada
Grace Paley	*The Loves of Shirley Abramowitz*	Tel Aviv University, JCC of Buffalo
Susan Sandler	*Companion Pieces*	Playwrights Horizons, NYC

1982–83

Crispin Larangeira	*Whispers*	1982 Berman Award
Marc Berman	*Albert Einstein Never Sang at the Met*	
Marcia Haufrecht	*On Bliss Street in Sunnyside*	Siesta Keys Actors Theatre, Sarasota, Florida
Sandra Perlman	*A Question of Voices*	
Richard Schotter	*The Wood Dancer*	Open Eye Theatre, NYC
Michael Taav	*Hard Knocks*	L.A. Theatre Works, L.A.
Philip Lombardo and Leo Garcia	*For Robert's Sake*	Siesta Keys Actors Theatre, Sarasota, Florida
Donald Margulies	*New and Recommended*	JRT, 1984 New York State CAPS grant
Crystal, Klein and Engquist	*My Heart is in the East*	JRT
Aviva Ravel	*Dispossessed*	
Betsy Julia Robinson	*A Platonic Affair*	
Susan Kander	*A Good Year for the Roses*	Equity Library Theatre, NYC
Alan Brody	*The Screening Room*	
Melba Thomas, Judd Woldin, and Muriel Robinson	*Goodbye and Good Luck*	

1983–84

Donald Wollner	*The Girl in the Taxi*	JRT
Susan Merson, Lynne Ahrens, and Margaret Pine	*Sarah K*	

Lynne Kadish	*Family Functions*
Bert Katz	*Jewish Kid*
Leonard Michaels	*I Would Have Saved Them if I Could*
Maggie Williams	*Doretta's Dream*
Jeffrey Sweet	*The Value of Names*

Edward M. Cohen, editor.

About the Editor

EDWARD M. COHEN is a playwright and director who has worked at the O'Neill Playwrights Conference, White Barn Theatre, Sarah Lawrence College, New York Shakespeare Festival, Manhattan Theatre Club, Playwrights Horizons, Leah Posluns Theatre in Toronto, and all over off-off Broadway. He is Associate Director of the Jewish Repertory Theatre, where he also serves as Literary Advisor and runs the JRT Writers' Lab. As Coordinator of Playwrights' Programs for the National Foundation for Jewish Culture, Mr. Cohen edited *Plays of Jewish Interest,* and coordinated the annual Berman Playwrighting Competition, the NFJC Travel Grant program, and the NFJC Conference for Playwrights.

Mr. Cohen's novel, *$250,000,* was published by G. P. Putnam's Sons in the United States and Arthur Barker Ltd. in England, and his stories have appeared in *Evergreen Review* and *Carleton Miscellany.* He is an alumnus of New Dramatists, a four-time fellow at the Edward Albee Foundation, winner of the John Golden Award, and recipient of a Literary Manager grant from the New York State Council on the Arts and a Directing Fellowship from the National Endowment for the Arts.